ONE WEEK LO ` `

Constitutions are suppose   ing st   for politics. Yet most die at a young age. Why is it tha   some constitu ons endu e, whereas others do not? In *The Endurance of National Constitutions*, Zachary Elkins, Tom Ginsburg, and James Melton examine the causes of constitutional endurance from an institutional perspective. Using both statistical and case study evidence, they argue that certain design features can sustain constitutions even in the face of seemingly lethal crises.

Zachary Elkins is an Assistant Professor in the Department of Government at the University of Texas at Austin. Professor Elkins's research focuses on issues of democracy, institutional reform, research methods, and national identity, with an emphasis on cases in Latin America. His work has appeared in leading journals such as the *American Political Science Review*, the *American Journal of Political Science*, and *International Organization*.

Tom Ginsburg is a Professor at the University of Chicago Law School. His books include *Rule by Law: The Politics of Courts in Authoritarian Regimes* (2008, with Tamir Moustafa) and *Judicial Review in New Democracies* (2003), which won the American Political Science Association's C. Herman Pritchett Award for best book on law and courts.

James Melton is a postdoctoral Fellow in political science at the IMT Institute for Advanced Studies in Lucca, Italy. His research focuses on aspects of democracy and democratization and he is currently working on projects related to constitutional design, voter turnout, and measuring democracy.

The Endurance of National Constitutions

ZACHARY ELKINS
University of Texas at Austin

TOM GINSBURG
University of Chicago Law School

JAMES MELTON
IMT Institute for Advanced Studies

CAMBRIDGE
UNIVERSITY PRESS

CAMBRIDGE UNIVERSITY PRESS
Cambridge, New York, Melbourne, Madrid, Cape Town, Singapore,
São Paulo, Delhi, Dubai, Tokyo

Cambridge University Press
32 Avenue of the Americas, New York, NY 10013-2473, USA

www.cambridge.org
Information on this title: www.cambridge.org/9780521731324

First published 2009

Printed in the United States of America

A catalog record for this publication is available from the British Library.

Library of Congress Cataloging in Publication data

Elkins, Zachary, 1970–
The endurance of national constitutions / Zachary Elkins, Tom Ginsburg, James Melton.
   p.   cm.
Includes bibliographical references and index.
ISBN 978-0-521-51550-4 (hardback) – ISBN 978-0-521-73132-4 (pbk.)
1. Constitutions   2. Constitutional law.   3. Constitutional history.   I. Ginsburg, Tom.
II. Melton, James, 1981–   III. Title.
K3165.E45   2009
342.02 – dc22   2009008474

ISBN   978-0-521-51550-4 Hardback
ISBN   978-0-521-73132-4 Paperback

To Jules, Amber, and Linh

[C]onstitutions are *made*, not found. They do not fall miraculously from the sky or grow naturally on the vine. They are human creations, products of convention, choice, the specific history of a particular people, and (almost always) a political struggle in which some win and others lose. Indeed, in this vein one might even want to argue that our constitution is more something we do than something we make: we (re)shape it all the time through our collective activity.

    – Hannah Fenichel Pitkin, *The Idea of a Constitution* (1987)

A permanent constitution must be the work of quiet, leisure, much inquiry, and great deliberation.

    – Thomas Jefferson to A. Coray (1823)

For if a constitution is to be permanent, all parts of the state must wish that it should exist and the same arrangements be maintained.

    – Aristotle, *Politics* IX (350 B.C.E.)

Contents

Preface

This book is the first from the Comparative Constitutions Project, a long-term research initiative we began several years ago with the goal of understanding the origins, characteristics, and consequences of written constitutions for most independent states. As part of this project, we have since identified and collected the texts of nearly all national constitutions from 1789 onward, and we are engaged in a systematic effort to code their contents along a wide range of dimensions. Readers interested in details of the project can find more information at www.comparativeconstitutionsproject.org. Logically prior to the collection of constitutional texts and a coding of their contents comes an accounting of when, exactly, the various documents came to exist and when they were replaced. This sort of census requires comprehensive historical information on the chronologies of national constitutions, including dates of birth, death, and amendment. In seeking genealogical data about, say, the whereabouts of the Ecuadorian constitution of 1830, we frequently came across veritable "obituaries" that reported the circumstances of death. It was not long before we were deeply engaged in questions of the mortality and endurance of these constitutions ourselves.

This book has its origins at the University of Illinois, where Elkins and Ginsburg were colleagues in the Political Science Department and the Law School, respectively, and where Melton received his doctorate. We are especially grateful to Peter Nardulli, Director of the Cline Center for Democracy at the University of Illinois, for his early and continuing support, friendship, and faith in our project, and to Richard Cline for his vision in endowing the Center and our efforts. Various other institutions have supported aspects of our project, and for that we thank Deans Heidi Hurd and Charles Tabb of the University of Illinois College of Law, Dean Saul Levmore of the University of Chicago Law School, Randy Diehl and Gary Freeman of the University

ix

of Texas, Alexander Thier of the United States Institute for Peace, and the National Science Foundation (Awards Nos. SES-0648288 and 0819102).

We have been privileged to have an outstanding group of students at the University of Illinois, University of Chicago, and the University of Texas work with us on the Comparative Constitutions Project over the years. Their assistance in helping to produce the raw materials for this book has been invaluable and we acknowledge each of them individually on the project website. Several students in and outside this group provided helpful research assistance for the book itself, and for that we thank Abby Blass, Justin Blount, Svitlana Chernykh, Adam J. Fleisher, Angelica Ghindar, Zoë Ginsburg, Michael Werner, and Emily Winston. Kalev Leetaru, of the Cline Center, provided inimitable assistance with the electronic archiving of texts and general information processing support.

Many audiences in law schools and political science departments have heard versions of the chapters here, and we are grateful to them all. An incomplete list of people to whom we are indebted for helpful comments includes Robert Barro, Omri Ben-Shahar, David Collier, Rui de Figueiredo, Manuel Delmestro, Rosalind Dixon, Brent Elkins, Nancy Elkins, Brian Gaines, Jacob Gersen, Mark Graber, Gretchen Helmke, Donald Horowitz, Gary Jacobsohn, Jai Kwan Jung, Dan Klerman, Maximo Langer, David Law, James Lindgren, Gabriel Negretto, Eric Posner, Mark Ramseyer, Kal Raustiala, Daria Roithmayr, Adam Samaha, Miguel Schor, Jeff Segal, Neil Siegel, David Strauss, Cass Sunstein, Michael Trebilcock, Tim Waters, Barry Weingast, and reviewers for Cambridge University Press. We are exceptionally indebted to John Carey, Jose Cheibub, and Henry Elkins, who read the entire manuscript and improved it immeasurably. We apologize to the many others whom we have not acknowledged here. Their collective wisdom renders the remaining errors inexcusable, and for those we bear sole responsibility. Finally, our thanks go to John Berger, our editor at Cambridge University Press, for his patience with a project whose life span, unlike most constitutions, lasted longer than it should have.

A new generation of Elkinses, Ginsburgs, and Meltons either came to be or passed major milestones during the process of writing this book. No doubt that they have left their mark on these pages somehow as well. Surely, our spouses – Jules, Amber, and Linh – have done so, through their patience, support, and sense of humor. To them, we give our deepest thanks and dedicate this book.

1

Introduction

In a series of exchanges with James Madison, Thomas Jefferson argued that constitutions should be rewritten every generation, declaring famously that the "dead should not govern the living."[1] Jefferson derided those who "look at constitutions with sanctimonious reverence, and deem them like the ark of the covenant, too sacred to be touched."[2] He even proposed an expiration date – one of nineteen years, a figure he came to from studying a set of actuarial tables.[3] Madison, having only recently shepherded the U.S. document through a sometimes contentious deliberation and ratification process, saw more merit in constitutional longevity. The two carried out their lively debate by mail in two very different contexts: revolutionary France, where Jefferson served as the inaugural U.S. ambassador, and the United States, where Madison was busy putting the new American charter into effect. Although those two countries seemed to be headed in a similar institutional direction as beacons of democracy in the late eighteenth century, their constitutional trajectory would be markedly different. Why is it that the inaugural constitution drafted in Philadelphia in 1789 has survived for 220 years and counting, whereas the French Constitution of 1791 lasted a little more than a year, to be followed in French history by fourteen more constitutions? Indeed, an old joke has it that a man goes into a library and asks for a copy of the French constitution, only to be turned away with the explanation that the library does not stock periodicals.

France, it turns out, is more typical than the United States with respect to constitutional life span. Our data show that most constitutions die young, and only a handful last longer than fifty years. At the extreme, the island of

[1] Thomas Jefferson to James Madison, September 6, 1789. See Hamburger 1989: 280.
[2] Letter to Samuel Kercheval, July 12, 1816.
[3] Thomas Jefferson to James Madison, September 6, 1789; Letter to Samuel Kercheval, July 12, 1816.

Hispaniola, home to the Dominican Republic and Haiti, has been the setting for nearly 7 percent of the world's constitutions and perennial governmental instability. Indeed, the life expectancy of a national constitution in our data is 19 years, precisely the period Jefferson thought optimal![4]

Investigating national constitutional histories shows a great diversity of patterns, with some countries and regions exhibiting great instability, and others, great stability. These patterns may vary over time within a particular country. The cases present puzzling contrasts. Why, for example, have the Brazilians followed the French pattern, writing seven charters since 1824, whereas the neighboring Argentines have made do with the same constitution since 1853, albeit with significant reforms in 1994? Why has the unwieldy Indian constitution persisted since 1948, whereas its neighbor Pakistan has written three such constitutions, each of which was suspended by military coup? Why, in short, do some constitutions endure, whereas others fail?

DESIGN VERSUS ENVIRONMENT

The answer to these questions seems obvious. Constitutional death, one might think, is epiphenomenal and merely reflects other changes that occur in a country's history. Some countries have led tumultuous lives since their initial constitution – with wars, coups, and crises of all kinds – whereas others have led less "interesting" lives, to use the Chinese euphemism. Surely, then, those historically volatile countries should have more unstable constitutional lives than those whose history is more tranquil. But, are the political, economic, and social histories of the United States, Argentina, and India really less combustible than those of France, Brazil, and Pakistan? How closely is constitutional change really tied to historical "shocks" and the larger environment? Are there other factors associated with the constitution itself that put the constitutional system at greater or lesser risk?

For us, these questions point to a distinction in the explanatory power of *design* versus *environmental* factors, a distinction with highly normative implications. Consider design factors as those having to do with the content and drafting process of the constitution itself and environmental ones as those pertaining to the international and national environments that host the constitution. The design versus environment distinction is roughly comparable to the classic behavioral debate in biology that pits the forces of *nature* versus those

---

[4] Calculated from a baseline survival model as the age before which 50 percent of constitutions will have died. See Chapter Six for further details.

of *nurture*. Like design, nature is relatively fixed for any individual organism, whereas nurture varies infinitely. However, the parallel breaks down in one crucial respect: the class of factors that is most malleable is reversed between the two domains. The design, or nature, of the constitution – unlike human DNA – is very much a product of human engineering, whereas the constitution's environment – unlike biology's nurture – is the less manipulable of the two sets of factors. This reversal shifts scientific priorities: with respect to both human and constitutional mortality, it is more imperative to understand those conditions we can do something about than those we cannot (the institutional scholar's version of the "serenity prayer"). So, although health professionals may gravitate toward studying the effects on mortality of remediable human behaviors like exercise and nutrition, and control for genetic predispositions, we do just the opposite. The hardwired genetic code of constitutions is ours (collectively) to engineer and thus worthy of extra attention.

In our theoretical approach, therefore, we are quite consciously open to the possibility that constitutional drafters can affect the durability of their designs. The alternative, perhaps prevailing, view is that constitutions are almost entirely at the mercy of *fortuna*, coming and going only as major world events wash them away. This latter view, it would seem, is based not only on the transformative power of wars, economic crises, and the like, but also on the widespread assumption that institutions are sticky, and constitutions the stickiest of them all. Consequently, many accounts of institutional change, such as those influenced by the concept of *punctuated equilibrium* in evolutionary biology (e.g., Krasner 1984), tend to emphasize environmental shocks over institutional structure. An understandable presumption with respect to constitutional change, then, is that exogenous shocks are a sufficient, perhaps even necessary cause. In his thoughtful book on Canada's constitutional history, Peter Russell (1993: 106) articulates this notion most emphatically: "No liberal democratic state has accomplished comprehensive constitutional change outside the context of some cataclysmic situation such as revolution, world war, the withdrawal of empire, civil war, or the threat of imminent breakup." Such a view, in which constitutional change is merely epiphenomenal, would seem to render constitutional design nearly irrelevant to constitutional mortality.

Nevertheless, our theory (which we introduce later) suggests several risk factors inherent in constitutions themselves that merit investigation. It is possible that the general expectation regarding the power of shocks is just that, an expectation – a highly intuitive one, perhaps, but one that has not yet been empirically validated. Some scholars have suggested as much, arguing that the literature on institutional change has underestimated the incidence of change unassociated with crisis (Cortell & Peterson 1999; Pierson 2004). In the case of constitutional change, any such error would be fully excusable, as no systematic empirical test of constitutional duration is on record as far as we know, and anecdotal evidence provides some examples that seem to confirm the power of environmental shocks in inducing change. However, linking a precipitating event to the time of death does not constitute a complete autopsy. In retrospect, it is easy to attach too much explanatory power to events simply because of their coincidence. A civil war that seems to have so obviously foretold the end of a constitutional system will seem lethal (to constitutions) only afterwards. Also, some events (e.g., political coups) are likely to result, to some degree, from underlying instability produced by constitutional provisions and, therefore, may be merely mediating factors. These possibilities imply two analytical strategies in assessing cause of death. The first is to identify and measure the effect of all crises, not just events in periods coinciding with constitutional demise. The second is to investigate the underlying structural causes of constitutional instability. These structural risk factors may be aspects of constitutions that render them more or less resilient than others, or some political, social, or economic conditions that render the state more or less hospitable to constitutional survival. The test of our theory follows this more comprehensive analytical approach. We seek, therefore, an opportunity to correct an imbalance in the attention paid to the environment at the expense of design in the study of institutions, of which constitutions constitute an important species.

None of this is to say that the environment is not worthy of study. Indeed, we cannot resist plunging into questions of environmental effects. Among the questions that we investigate: what are the consequences for constitutional change following a shift from democracy to authoritarianism, or vice versa? Are newly installed democrats and new authoritarians equally likely to replace the existing constitution? Does it matter whether the constitution that transitional actors would replace was originally written by democrats or by dictators? What about constitutional change within stable democratic and authoritarian regimes: is the constitution equally stable under these two systems? What also are the various effects of major state events such as a defeat in war, a loss of territory, or a severe economic crisis? Do they all imperil constitutions?

And what of time? Have constitutions become more stable since the early 1800s? If so, which risk factors, if any, have waxed or waned to produce these trends? Does the age of the state matter? Burke, Rousseau, and Hegel were famously skeptical of the positivist notion that we can implant constitutions in newly formed states, suggesting instead that institutions need to grow organically. Are inorganic constitutions in new states any more brittle than those of countries with more settled institutional customs? Do we observe any effects of birth order, such that a state's second-, third-, and fourth-born constitutions are increasingly more stable? Apart from these questions regarding the age of the international system or its states, are there aging effects with respect to the constitution itself? We know that marriages, to which constitutions might arguably be compared, show a very distinct pattern in the *hazard rate* across time: these unions enjoy an initial honeymoon period of low risk, only to become especially combustible at the age of six years or so, after which they grow increasingly stable (Aalen and Gjessing 2001). Are constitutions like marriages in this sense? Do they exhibit any discernible patterns of decay or crystallization as they age? All of these are intriguing questions in their own right – and we seek to engage them – but they are subsidiary to our central issue regarding the effects of constitutional design on constitutional endurance.

WHAT GOOD IS CONSTITUTIONAL ENDURANCE?

Before exploring the determinants of mortality, we consider the normative question: how long *should* constitutions last in a democracy? Surely, longevity is not desirable as an end in and of itself and, as Jefferson suggested, it may even be pathological. Chapter Two explores the merits of Jefferson's conjecture and Madison's response, as well as other theoretical and practical arguments for and against durable constitutions.

Often, normative discussions of this kind have a rather abstract quality, which sometimes allows would-be Madisons and Jeffersons to talk past one another. We regard many of the claims and assumptions in this particular debate as eminently testable. Chapter Two, therefore, also evaluates empirically a series of hypotheses implied by the various claims. Among other questions, we consider whether endurance is associated with important social and political goods, such as democratic participation, economic development, national unity, and political stability, and whether constitutional replacement can be said to update otherwise anachronistic or outmoded institutions. We also explore empirically the critical question of whether periodic replacement of the constitution impedes its ability to serve as a constraint on ordinary law and practice, a central function of constitutions. Our findings on these questions are mixed, with support for both Madison and Jefferson, and their followers. Nevertheless, we are most struck by a general finding that most of the purposes that are ascribed to constitutions, such as entrenching fundamental principles or providing normative guidance for the polity, seem to improve with age.

WHAT IS A CONSTITUTION?

Our approach assumes that we can identify a set of laws as the "constitution" in a comparable manner across centuries and continents. Chapter Three grapples with this crucial conceptual question of constitutional definition. For many, constitutions have become shorthand for political institutions more generally. Recently-written constitutions such as Brazil's 1988 document, which attempt to constitutionalize nearly every aspect of public life, have not helped to circumscribe the definition. Other countries such as Britain, Israel, and Saudi Arabia have unwritten or uncodified constitutions. To add even more confusion, countries such as New Zealand and Canada accumulate a set of important documents over a period of years until, at some point, scholars determine that the collection is too important *not* to be a constitution, whether or not the texts were consecrated as such. Constitutions also evolve through ongoing interpretation, such as by high courts engaging in constitutional review or legislatures interacting with executives. Finally, societies have unwritten norms of political practice that bear an ambiguous relationship with the formal written text. The scope of the unwritten constitution poses daunting challenges to comparative research, and we acknowledge the importance of such norms, but, ultimately, we defend the idea that the written constitution – a product of unique and discrete social practices – is itself an object worthy of study.

Chapter Three also provides a methodological introduction to the data on which this study is based. As noted, our data cover the constitutional history of every independent state from 1789 to 2005, a period that includes 935 different constitutional systems for more than 200 different nation states, both past and present. Defining constitutional life span is not always a straightforward task given the frequency of constitutional amendment – some of which sometimes entail significant revisions – alongside the phenomena of constitutional suspension, reinstatement, and replacement. In introducing our census of constitutions, we are then in a position to engage in a set of empirical tests of the validity of our conceptual approach. These tests include an analysis of the gap between the written text and de facto constitutional practice, an assessment of the degree of change in content associated with constitutional replacements versus amendments, and an exploration of the coincidence of constitutional change and regime change, two closely related but empirically distinct concepts. As in Chapter Two, our approach to Chapter Three is to contribute a set of empirical findings to a persistent debate that mostly operates at an abstract level.

A THEORY OF CONSTITUTIONAL CHANGE

To understand the effect of design on constitutional mortality, one needs to understand what constitutions do and what pressures, exactly, lead to their demise. This book elaborates just such a theory of constitutional formation, adjustment, and endurance. Our theory operates on two very different levels in terms of causal proximity. At its most proximate, our theory describes the process of constitutional crisis and death. This is the constitutional equivalent of a description in a medical textbook of the breakdown of vital organs, complete with detailed micro information about tissue and cells. At a more remote level, however, our theory needs to connect these processes to genetic predispositions, activities, or conditions that might increase the risk of breakdown. It is one thing to describe the physiological details of cancerous cells and their threat, and still another to connect the onset of cancerous tumors to human behavior and genetic code. The same is true of constitutional mortality. We recognize the importance of both levels of theory and devote a full chapter to each.

Chapter Four presents our physiological theory of constitutional change. Because we recognize that constitutional change is a subspecies of institutional change (though a very important subspecies), the discussion is informed by the rationalist tradition in institutional analysis and, in particular, the growing literature on self-enforcing institutions. We assume that constitutions are bargains among elites that are meant – at least by their authors – to be enduring. Unlike normal contracts, however, there is no external guarantor who will enforce the agreement, independent of the parties. A constitution will be maintained only if it makes sense to those who live under its dictates, so a crucial quality of any successful constitution is that it be self-enforcing. This means that those *within* the constitutional bargain must have a stake in the successful implementation of the document for it to endure. Even though constitutional bargains may have relative winners and relative losers, they will endure to the extent that parties believe they are better off within the current constitutional bargain than in taking a chance on, and expending resources in, negotiating a new one.

Our model of endurance also imagines that a political bargain, once adopted, will be stable so long as it is not subject to either endogenous or exogenous shocks, such as financial crises, armed conflict, or the death of a long-serving leader. Such shocks change the calculus of costs and benefits for parties considering whether to remain in the constitutional bargain. In the real world, however, such shocks are endemic: currencies plunge, invasions occur, and new technologies are invented that empower some actors, but weaken others. The question then becomes whether there are any features of the constitution that can render it more resilient in the face of shifting conditions. We focus on three such features: constitutional flexibility, the inclusiveness of the constitution, and the level of detail and scope of coverage in the constitution, which we call specificity. Chapter Four describes these concepts, how they interact, and how they facilitate endurance. *Flexibility* represents the constitution's ability to adjust to changing circumstances, and is captured in the empirical analysis by the ease of formal and informal amendment. Constitutions can be changed through both formal processes as well as interpretative changes that update the understanding of the text among relevant actors. *Inclusion* captures the degree to which the constitution includes relevant social and political actors, both at the time of drafting and thereafter. Inclusion facilitates both enforcement of the constitution as well as investment in its endurance. *Specificity* refers to the breadth of coverage and level of detail of constitutional provisions, and we explain why it is that detailed documents may be more enduring than general framework documents so celebrated in American constitutional thought. These three features, we believe, are crucial for facilitating constitutional endurance.

Chapter Five develops the behavioral component of our theory. There, we connect the processes of constitutional negotiation and renegotiation to the predispositions of constitutions and the conditions under which they live. These hypotheses regarding factors of design and environment follow directly from our physiological theory, and we develop their connection to constitutional replacement in some depth. A venerable maxim in political science – the rule of three – recommends that analysts restrict the number of explanatory factors to three (Achen 2002). We violate this rule reluctantly by looking at a wide range of factors, but do so with good reason. First, given that our epidemiological analysis forges new ground, our intent is to report the effect of a host of factors that are of interest to us, and, perhaps, to suggest others undeveloped in our account, which may be explored more fully by future researchers. Second, given the prevailing view that environmental factors are fully determinative of constitutional mortality, we are interested in assessing the impact of constitutional design above and beyond a full set of competing environmental hypotheses.

THE EMPIRICAL APPROACH

We take an explicitly multi-method approach to testing the empirical implications of our theory. The central line of attack is an epidemiological one, set forth in Chapter Six, in which we explore patterns in the mortality of almost the full population of national constitutions since 1789. This analysis provides valuable insights, but is limited in ways we describe shortly. The basis of the epidemiological analysis is a set of original data – the *Comparative Constitutions Project* (CCP) data – which we began collecting in 2005. The data set records a large set of characteristics of each and every constitution written since 1789. The project has entailed considerable investment in unearthing the constitutional chronology of states (e.g., identifying years of constitutional amendment, replacement, suspension, etc.), collecting the texts for each constitutional change, and coding the relevant characteristics of these documents. Our analysis of the endurance of constitutions represents our first comprehensive use of these data. These data provide some important opportunities, not only for its wealth of information regarding constitutional design, but also because of the expansive scope of the sample.

We became more appreciative of these advantages when we stumbled upon the classic study of mortality in ancient Rome by Durand (1960). With an exceptionally clever research design, Durand analyzed data on the dates of birth and death on tombstones found in various Roman ruins. Understandably, Durand was sensitive to issues of selection bias in the sample, particularly with respect to gender and class. Even with this very truncated set of data, Durand was able to tell us a great deal about baseline mortality rates and differences in mortality between different segments of the Roman population.

In our case, we are fortunate to have public records of the birth and death of most of our subjects as well as a wealth of historical information about many of them. Not only that, but we believe that we have identified the complete universe of cases, not just a reasonable sample. We thus take the ambitious step of analyzing constitutional endurance across all cases. We recognize that constitutions are born and die in a wide range of circumstances, and our global approach will fail to account for many individual cases. On balance, however, the global approach allows us to draw broad conclusions about constitutions, which apply across many countries and eras.

In a second line of attack, we devote Chapters Seven and Eight to case studies that explore what we have come to think of as *autopsies* and *family histories*. The autopsies explore very carefully the demise of particular constitutions, whereas the family histories focus on a country's series of constitutions. Much of the evidence we consider in these chapters is in the form of what Brady and Collier (2004) have called *causal process observations* (as opposed to *data set observations*). The focus on a particular case (or series of cases) of constitutional replacement allows us to examine the sequence, timing, and relevance of various risk factors and to assess cause of death more precisely.

In our design of the case study research, we examine two different samples that we draw sequentially using first a "most similar systems" design (Chapter Seven) and then a "most different systems" design (Chapter Eight). We sample countries (not constitutions) and explore both the patterns of constitutional endurance *across* countries as well as the variation in endurance *within* countries. The latter within-country analysis provides added analytical leverage by multiplying instances of constitutional mortality while effectively controlling for a host of environmental and genetic factors. The across-country analysis compares national trajectories and allows us to look more systematically at issues of sequence and legacy. Although we take a rather structured approach to the set-up of the case-oriented material (with an eye towards hypothesis testing), our hope is that the case studies take on a less didactic narrative style with the more general purpose of illuminating the concepts and processes invoked in our theory.

CONCLUSION

Written constitutions are central institutions in the political order and powerful symbols of statehood. As a normative matter, most designers and scholars seem to assume that they should endure. Yet, in many times and places, constitutions are remarkably ephemeral. Establishing an enduring constitutional scheme appears to be quite difficult, particularly in new democracies outside of Western Europe and North America. This instability may have real consequences in an era in which constitutions are centerpieces of political reconstruction (Arjomand 2007) and foreign policy (Elkins, Ginsburg, and Melton 2008; Feldman 2005).

Alas, we have, to date, very little knowledge about how to create more enduring constitutions (Negretto 2008; Ordeshook 1992; Sutter 2003; Weingast 2006). This book is a modest effort to bring the issue of constitutional endurance to the fore. By documenting the phenomenon of constitutional mortality and examining the various environmental and design factors that influence constitutional life span, we hope to answer some questions, but, at the same time, raise others for further analysis in comparative constitutional studies.

Our central point is a simple one: design choices matter. Our evidence confirms that scholars have been right to respect the influence of environmental crises and conditions on constitutional change. However, up to certain thresholds, more flexible constitutions that include a wide range of social actors and provide some amount of detail seem to endure longer than those that do not. These choices may also make constitutions more democratic, although this is not our overriding normative concern. Indeed, as we shall see in the next chapter, it has been argued that endurance may have some positive consequences independent of the content of constitutions. Regardless, we expect that constitutional designers will continue to struggle for a stable anchor for politics in a world of constant change, and we hope that this book will provide some perspective on this struggle.

2

How Long Should Constitutions Endure?

The bicentennial of the 1787 Constitutional Convention in Philadelphia was met with much fanfare. Historians penned suitably reverential retrospectives, Independence Hall allowed its visitors to sign (virtually) the constitutional text themselves, and media outlets everywhere used the opportunity to revisit the founding and evolution of the document. Some observers, however, were not so buoyant in their reactions. In a typically iconoclastic piece, Thurgood Marshall (1987: 5) suggested that Americans were less indebted to the framers than "to those present who refused to acquiesce in outdated notions of 'liberty,' 'justice,' and 'equality.'" Despite Marshall's dissent, the majority opinion seems to amount to a vindication of Madison's call for the preservation of the Philadelphia bargain. But, after 200 years of constitutional births and deaths around the world, we are in a position to address some intriguing counterfactuals. Would the United States (and any other country) be better off had it wholly replaced the Constitution with an upgraded document? Would the country have been as prosperous, as democratic, as stable? Would our higher law "fit" the norms and customs of today's citizens better? Would the substituted document have the same degree of sanctity and inviolability as higher law? What would be the implications for national identity or the economic and political institutions that have grown around the older document? In this chapter, we revisit the original arguments of Jefferson and Madison, as well as those of like-minded theorists, and evaluate the various claims against the historical record.

THE JEFFERSONIAN POSITION

Jefferson's proposal of an expiration date initially seems unrealistic and most of his contemporaries – to the extent they were aware of it – likely viewed it as nothing more than a thought experiment. In general, the participants in Philadelphia in 1787 assumed that constitutions by their nature ought to be permanent, a position rooted in an understanding of the English Constitution as being ancient and immutable (Hamburger 1989: 241, 263, 275 n. 123).[1] Moreover, a sunset clause arguably constrains future generations as much, and perhaps more, than does presumed permanence. Why should citizens artificially abandon a well functioning constitution simply because it has reached a certain age? It is unclear exactly what Jefferson contemplated would happen upon the expiration of the current laws (Yarbrough 1998). As Strauss (2003: 1727) points out, reverting to yet earlier laws (one possibility) only compounds the problem, as the dead governors of the living would be replaced by the even more dead.

Yet, sunset clauses have a long tradition in public law, dating back to at least the Roman concept of the mandate. The *Athenian Stranger* argued that some laws should be accompanied by a period of experimentation, say ten years, after which they would become immutable, requiring unanimity to overturn (Schwartzberg 2007: 62). Some amendment provisions in constitutions take the opposite tack: immunizing the document from revision for a period of time following promulgation (for example, Spain 1812). The U.S. drafters took this approach when they proscribed any ban on the slave trade until 1808 (a period that coincidentally corresponded precisely with Jefferson's ideal of nineteen years from the founding).[2] Akhil Amar (2006: 295) suggests that many founders may have wished also to sunset the hard-won agreement to treat states equally regardless of size when apportioning the Senate – a proposal that, to the chagrin of contemporary and subsequent critics of the document, did not materialize. A more explicit Jeffersonian position was reflected in the ill-fated French Constitution of 1793, which emphatically refused to entrench itself and declared that no generation could subject future generations to its laws.[3]

Inspired in part by Jefferson, as well as some state constitutions pre-dating the U.S. Constitution, some fourteen American states to this day require the people to be consulted on a regular basis by the legislature as to whether to call a constitutional convention (Rees 2007: 266; Samaha 2008; Williams 1996, 2000).[4] A

---

[1] Of course, the founders were gathered with the purpose of altering – quite fundamentally, as it happened – their country's first set of founding laws.

[2] U.S. Constitution, Art. I, Sec. 9, cl. 1. This is an example of a transitional clause used to secure the constitutional bargain. Other examples include the Interim Constitution of South Africa, which contained a provision entrenching a grand coalition government for five years after the first democratic election. See Klug (2000: 115).

[3] Declaration of Rights of Men and Citizens (1793), Art. 28 ("A people have always the right of revising, amending and changing their Constitution. One generation cannot subject to its laws future generations.")

[4] E.g., Constitution of Maryland 1851, Art. XIV, Sec. 2 (calling for sense of the people resolution every ten or twenty years). As of 1982, eight states submit this question to the people every twenty years; one state holds a vote every sixteen years; four states vote every ten years; and one state votes every nine years (Sturm 1982: 83; Martineu 1970). The state constitutions of

more recent comparative example is the late Fijian Constitution of 1990, which required review every 10 years.[5] Similarly, Micronesia's Constitution adopts the American state mechanism of regular consideration of constitutional conventions.[6] Papua New Guinea's Constitution calls for a General Constitutional Commission to review the workings of the document after three years.[7] The 2005 Constitution of Iraq calls for a one-time special committee to propose amendments, a feature designed to correct errors in the bargaining process.[8]

This return to the well of contemporary popular sovereignty is mirrored in the periodic ritual of elections. The critical difference is that elections renew the personnel that fill government posts, not their powers or even the existence of the posts themselves. Many states have adopted limits on the number of terms that a representative can serve, responding to popular frustration with the advantages of incumbency. Like expiration dates for laws, limits on terms strike a difficult balance between two threats to representation: the inertial power of the status quo and the illiberalism of forbidding the continuation of the status quo. Term limits for officeholders may provide an even more extreme institutional limitation on choice than those proposed by Jefferson for laws. Presumably, Jefferson contemplated only a new round of deliberation, not one that would have prevented the electorate or their delegates from sustaining the old constitution by popular acclaim.

Indeed, one wonders, if Jefferson's conjecture had been implemented, whether compulsory redeliberation would in fact produce different results from what we already observe. Given what we have learned about cognitive processes in recent years, one might be skeptical that Jefferson's redeliberation would produce anything other than a routine blessing of the previous rules, much as we typically use the opportunity afforded by elections to reinstate incumbents. We are endowed with a status quo bias that causes us to stick with earlier choices, often without conducting a full evaluation of the merits (Samuelson and Zeckhauser 1988: 8; Sunstein 2000). Another relevant bias is loss aversion, the preference for avoiding current losses over seeking unrealized gains, which may prevent those with a current distribution of gains from agreeing to modify institutions (Kahneman et al. 1991: 194–9). In the language of calculus, these inertial factors may, under certain circumstances, keep us at a *local maximum* in the distribution of institutional outcomes and discourage our ascension to a *global maximum*.

Massachusetts, New Hampshire, and Connecticut had related provisions prior to the adoption of the U.S. document.

[5] Art. 161.

[6] Art. 14, Section 2. East Timor's Constitution of 2002 has the interesting provision that six years must pass between amendments. Constitution of East Timor, Art. 154(2) (2002).

[7] Constitution of Papua New Guinea, Art. 260 (1975).

[8] Art. 137.

It is possible, of course, that a country's founders may stumble upon a global maximum right from the start. One suspects, however, that constitutional products are more likely to be *beta* versions that, like most technology, will benefit from a comprehensive overhaul. Moreover, even if a constitution represents a global maximum at the time of drafting, over time that same constitution may become suboptimal and require replacement as power distributions shift and viable alternatives arise. At the risk of flattering our own professions, one would expect that legal scholars and political scientists have managed to improve (or at least better understand) constitutional technology since the eighteenth century models. But, we need not rely on scholars; surely two hundred years of living with modern constitutions has taught citizens and political actors something about constitutional strengths and weaknesses.

Given the possibility of a suboptimal starting point and the existence of powerful inertial forces, one can make a case in favor of forcing the polity to *re*engage with fundamental principles. Surely the existence of biases that push us toward retaining current institutions is not an argument for *avoiding* reconsideration of them. Inferior products abound because of the difficulties in coordinating users and overcoming adoption costs. To cite a classic, if perhaps clichéd, example of the use of suboptimal but persistent technology, it is worth recalling that we continue to type – including our composition of this book – using the relatively inefficient QWERTY keyboard layout (David 1985). Suboptimal political institutions are arguably less tolerable than is a suboptimal keyboard. Accordingly, regulations like Jefferson's sunset clause that disturb these sort of *low equilibrium traps* deserve serious consideration. Indeed, there may be merit in precommitting ourselves to cast our eyes higher and to consider the possibility of global, rather than local, maxima.

Technological advancement and enhanced representation, then, are two potential outcomes of periodic replacement. Another has to do with the value of the constitutional design process itself. Jefferson's view was rooted in a deep commitment to self-government as an end. He saw democracy as more than mere delegation to periodically approved representatives; rather, self-government was an ennobling and a civic virtue in and of itself, in which a free people exercised innate power.[9] In this, Jefferson's view is consonant with scholars (e.g., Ackerman and Fishkin 2005; Fishkin 1991) who describe the benefits of a deeper, more deliberative, democracy. Jefferson, moreover, suspected that stability in government would induce corruption, which he diagnosed as the downfall of the ancients (Yarbrough 1998: 106). Only the

---

9 Letter to John Adams, October 28, 1813, in Adams-Jefferson Letters 387–92. See discussion in Yarbrough (1998: 102).

spirited exercise of popular will, beyond regular selection of representatives through elections, could reinvigorate and sustain republican government. No doubt this orientation informed his early romantic attachment to attempted revolutions, from the French Revolution of 1789 to Shays' Rebellion in the United States.[10] Some of the benefits of a spirited return to basics are evident in modern constitutional drafting exercises. In Brazil, the constitutional convention of 1987–1988, which inaugurated a transition to democracy, triggered a wide-reaching national debate over institutional choices, in particular the choice between parliamentarism and presidentialism. Similarly, Thailand's 1997 Constitution resulted from extensive public debate and participation, creating institutions that endured even after the formal constitution fell in a coup (Ginsburg 2009). To the extent that civic engagement in the building and maintenance of government institutions is healthy, cases like Brazil and Thailand engender some sympathy for Jefferson's proposal.

Later in his life, Jefferson mellowed and reacted less favorably to armed rebellions, such as the Whiskey Rebellion (Yarbrough 1998: 115). Certainly by the time he took office as President, his views of armed resistance to government had shifted in favor of institutional alternatives such as constitutional amendment, and he eventually dropped his perfectionist insistence on continuous reinvention. As he wrote:

> I am certainly not an advocate for frequent and untried changes in laws and constitutions. I think moderate imperfections had better be borne with; because, when once known, we accommodate ourselves to them and find practical means of correcting their ill effects. But I know also that laws and institutions must go hand in hand with the progress of the human mind. As that becomes more developed, more enlightened, as new discoveries are made, new truths disclosed and manners and opinions change with the change of circumstances, institutions must advance also and keep pace with the times. We might as well require a man to wear still the coat which fitted him when a boy as civilized society to remain under the regimen of their barbarous ancestors.[11]

In this more reflective Jeffersonian moment – coming several years after his proposed expiration date for the U.S. Constitution – we see some sense of the

---

[10] As Jefferson famously remarked about the Shays' Rebellion, "a little rebellion, now and then, is a good thing, and as necessary in the political world as storms are in the physical." Letter to James Madison, January 30, 1787. In another odd calculation, he noted that one rebellion in 13 states during the first 11 years of the country amounted to a rate of one per state every 150 years, and "no country should be so long without one." Letter to James Madison, December 20, 1787.

[11] Letter to Samuel Kercheval, 1816; in Jefferson, 1930.

balance between commitment and flexibility. Jefferson's notion of fit provides clues as to when we ought to jettison existing institutions. We will return to this theme of fit later.

MADISON'S CAUTION (AND RELATED ARGUMENTS)

Against the virtues of periodic constitutional renewal, one can marshal theories that support endurance. Certainly, Madison was quick to engage his friend's proposals and provide a forceful counterpoint. We describe Madison's response and related considerations.

Habits of Obedience

One response to Jefferson might be considered Burkean, even though it traces back to at least Aristotle's *Politics*. Aristotle argued that the strength of law lay in citizens' habits of obedience, which are the force that gives law power. Instability in law, he argued, can weaken the notion of law itself (*Politics* II.8; see Schwartzberg 2007: 62). He recognized, to be sure, the need for ongoing interpretation in the context of the application of law, a feature demanded by the general character of legal rules. But, frequent change in fundamental rules would seem to undercut the ability of law to inculcate habits of obedience.

Madison picked up on this theme in Federalist 49, rebutting Jefferson's critique of entrenchment in *Notes on the State of Virginia*: "as every appeal to the people would carry an implication of some defect in the government, frequent appeals would, in a great measure, deprive the government of the veneration that time bestows on everything, and without which perhaps the wisest and freest governments would not possess the requisite stability." Veneration is the first casualty of reinvention. One is certainly right to wonder about the implications of excessive veneration (Levinson 1988). However, as we argue in Chapter 4 and elsewhere, veneration of (or at least attachment to) the constitution can be very useful in helping citizens to overcome the coordination costs of defending and enforcing the constitution. Enforcement, as we will emphasize, is a guarantor of sorts of constitutional endurance. If endurance, in turn, enhances attachment to the constitution, the combination yields a virtuous cycle. There are other ways to increase citizens' attachment to the constitution, but as we will see, endurance is most certainly one of them. This virtuous cycle of attachment-enforcement-endurance is one of the persistent themes of this book and one we will return to frequently. For now, we simply posit the possibility that endurance breeds this mix of habits of obedience and attachment to the law that may be mutually reinforcing.

Issues of Process and Timing

Madison also worried about the dangers of engendering conflict and partisanship through calling into question fundamental rules:

> The danger of disturbing the public tranquility by interesting too strongly the public passions, is a still more serious objection against a frequent reference of constitutional questions to the decision of the whole society. Notwithstanding the success which has attended the revisions of our established forms of government, and which does so much honor to the virtue and intelligence of the people of America, it must be confessed that the experiments are of too ticklish a nature to be unnecessarily multiplied. We are to recollect that all the existing constitutions were formed in the midst of a danger which repressed the passions most unfriendly to order and concord; of an enthusiastic confidence of the people in their patriotic leaders, which stifled the ordinary diversity of opinions on great national questions; of a universal ardor for new and opposite forms, produced by a universal resentment and indignation against the ancient government; and whilst no spirit of party connected with the changes to be made, or the abuses to be reformed, could mingle its leaven in the operation. The future situations in which we must expect to be usually placed, do not present any equivalent security against the danger which is apprehended.[12]

Madison here ties constitution making to crisis, and is concerned that constitutional reform without crisis may become overly tainted with both self-interest and passion. As a descriptive matter, Madison is surely correct in his observation that constitutions tend to be written following catastrophic events (although, as we shall see, this coincidence has been overstated). And, certainly, in the absence of a crisis, the risk of the ordinary politics of self-interest intervening seems plausible. But, crises have risks of their own. Although the urgency of the situation can, of course, repress passions and encourage agreement, it can also prevent rational consideration of alternative institutional arrangements (Brown 2008; Horowitz 2002; Elster 1995).[13] Surely, one would not make lifelong personal commitments in times of personal crisis. There is also the possibility of focusing on past experience rather than looking forward to future problems (Scheppele 2008). Critics of the Weimar Constitution, for example, have noted that the document was drafted in the aftermath of World War I

---

[12] Federalist 49. See discussion in Yarbrough (1998: 117–124).

[13] Hume made a slightly different point about manipulability: "[W]ere one to choose a period of time, when the people's consent was the least regarded in public transactions, it would be precisely on the establishment of a new government. In a settled constitution, their inclinations are often consulted; but during the fury of revolutions, conquests, and public convulsions, military force or political craft usually decides the controversy." Hume, 1777.

and hence contained very few checks on emergency powers – which ultimately contributed to the rise of Hitler's dictatorship through constitutional means (Skach 2005). Nevertheless, Madison reminds us that crises can bring a healthy urgency to constitution making, and Jefferson's pluralist redeliberation might just be cacophonous. There is, in short, a risk of ending up with worse institutions than those that previously governed. In light of such risks, gradual change – a theme associated with Madison's contemporary, Edmund Burke – would seem far safer.

Ancillary Institutional Development

The emphasis in Burke and Aristotle on habits of obedience can be translated into modern institutional language. Written constitutions do not specify all the details of their institutions. Even if they did, it seems quite clear that simply stipulating the organization and relationships among governing institutions is not enough to ensure their implementation. A certain degree of habituation must occur before the institutions can take shape. These processes take time, and exhibit what we might call constitutional particularity (an analogue to the concept of asset-specificity in economics), a quality of being organically related to the constitutional schemes they inhabit.

To illustrate, consider one set of institutions nowhere mentioned in the American constitution: political parties. As Madison's quote above makes clear, the founders distrusted political parties and failed to foresee their imminent rise (Ackerman 2005). Yet, by all accounts the existence of parties has a constitutional character, facilitating the operation of many of the formal institutions of government. The existence of parties has since become a constitutional norm, so that more recent constitutions spend some time on their definition and regulation. Whereas fewer than 10% of constitutions in force in 1875 mention parties, over 80% of those in force in 2006 do so.[14] Political parties are also organically related to the constitutions they inhabit. U.S. political parties, for example, reflect the country's federal structure and the rules of competition laid out in the Constitution. The presidential selection system in the U.S. Constitution, at least as originally drafted, failed to anticipate the rise of political parties, and provided that the Vice-President would be the second highest vote-getter in the presidential election. Successive elections in 1796 and 1800 showed the dangers of this scheme (Ackerman 2005). The Twelfth Amendment, which rendered the system manageable (if not ideal) by requiring candidates for the two offices to run in separate contests, recognized and

[14] Data from the Comparative Constitutions Project.

consolidated a central role for parties. One could imagine that an abrupt shift in such rules, or those governing the election of the legislature, would propel changes in the party system again.

Of course, some might see the prospect of such a change in the party system as unproblematic, maybe even desirable. However, a large institutional infra-structure has developed alongside the U.S. Constitution and the investment in these institutions has been considerable. Such institutions might include the central bank, ministries, interest groups, or legislative committees – institutions that make for effective governance, yet, may not be mentioned in the consti-tution at all. Although the development of this infrastructure may proceed outside the constitution, it often requires a stable constitutional environment. One of the reasons that the U.S. Constitution works (legitimate critiques notwithstanding) is that political life has grown around it and adapted to its idiosyncratic edicts.

Constitution-particular institutions will tend to reinforce existing political arrangements. As these collateral institutions develop, they develop constituen-cies that invest in their processes and structures, and will resist efforts to over-turn or modify basic structures too drastically. These constituencies also have a crucial stake in enforcing the constitution, potentially restricting sovereign power. Tying actors' hands with respect to the rules of the game compels them to compete with more democratic methods. Periodic changes in the fundamental rules, on the other hand, might encourage opportunistic elites to engineer institutions for their short-term benefit. For example, the practice of gerrymandering electoral districts by the party in power is common to many constitutional democracies, and represents the kind of cycle of mischief that constitutions seek to prevent by taking contentious issues off the table.

Constituting the Polity

Besides the important and well-recognized role constitutions play in defining and limiting government structures, many believe that constitutions play a critical role in *constituting* the polity. By serving as a national symbol, consti-tutions can help instill in the citizenry a sense of shared identity (Breslin 2009; Murphy 1993). This function is central to Americans' view of their Constitu-tion, and may be especially important in democracies without a monarchy or other historical symbols to represent the state's sovereignty and build a "national myth," in Anderson's (2006) sense of a peoples' collective history. A strong attachment to a shared identity and the state is especially a concern in multiethnic states in which the state competes with other groups for loyalty. If citizens do not have a commitment to, or cannot agree on, the sovereignty of the state, then the very basis for participation and citizenship unravels (Linz and Stepan 1996; Rustow 1970). As Dahl (1989: 207) puts it, "the criteria of the democratic process presuppose the rightfulness of the unit itself." In states in which commitment to the state is in question, an enduring constitution can become an important source of national unity. Many of these democracies, moreover, are *new* democracies. In such states, which do not have a long history that can be packaged as a set of unifying myths such as a royal family, a coat of arms, and all the trappings and symbols of nationhood, constitutional endurance can be particularly useful in fostering national unity.

It is possible that the U.S. Constitution, with its almost eerie degree of veneration, serves this very purpose. Those concerned with describing the content of American national identity have noted the distinct place of *consent* over *descent* (Sollors 1986). The United States is built on the agreement about a set of political ideas, more than it is on a set of ethnic or cultural characteristics. Levinson (1988: 95) surveys this widely held view, quoting Whittle Johnson: "To be an American means to be a member of the 'covenanting community' in which commitment to freedom under law, having transcended the 'natural' bonds of race, religion, and class, itself takes on transcendent importance." For Samuel Huntington, the implications of the covenanting bond are profound. Abrogating the constitution, in his mind, would "destroy the basis of community, eliminating the nation and, in effect, returning its members – in accordance with the theory on which that nation was founded – back to a state of nature" (Huntington 1981). We hasten to add that this sort of "national religion" based on constitutional ideas has by no means coincided with the end of racial intolerance or the marginalization of groups by race, religion, or national origin. Indeed, we are as skeptical as any about the powerful role of national identity and the symbols that foster it. However, a strong attachment to the U.S. constitution has, quite remarkably, coincided with a degree of unity in the post–civil war United States regarding the "rightfulness of the unit." There is no difference among the various ethnic groups in the United States in the degree to which citizens express either their pride to be Americans or their identity as Americans (Elkins and Sides 2007). Whether or not this is directly relevant to the challenges to democracy in other multiethnic states, it does suggest that the constitution that persists and endears itself to the citizenry can potentially form the basis of national unity.

Economic Welfare and Endurance

A separate rationale for endurance comes from the economic sphere. Since the dawn of modern social theory, scholars have been concerned with the relationship between constitutions and capitalism (Weber 1977; Persson and Tabellini 2003). Clearly, constitutions provide a substantive basis for regulation of economic activity, and so we ought to expect that constitutions that, for example, protect property rights and create structures for the enforcement of contracts will facilitate economic development (North and Weingast 1989).

Weber's point, however, was broader than suggesting what substantive rules ought or ought not to be in a constitution. For Weber, two crucial features of rational law help to provide predictability for capitalists to order their affairs. First, law is *general*, in that it covers a large set of like situations efficiently. Second, implicit in his notion of rational law is the idea of *endurance*. Law works not only because it is general, but because it provides a stable and enduring set of rules. Even rules written at an appropriate level of generality would lose their rationality if they are frequently rewritten.

Presumably, stability in rules operates somewhat independently of their content (Fuller 1977). To be sure, economists might be skeptical that constitutions that actively discourage nonstate economic activity, such as by nationalizing industry or providing for very high tax rates, will produce long-term economic growth. But, within a certain range of regulatory schemes, longevity may help produce growth because it will allow firms to operate under a stable set of rules. This is particularly true with regard to foreigners, who rely on constitutional and legal provisions for signals as to government policy, and may be unable to avail themselves of locally based informal enforcement schemes to have contracts upheld. In short, constitutional stability may provide the necessary predictability for markets to flourish, in which case we ought to observe a correlation between constitutional duration and long-term investment and growth.

Summarizing the Debate

We are left with a series of equally plausible and desirable outcomes on either side of the normative debate about endurance. On Jefferson's side, the consequences of constitutional replacement include increased representation, a more participatory public regarding higher law, and upgrades to suboptimal or outmoded institutions. Arguments on Madison's side include a role in facilitating precommitment, binding a sometimes diverse and multitudinous citizenry, fostering the development of ancillary institutions, and a potential instrumental benefit in facilitating investment and economic activity. In most respects, the debate reduces to the perennial tension between flexibility and commitment. There is rarely any one-size-fits-all resolution to this tension; answers will depend upon one's particular desiderata and the characteristics of each constitution. Many of the arguments just listed are testable, however, and the rest of this chapter advances data and analysis that do just that.

EVALUATING THE CONSEQUENCES OF ENDURANCE

The Jefferson-Madison letters are highly speculative. Writing at the birth of what is often considered the first modern constitution, they could appeal to very little relevant evidence. Granted, countries had operated with basic laws and treaties, which are certainly analogous, and the American colonies and, states had operated with a set of constitutions prior to 1789. Nonetheless, the Jefferson-Madison claims about the merits of endurance are largely asserted *a priori*. What do more than two hundred years of constitutional experience tell us about the merits of constitutional longevity? Curiously, we cannot cite any systematic evidence from the literature on the relationship of constitutional endurance to any of the normative claims cited earlier. Indeed, despite the massive volume of work on the endurance of democratic regimes, the consequences of constitutional stability are largely undocumented. This section attempts to fill this gap by providing a baseline set of empirical findings.

The Jeffersonian Claims

We begin with an evaluation of the Jeffersonian claim about the benefits of technological progress: namely, that periodic replacement of the constitution provides a welcome update to institutions deemed to be outdated or suboptimal. For a variety of reasons, one would expect that replacements might bring improvements in design, especially as scholars, citizens, and leaders learn from their own experience and that of others. This view is one of progressive evolution, in which constitutions continuously improve over time in their adoption of new technologies of governance.

Of course, wholesale replacement may not be necessary to incorporate technological advances. However, because of the difficulty of many amendment procedures and the constraints of the original document's basic footprint, amendments are not an easy path toward comprehensive reform. Nevertheless, a review of the constitutional chronologies of some countries suggests that replacement may not represent much of an advance either. Instead of institutional "progress" through replacements, at least two alternatives seem plausible. One is what we term institutional *churn*, in which states replace their constitutions frequently but remain anchored to the same institutional choices. Socialist countries like China reflect this model, as did the Dominican Republic under the Trujillo dictatorship and other periods in its history. Venezuela, whose nineteenth-century constitutions rarely lived longer than six or seven years and differed very little from one another, seems also to have exhibited this pattern. Another plausible pattern is *cycling*, in which a country caught in the grip of two competing and irreconcilable groups will bounce back and forth between constitutions according to which group is in power. Again, we can turn to nineteenth-century Latin America, where a number of countries seem to have experienced this roller coaster, with constitutions marking the rise and fall of groups on opposite sides of issues such as the degree of centralization, the structure of executive-legislative relations, or ideology. Haiti's liberal Constitution of 1843, for example, was overturned in 1849, but served as the basis for the constitutions of 1867 and 1879. Similarly, the 1854 and 1858 constitutions of the Dominican Republic would be the touchstone for authoritarians and liberals for much of the remainder of the nineteenth century. In these environments, constitutional transitions reflect a transfer of power from one set of elites to another, and largely parallel ordinary turnover in democratic polities. Such constitutions amount to mere maps of policy and internal regime organization, without a long-term stabilizing function and without the progress that the Jeffersonian argument envisions.

One can gain some understanding of these effects by exploring patterns in the similarity of constitutions over time. Our approach is to construct a measure of similarity between any two constitutions, historic and contemporary, using our database of more than six hundred characteristics of constitutions. In this regard, we are faced with the delicate task of selecting the attributes with which to construct the measure. A related choice involves how deep down the decision tree to go. We can compare whether two constitutions make the same choices on any given list of provisions or we can compare whether two constitutions address the same issues. We employ the latter here: that is, a measure of which topics, regardless of the choices within those topics, are included in a constitution. Such a measure – call it a measure of inventory similarity – is composed of a series of binary indicator variables about whether topic x or y is covered in the constitution (e.g., does the constitution deal with the environment, telecommunications, etc.?).[15] We exclude from this list many subtopic questions that should be understood as making rather refined distinctions between constitutions. For example, we include whether the constitution contains provisions about the selection procedure for the lower (or only) house of the legislature but exclude the details about the specific selection mechanism. We also sought to choose topics that were relatively broadly distributed across time and space, although not so universal as to lack variation. The goal is to identify topics at a broad level and thus measure general areas of coverage in constitutions. The set of such variables delimits the *scope* of a constitution – a variable in its

---

[15] See the appendix for a full list of provisions that constitute the raw ingredients for both this measure of inventory similarity and the measure of scope, which we introduce later.

own right, as we will see in later chapters. Here, we simply want to ascertain the degree to which two constitutions cover the same topics. The measure is calculated by summing the number of topics for which the two constitutions agree (that is, that they both omit or include the topic) and dividing by the number of topics in the set. Accordingly, two cases score a 0 if they do not match on a single topic and a 1 if they match on every topic.[16] We calculate this measure of similarity for every country-year in the data set in which the constitution changed either by amendment or replacement.[17] The result is some 130,872 unique pairs.

The measure ranges from 0 to 1, in which any two constitutions address 0 percent and 100 percent of the same topics, respectively, and has a mean of 0.65. In observing countries with a series of constitutional replacements, we were able to identify what looked clearly like cases of churn (e.g., the Dominican Republic under Trujillo), cycling (Ecuador), and evolution (Brazil). To assess the issue of *progress* more comprehensively, it is useful to compare the U.S. Constitution, which of course has never been replaced, to the pattern of reform among Latin American constitutions, which have been replaced frequently. As is well known, early Latin American constitutions drew inspiration from the U.S. model, adopting its brand of presidentialism and many of the same rights and prerogatives for citizens and political actors. The question is whether the Latin American constitutions have evolved from this model through periodic replacement. Figure 2.1 plots the similarity of each Latin American constitution in the year of its promulgation to the U.S. Constitution circa 1789.

The figure suggests a steady decrease in overall similarity to the U.S. document over time, with a sharp decrease following World War II. Latin American constitutions, not too surprisingly, have moved significantly away from the aging U.S. model. It is possible that, in so doing, they have shed some of suboptimal elements of the U.S. document and perhaps tailored their institutions more carefully to the local environment. It could also be, however, that these countries have chased new institutional fashions that do not necessarily

---

[16] One could conceivably construct a measure across every attribute in the data, but one thereby runs the risk of over-weighting topics for which there are multiple questions in the survey (e.g., the 10 questions on executive decrees or the 46 questions on legislative electoral systems). If one constitution does not provide for decrees and another one does, it makes little sense to probe deeper and deeper into the details of decrees to distinguish them. Indeed, doing so (that is, looking for difference across some ten items on an executive decree) would lead us to believe that the constitutions differ more than they actually do. Another approach would be to focus on common constitutional elements such as rights (nearly all constitutions include at least some rights).

[17] Further detail on the content of the measure is available in the online Appendix at www.comparativeconstitutionsproject.org.

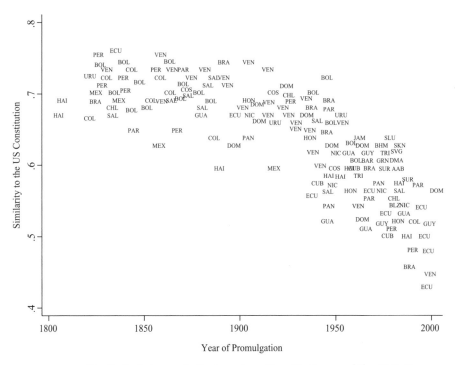

FIGURE 2.1. Similarity between Latin American Constitutions and the U.S. Constitution, over Time.

represent advances. A review of the survival of a number of distinctive components of the U.S. model sheds some light on this question.

Consider, for example, the fateful decision in Philadelphia to apportion the Senate equally among states, regardless of population. As we know, the result of the great compromise has drawn criticism from the day of its enactment, criticism that has hardly abated since. In just the last decade, three prominent scholars have written books critical of the U.S. Constitution and have listed the Senate apportionment scheme highest on their list of flaws (Dahl 2001; Levinson 2006; Sabato 2007). The four federal countries in Latin America – Mexico, Venezuela, Argentina, and Brazil – all adopted in their early constitutions a bicameral legislature with a U.S.-style apportionment scheme for their upper house. Each of these countries has since replaced their constitution several times; Argentina has had three constitutions, Mexico and Brazil seven, and Venezuela a staggering twenty-six. Of the four countries, Argentina and Brazil have retained an upper house apportionment with a fixed number of senators per state, whereas Venezuela recently adopted a unicameral

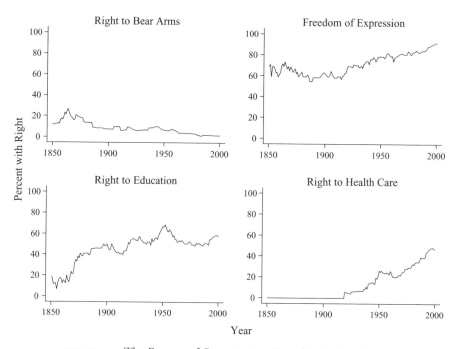

FIGURE 2.2. The Percent of Constitutions Providing Select Rights.

legislature selected through a mix of multi-member and single-member districts and Mexico has adopted a similarly mixed electoral system for the upper house in which some Senators are elected at large and some from the state. We should note that Mexico's revision was a result, not of constitutional replacement, but of amendment. We see, then, two countries which after multiple replacements have not overturned an allegedly suboptimal apportionment scheme, one that has (but only after twenty-five previous iterations), and one that made the improvement without recourse to constitutional replacement.

Nevertheless, other aspects of the U.S. model in Latin American constitutions have been "modernized" through a steady process of replacement. Rights such as those to bear arms and the non-quartering of soldiers – protections that many drafters of contemporary constitutions probably now see as anachronistic, if not suboptimal – have been eliminated. Figure 2.2 plots the percentage of all constitutions granting the right to bear arms over time, among other rights (about more, shortly). At its peak in the 1860s, nearly twenty percent of constitutions – almost all of them in Latin America – provided the right to bear arms. By the end of the World War II era, fewer than ten percent of constitutions did so, and by 2000, the United States, Mexico, and Guatemala were alone in providing this right. Consider a third controversial provision of the U.S. Constitution, life tenure for federal judges. That provision, also once a mainstay of Latin American constitutions, is increasingly rare among modern constitutions across the world, including those in Latin America (Ginsburg 2003). Modern constitutional designs lean almost exclusively toward long fixed terms or maximum age limits as alternative mechanisms to ensure judicial independence, thus solving, according to some, the potentially serious flaws of judicial life terms. We should emphasize that not all will see these prior institutions as suboptimal. Indeed, all three likely have as many (if not more) sympathizers as they do critics, at least among Americans. We note only that these three institutions – equal representation for states in the upper house, the right to bear arms, and life tenure for judges – are rarely adopted by today's constitutional drafters, perhaps for good reason. This might represent a kind of collective evolution, resulting from cross-national learning processes over time.

Technological innovation works by addition as well as subtraction. In addition to weeding out irrelevant rights and institutions, designers writing replacement documents have the opportunity to implant others. Nowhere is this more obvious than in the area of rights. As is well known, the menu of "required" rights has expanded dramatically since the days when the negative rights enshrined by the U.S. founders seemed complete. Second and third generation rights, the positive rights, are now included in international covenants as well as most national constitutions. Returning to Figure 2.2, we can observe trends in the adoption of three more rights: freedom of speech, the right to education, and the right to health care. Taken together, this chart summarizes the weeding out of a soon to be strictly *North* American right (bear arms), the continuing prevalence of a negative right (freedom of speech), and the adoption of second- and third-generation positive rights (right to education and right to health care, respectively).

This close look at the institutional trajectory of countries undergoing periodic constitutional replacement (in particular, those in Latin America) yields mixed normative results. Some cases of clearly pathological replacement (e.g., churn and cycling) are evident. Overall, however, if Latin American countries were spinning their constitutional wheels in the 1800s, they did not do so forever. Rather, the process of periodic replacement has resulted in some decided institutional modernization in the post–World War II era. Whether the benefits of these institutional advances outweigh the disadvantages of constant renewal is a more complex question. Of course, these countries might just as easily have made these changes through amendment as through replacement. As we noted, Mexico, to a large extent, has incorporated broad changes to its

1917 Constitution in this way. Many constitutions, however, include extremely difficult amendment procedures that make such changes difficult, a problem whose implications for endurance we turn to in depth in Chapters 4 through 6.

The Madisonian Claims

We turn now to an evaluation of the Madisonian claims and consider first the unifying, or constitutive, function of constitutions. The claim is that a stable, and consequently venerated, constitution will help to unify an otherwise fragmented society. The presence of such a strong covenant has seemed to serve this function in the United States, but, what about elsewhere? It is always hard to assess citizens' attachment to the state – or any identity, for that matter – but public opinion data provides at least one window onto such. Elkins and Sides (2007) look at the problem in fifty-one multiethnic states and compare the responses of members of the different constituent ethnic groups in those states to questions regarding their attitudes towards the state. Their question is whether certain institutional arrangements are more or less successful in inculcating a national identity among minorities. They find that whereas particular institutions such as federalism, proportional representation electoral systems, and democracy itself – powersharing institutions that are thought to incorporate minorities – have little bearing on a minority citizen's pride in the state, the duration of some of these arrangements matter. For example, an accumulated history of stable democracy tends to increase the national attachment of both minorities and majorities, whereas contemporary levels of democracy matter little. Recognizing that the causal direction is likely recip-rocal, we might imagine that that constitutional endurance works in the same way, so that durable institutions engender increasing loyalties and vice versa.

Next, we consider the claim of increasing fit. The claim is that longevity may affect the degree to which the de facto and de jure constitutions align. Constitutions – especially aspirational ones – may take a while to be fully implemented, so over time we may expect observable measures of the execu-tion of the constitution to match its formal provisions better. Alternatively, as written constitutions endure, they may give rise to informal understandings that diverge from the formal text. Interpretations of the constitution by judges and political actors may lead to new constitutional rules for which the formal text may have only a loose semiotic relationship. If so, our measure of the con-gruence between the formal text and de facto practice may show divergence over time (Strauss 1996).

Figure 2.3 displays the difference between de jure constitutional provi-sions and de facto practice for two aspects of constitutions: the level of

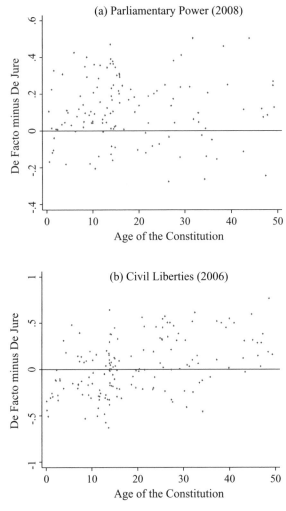

FIGURE 2.3. Difference Between De Facto and De Jure Constitutional Law, by Age of Constitution.

parliamentary power and the protection of civil liberties. To measure parliamentary power, we rely on the index developed by Fish (2006; Fish and Kroenig 2009), which is based on a set of 32 items scored by country experts circa 2007. Because experts are presumably versed in the operation of legislative power as it is manifest (hence the advantage of surveying country experts), we can treat this as a de facto measure. We then match the elements from the Fish and Kroenig (2009) survey to items in our own data in the Comparative

Constitutions Project (CCP) and are able to produce a de jure measure of legislative power for each constitution by taking the mean of the 32 binary elements. A score of 1 on either of these scales indicates the maximum amount of legislative power. For civil liberties, we rely on an index of de facto protection created by Freedom House (2006) and compare it with a comparable set of de jure indicators from the CCP.[18]

The graphs in Figure 2.3 plot the mean de facto/de jure difference for Parliamentary Power and Civil Liberties against the age of the constitution for approximately 150 and 187 cases, respectively. Higher numbers on the y axes indicate more de facto power or rights, respectively, than de jure; points close to the $y = 0$ line indicate a close fit between de jure and de facto law for the two domains. Rather than increased fit over time, what we see is that legislatures assume more power as the constitution ages and that respect for rights exceeds their provision in the constitution. To the extent that one believes that alignment between the de facto and de jure constitution is a good thing, the observed gap may be troubling. But, it is noteworthy that the divergence seems to be in the direction of greater protection of civil liberties, and greater levels of parliamentary power. Constitutions may be floors, but not ceilings on the provision of rights or power. This finding provides some support for Strauss's (1996) conjecture, and suggests, in an admittedly cursory fashion, that citizens and political elites may be learning to adapt to and manipulate the constitutional rules to achieve democratic goals.[19]

Finally, we consider some of the instrumental benefits of longevity in the form of a set of variables measuring political and economic "prosperity." None of these variables should be considered outcomes of longevity any more than individual health should be treated as the cause of individual fortunes: very likely, the relationship is reciprocal. Nonetheless, it is interesting to explore their correlation as a preamble to our epidemiological analysis later in the book. Figure 2.4 plots the average per capita Gross Domestic Product (GDP), democracy, political stability, and crisis propensity for all constitutions (current and historical) in the *n*th year of their life.[20] The data suggest that endurance is positively associated with GDP per capita, democracy, and political stability and negatively associated (albeit moderately) with crisis propensity. The

[18] For further description of how the de jure and de facto indices were created for these figures, see the online Appendix at www.comparativeconstitutionsproject.org.

[19] One might think that the observed relationship in Figure 2.2 is caused by the presence, or absence, of democracy, but actually, the relationship is even stronger when controlling for democracy.

[20] Data from World Bank (GDP); Polity II (democracy); the International Country Risk Guide (political stability); and the CCP chronology. Information on the crisis variable is found in the online Appendix at www.comparativeconstitutionsproject.org.

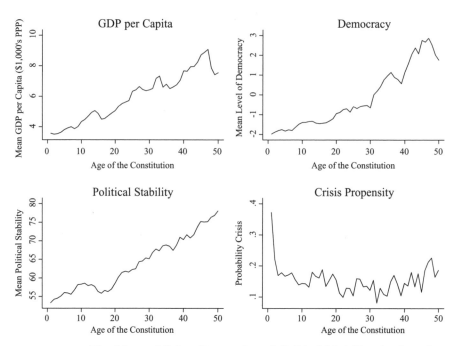

FIGURE 2.4. The Mean of Select Economic and Political Variables, by Age of Constitution.

drop in crisis propensity appears to coincide with the fourth or fifth year of life and vacillate at a low level thereafter. On average, countries are richer, more democratic, more politically stable, and experience fewer crises, as their constitution ages.

Another way to think about these effects concerns the relationship between democratic and constitutional stability. Admittedly, the relationship between regimes and constitutions is a complicated one, at least to analyze. One can ask whether constitutions that are born democratic are more likely to survive, or whether the level of democracy – or changes in such – trigger constitutional change. We take these questions up in subsequent chapters. Here, we consider whether stable democracy requires constitutional stability. If we call cases of stable democracy those states that go a generation (say, thirty years) without breakdown, we find that this outcome is strongly associated with constitutional stability. The 30 democratic regimes that have persisted uninterrupted for more than thirty years replace their constitutions, on average, once every 42 years. By contrast, the 73 authoritaritan regimes that have lasted more than thirty years replace their constitutions once every 16 years. In fact, with the exceptions of Finland, Sweden, and Switzerland,[21] no country has experienced more than fifty years of continued democracy while replacing their constitution along the way.

Of course, we recognize that these statistical associations do not demonstrate any causal relationships. One might argue, with some plausibility, that aspects of democracy, human rights, and other political goods are likely to *contribute* to constitutional endurance as much as they are caused by it. Countries where politicians protect human rights and provide public goods are less likely to experience the shocks and crises that can lead to constitutional demise. Additionally, each of the outcomes assessed here has multiple causes, and these other causes could be highly correlated with the variables of interest, leading to spurious associations. These issues are, of course, relevant to the task of sorting out the predictors of endurance – the purpose of this book – and we thus return to some of these issues in the next several chapters.

CONCLUSION AND DISCUSSION

The grand Jefferson-Madison debate, however rhetorically appealing, leaves the impression that the merits of longevity can be judged unconditionally. Even Jeffersonians, however, would agree that *some* constitutions deserve a longer lease on life, whereas Madisonians would recognize that *some* constitutions should be euthanized. Indeed, when we observe how Jefferson and Madison themselves behaved with respect to constitutional preservation, their debate appears to have been highly abstract. The preservationist Madison, for his part, played an instrumental role in hastening the death of the Articles of Confederation. Indeed, Madison's Virginia Plan, as many of his fellow delegates noted with alarm, was clearly intended to replace, not amend, the Articles. Or consider Jefferson. In splendid irony, the modernist Jefferson was in a perfect position to implement his sunset suggestion, having served as president during his proposed expiration date of the Constitution, nineteen years after it began operation in March 1789. Jefferson, however, ably preserved the constitutional bargain while president.[22] The dead, so Jefferson appears to have concluded, *should* rule the living in the case of the U.S. Constitution.

---

[21] Finland, Sweden, and Switzerland each have long lasting democratic regimes, but, their current constitutions have been alive for only 10 years, 35 years, and 10 years, respectively. However, each country's previous constitution lasted significantly longer than 50 years.

[22] No wonder then that Jefferson was accused of "pliability of principle" by John Quincy Adams, and worse by his political opponents Hamilton and Burr. Bailyn 2003: 38.

What seems like hypocrisy on the part of Madison and Jefferson is surely a matter of conditional claims. Whatever the general merits of longevity are, the optimal life span in any individual case will depend, in part, on the particular constitution and the nation it is to serve; simply put, some constitutions will age better than others. In that sense, the Articles of Confederation and the 1789 Constitution may well represent two bargains that have each enjoyed optimal life spans, anomalous to any general expiration date.

We can speculate about what sorts of constitutions will survive longer and, from a positive perspective, do exactly that in the rest of this book. From a normative perspective, however, it makes sense to note simply that – whatever the merits of longevity – *some* constitutions ought to be euthanized, whereas others ought to be preserved. Happily, as we describe in more detail in Chapter 4, many of the factors that predict longevity are also healthful from a normative perspective. To anticipate that discussion, two such important factors have to do with the *fit* of the constitution with the society it governs and the process of change.

With respect to fit, certainly no one would suggest that a constitution continue in effect if its provisions are grossly out of step with society. Constitutions are designed to stabilize and facilitate politics, but, there is certainly the possibility that constitutions can outlive their utility and create pathologies in the political process that distort democracy. Such constitutions surely deserve replacement. We are reminded of Hegel's derisive view of such documents: "How blind they are who may hope that institutions, constitutions, laws which no longer correspond to human manners, needs and opinions, from which the spirit has flown, can subsist any longer; or that forms in which intellect and feeling now take no interest are powerful enough to be any longer the bond of a nation!" (Hegel 1964: 244).

A tragic example of poor fit is the 1926 constitution of Lebanon, supplemented by the so-called National Pact of 1943, which divided power among confessional groups. A 1943 amendment provided that the sects would be represented in an equitable manner "as a temporary arrangement."[23] Under the National Pact, the president of the country would be a Maronite Christian, the Prime Minister a Sunni Muslim, and the Speaker of the Parliament a Shiite; Parliament would have a 6:5 ratio of Christians to Muslims. The idea was that a confessional basis for politics would gradually promote national unity. The arrangement was stable for some decades, but, ultimately, demographic change meant that the rigid Christian-Muslim ratio of political power became undemocratic, and the constitution no longer fit the society. The

---

[23] See Constitution of Lebanon, Article 95 (1946).

Lebanese Constitution died in a bloody fourteen-year civil war beginning in 1975. Surely a firmer sunset provision might have prevented the nominally temporary arrangement from breaking down in such a horrific manner.

One can even make a plausible case, as Dahl (2001), Levinson (2006), and Sabato (2007) have, for a comprehensive review – if not abrogation – of the bargain struck in Philadelphia in 1787.[24] Complaints about the U.S. document range from the fundamental, such as the undemocratic nature of the Senate and the pathologies of the electoral college, to more minor issues such as the use of male pronouns or the apparent restriction, in Article II, of candidates for president to those alive "at the time of the adoption of this Constitution" (Samaha 2008). Dahl, Levinson, and Sabato may identify real improvements but, by comparative standards, the U.S. Constitution fits (and fits very well). In other constitutions, the spirit has clearly flown, and, whatever the merits of endurance, these charters should be replaced.

Or, consider the manner of constitutional revision. Certainly it matters how constitutional replacement occurs. Who can defend a skeptical Madisonian view of constitutional replacement, if replacement is undertaken at the initiative and encouragement of a large majority of the citizenry? By the same token, who is to stand in the way of the jettisoning of a constitution foisted on the country by a small group of authoritarian actors? Certainly, the way constitutions come to be and the way they are replaced should have some bearing on how we view longevity as a normative matter.

On balance, our sense is that enduring constitutions are good for young democracies. Endurance allows the polity to grow into the institutions of government, but also adapts the constitution to its own needs. It allows for a stronger sense of civic unity important in multiethnic states and seems to provide a more solid foundation for economic prosperity and democratic stability. Still, our argument is quite conditional. Institutions adopted at time one need not automatically fit the society at time two, as various social, economic, and technological changes occur. When a society grows out of sync with its constitutional arrangements, pressure to renegotiate can become severe. Jefferson's metaphor of a grown man wearing his boyhood coat is apt here: when a constitution no longer fits its polity, it is altogether appropriate that the constitution be shed, lest it stunt the growth of the nation inside it.

[24] Such proposals have precedents. See Lieber (1865).

3

Conceptualizing Constitutions

INTRODUCTION

Walter Murphy, one of the most distinguished scholars of constitutional law, is fond of interrupting conversations about "constitutions" with the pointed interjection, "you mean the text, right?" To pre-empt this valuable intervention, we reiterate that we do indeed mean the text, specifically the written constitutional charter of independent countries. Ours is the (wo)man-on-the-street's idea of the constitution and very close to S. E. Finer's (1979: 15) canonical definition of constitutions as "codes of rules which aspire to regulate the allocation of functions, powers and duties among the various agencies and offices of government, and define the relationship between these and the public." Nonetheless, it is a delicate step to refer to such texts as *the* constitution in a particular country. We do so only partly for convenience, for we believe that the written text – although in some cases incomplete or even misleading – often forms the core of the *formal* constitution for most states. A focus on the formal constitution has its limits, as we will be the first to attest. Certainly, not all that is constitutional is written, and not all that is written is constitutional. However, a focus on the text pays extraordinary dividends both in terms of analytic leverage and in understanding change in the broader constitutional order. In this chapter we evaluate these potential dividends against what may appear to be substantial costs.

It is worthwhile at the outset to clarify the relevant criteria by which to evaluate our choice of concepts. A basic concern is one of transparency and mutual intelligibility. We certainly do not wish to disappoint the reader who has opened this book hoping to see documentation of the rise and fall of constitutional norms, theories, interpretive precedents, or any such extra-textual element. But, given the geographic and temporal scope of our inquiry, we also face a reasonable question of conceptual and measurement comparability.

The critical question is whether our understanding of the *constitution* of a particular country, and the criteria that we use to identify it empirically, travels well from one context to another. That is, does the question, "what is the written constitution of country x in year y?" generate basically the same kinds of answers across cases spanning the range of x and y? Note that this standard of analytic equivalence does not require that written constitutions function exactly the same way or contain the same set of provisions across spatio temporal contexts. Quite the contrary. Any such differences would conceivably be among the set of factors that one might posit as predictors of constitutional longevity, which is our focus in this book.

A further issue concerns the question of the written constitution's role in the larger constitutional order. If we are brazen enough to omit the word *written* when discussing the constitution, the reader might reasonably infer that the written text, if not *central* to the constitutional order, is at least representative of such. To be sure, the text's relationship to the larger constitutional order may not be relevant; certainly, written constitutions could be interesting enough in their own right (Brown 2001). However, we suspect that their role in the constitutional order is often (but not always) quite prominent and, thus, a focus on the written text speaks volumes about a more expansive conception of the constitution. At a minimum, focusing on the written text is a crucial first step that facilitates further work by those interested in the more expansive conception.

The chapter evaluates our choice of concept along these criteria. It begins by exploring the highly contested conceptual terrain of *constitutional identity* (Jacobsohn 2006) and describing the limits and alternatives to a *thin* understanding of the concept, such as ours. We do so less to justify our particular focus than to examine, with quite open minds, the role of the written constitution. Indeed, toward this end, a thorough accounting of the rise and fall of written constitutions, together with their content, can be enlightening. We follow our conceptual discussion by turning to the concrete. We define the written constitution and introduce the universe of cases that we have uncovered based on this operational definition. We conclude the chapter with an empirical evaluation of the role of the written constitution in the larger constitutional order. The empirical analysis focuses on three questions in particular: (1) the degree to which the provisions in written charters are representative of *de facto* law, which we began to examine in Chapter Two; (2) the substantive difference between constitutional *replacements* and *amendments*; and (3) the association between regime change and constitutional change. Our data allow us to make an original contribution to these very central questions, questions provoked by any study of formal institutions.

CONSTITUTION-AS-FUNCTION VERSUS
CONSTITUTION-AS-FORM

The principal divide regarding the use of the term *constitution* has to do with its reference to either certain functions (however achieved) or a certain form (whatever its function). The constitution in the first connotation comprises those elements (e.g., laws, theories, and interpretations) that perform what are traditionally understood as "constitutional" functions. The constitution in the second connotation refers to the formal written charter, a document that has become nearly universal among modern states.

To understand the first conceptualization, that of constitution-as-function, we should clarify what scholars view to be the traditional purposes of constitutions (Breslin 2009; Elazar 1985; Finer 1988). Arguably, the most important role of constitutions is to limit the behavior of government. Constitutions generate a set of inviolable principles and more specific provisions to which future law and government activity more generally must conform. This function – which, as if to highlight its centrality to the concept, is commonly given the namesake *constitutionalism* – is vital to the functioning of democracy. Without a commitment to higher law, the state operates for the short-term benefit of those in power or the current majority. Those who find themselves out of power may find that they are virtually unprotected, which in turn may make them more likely to resort to extra-constitutional means of securing power. By limiting the scope of government and precommitting politicians to respect certain limits, constitutions make government possible (see Przeworski 1991; Sunstein 2001; and Weingast 1997 for a broader discussion of this rationale).

A second function that constitutions serve is the symbolic one of defining the nation and its goals. A constitution operates as a device that declares the legitimacy of the perhaps fledgling or otherwise rudderless state and sets aspirations toward which the polity can set steer. This state building function of constitutions is particularly important for young states, whose citizens have strong ethnic or communal identities that may compete with their loyalty to the state. The constitution functions not so much as a set of rules as an ongoing set of practices that define the political unit. As Hanna Pitkin (1987: 169) put it, "our constitution is less something we have than something we are. This sense of 'constitution,' then, is activating and empowering, calling us to our powers as co-founders and to our responsibilities." It is in this sense that Peter Russell (1993: ix) worries that Canada – having patched together scraps of laws enacted in coordination with Great Britain – has fallen short of "constituting itself as a people."

A third and very practical function of constitutions is that they define patterns of authority and set up government institutions. Even a dictatorship needs established institutions through which to govern. Defining institutions allows those in charge to focus on the substance of government policy, rather than arguing over fundamental rules of the game. This function differs from the *constitutionalist* function of limiting government. Although the mere process of defining an institution involves *some* constraints on its behavior, these organizational maps are conceptually distinct, albeit subtly, from the *substantive* and entrenched limits on government action incorporated into the notion of constitutionalism.

No doubt these three items do not exhaust the functions of constitutions and other commentators might include many more (see Breslin 2009). The point, however, is that any consensus on the functions of a constitution marks the point after which *thicker* conceptions part ways with narrower conceptions. Thicker functional definitions identify the constitution as comprising those rules or understandings that purport to accomplish the functions just described. More circumscribed definitions limit the term to encompassing only the founding charter – that is, the nominal constitution – regardless of whether it adequately serves these purposes. Consider, thus, the functional definition offered by Walter Murphy (2007: 13):

> I shall use *constitution* [italics in original] interchangeably with what the Basic Law of the Federal Republic of Germany and the Constitutional Court refer to as the "constitutional order": the nation's constitutional text, its dominant political theories, the traditions and aspirations that reflect those values, and the principal interpretations of this larger constitution.

The notion of the *constitutional order* here is a useful synonym for constitution-as-function, denoting the larger set of constitutional elements including, but not limited to, the written text. A more subtle, but still parallel, labeling approach is to use the "big-C" and "small-c" versions of the word, in which the proper noun Constitution is reserved for the text (Brennan and Pardo 1991; Harris 1993; Michelman 1998; Palmer 2006) and the lower-case spelling refers to the broader constitutional order.

Whatever the label, the distinction is clear enough to most scholars. In the functional definition, the *constitution* equals the constitutional order; in the formal definition, the *Constitution* constitutes one element, albeit a very central element, of the larger constitutional order. Our own usage is to reserve the upper-case term for references to particular constitutions. As Murphy's definition elaborates, the functional constitution includes the collection of legal theories, norms, customs, and understandings that make up some intersubjective consensus about what constitutes the fundamental law of the land. Any terminological confusion results from the tendency of scholars to lapse into the use of the shorthand *constitution*, as both Murphy and we do, albeit with altogether different referents. Our conception may be more in tune with the vernacular conception of the constitution (few citizens, when asked, would likely speak of norms and the like when asked to identify their country's constitution), but perhaps more out of sync with the understanding of some comparative scholars. For example, Persson and Tabellini's (2003) widely read work, *The Economic Effects of Constitutions*, assumes a functional understanding of constitutions. Part of the authors' focus is on electoral systems, the specifics of which are largely absent from written constitutions (in fact, only 19 percent of written constitutions since 1789 have specified the details of the electoral system for the lower house of the legislature).[1] Persson and Tabellini are not alone. The functional approach goes back at least to the venerable British constitutional scholar Albert Venn Dicey: "Constitutional law, as the term is used in England, appears to include all rules which directly or indirectly affect the distribution or the exercise of the sovereign power in the state" (Dicey 1960: 23).

The distinction here is, on one hand, merely semantic. Like other scholars, we recognize the importance of elements other than the written charter in the larger constitutional order. Therefore, although we employ the shorthand *constitution* at times, we try to add the modifier *written* when possible (although, as we shall soon see, even that modifier may not be precise enough!). But, even the occasional use of the shorthand suggests the possibility that we elevate the written charter over other instruments in some hierarchy of the constitutional order. We are, in truth, especially intrigued by the written charter and view it as worthy of study in its own right. Written constitutions are a discrete social phenomenon, the product of self-conscious acts of purposive institutional design. Nonetheless, we harbor no illusions that written constitutions necessarily represent the larger constitutional order or that they are necessarily consequential in practice. Rather, these are empirical questions that are central to an understanding of constitutional identity. To this end, we appeal to our data on the written charter with an eye toward locating its role in the larger constitutional order.

THE ELEMENTS OF THE CONSTITUTIONAL ORDER

What elements comprise the constitutional order and how does the role and content of the written charter compare to those of the order's other constituent parts?

---

[1] Data from the LHELSYS variable from the Comparative Constitutions Project.

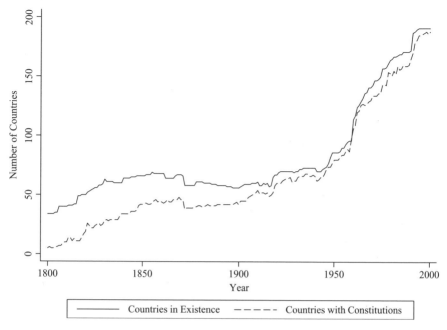

FIGURE 3.1. The Universe of States and Constitutions.

The Written Charter

As Figure 3.1 indicates, the practice of adopting a document entitled the Constitution or Basic Law is coincident with the rise of modern states. The United States, France, and Poland wrote what many take to be the first modern versions of these documents as the eighteenth century came to a close. Before then, a standard written instrument for serving the purposes we list previously had not taken hold. Certainly, other foundational documents served these ends (for example, the Magna Carta) and at least since Aristotle, the word "constitution," in its various translations, has been invoked to refer to the higher law of political jurisdictions. Aristotle, indeed, analyzed constitutions from Greek city states in the *Constitution of Athens, Politics*, and *Nicomachean Ethics*. Nevertheless, no universal model existed until the rise of the modern state at the turn of the 18th century.

The development of a modern standard was rapid and thorough. In the space of fifty years or so in the early nineteenth century, constitutions had become a thoroughly necessary chapter in the script of independent states. For new states founded after 1789, particularly in Latin America, the writing of a constitution came to be seen as obvious. Such states are under especially strong pressures to proclaim and legitimize their sovereignty. But, for others, especially those in Western Europe, the allure of this new form of contracting was considerably less seductive. For states that had functioned well enough without a constitution for years, to follow fashion and write such a document might have seemed unnecessary, if not slavish. Of course, seismic interruptions in the politics of these states (for example, a loss of sovereignty to a foreign invading power, a social revolution, or a coup) would in some ways create opportunities and challenges that are analogous to those of new states. However, it seems clear that pre-1789 states and post-1789 states faced different pressures to constitutionalize.

An examination of the chronology of constitution writing provides a better sense of some of these forces. With these data, one can very easily document the *neo natal* constitution making of post-1789 states as well as the adolescent or even mid-life adoptions of constitutions of the pre-1789 states. The panels in Figure 3.2 plot three survival curves – understood in this context as the proportion of cases not to have adopted a constitution before a given amount of time – for different populations and for different time periods. Each panel indicates, arrayed along the vertical axis, the probability that a country will *not* have adopted a constitution before the particular age arrayed along the horizontal axis. Panel (a) of Figure 3.2 plots the rate of non-adoption starting in the year of their emergence as sovereign states for states forming prior to 1789 and for states forming after 1789. The plot demonstrates quite clearly the disparity in the adoption of the constitutional form between states forming pre- and post-1789. Of those states that formed prior to 1789, fifty percent went more than 300 years without a formal constitution. Meanwhile, states that formed after 1789 adopted their first constitutions almost immediately upon birth. In fact, by the second year of life a full 85 percent of post-1789 states had adopted their first constitution, and by five years, almost 95 percent of them had such instruments. Panel (b), which plots the rate of non-adoption after 1789 for states formed prior to that year demonstrates the accelerated shift to constitutionalization following 1789, the critical year in which the U.S. constitution came into force, followed almost immediately by the French document two years later. While the move towards constitutions was rapid, a fair percentage of these states (40 percent) remained without a constitution through the end of the 19th century. Prominent examples include China, Thailand, and Iran. In Europe, the adoption rate was much higher than for other pre-1789 states. Only two states in Europe that existed prior to 1789 adopted constitutions later than 1850. Both of these (Monaco in 1911 and Andorra in 1993) are city-states and understandably atypical. On average, European states that existed prior to 1789 promulgated constitutions twenty-nine years after that year. Clearly, constitution making has become an essential symbol of the modern state, and only a handful of outliers fail to adopt.

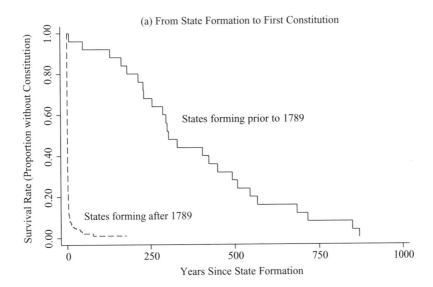

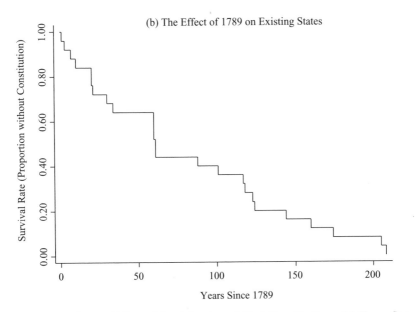

FIGURE 3.2. Survival Plots of the Adoption of First Constitutions: (a) From State Formation to First Constitution (all states). (b) From 1789 to First Constitution (pre-1789 states).

Other Texts

A focus on the formal encoded charter runs the risk of ignoring important, seemingly *constitutional* laws. Many countries, for example, enact a parallel set of *organic laws* or *institutional acts*, which serve a constitutive or organizational function and are practically, if not formally, unamendable. In other words, nonconstitutional documents can play similar functions and could, under a functionalist definition, be considered part of the Constitution writ large. Mathew Palmer (2006) has adopted precisely such an approach in describing the Constitution of his native New Zealand, and Ernest Young (2007) adopts a similar functional approach to describing the United States "Constitution Outside the Constitution." (See also Ackerman 2007, Levinson 1988: 33–36; Rubenfeld 2001a; Tribe 2008.) Young includes such materials as the Clean Water Act, as well as legal decisions of the U.S. Supreme Court. Similarly, William Eskridge and John Ferejohn (2001) focus on *super-statutes* such as the Civil Rights Act of 1964, which seem to be for all practical purposes entrenched. Members of the U.S. Supreme Court have treated the Federalist Papers as decisive on certain constitutional questions.[2] Finally, Lincoln very famously subordinated the written Constitution itself to the Declaration of Independence, depicting the latter as a golden apple within the former's silver frame.[3] Admittedly, it seems convenient for Lincoln to have done so, as it helped to legitimize his transgression of the Constitution, but, his elevated view of the Declaration had formed long before his presidency and few would quibble with his constitutionalization of the venerated Declaration.[4]

In a critical sense, one might argue that such quasi-constitutional documents differ from the formal constitution. Although these other laws share some attributes of a constitution in that they define patterns of authority and establish institutions, they lack some quintessentially constitutional qualities. For one thing, such measures are usually not adopted in the formal and deliberate manner that typically (although certainly not always!) characterizes the process of constitution making. More importantly, even in those countries where organic lawmaking is entrenched, such laws can usually be abrogated more

---

[2] *Printz v. U.S.*, 521 U.S. 898, 971 (1997) (Souter, J. dissenting) ("it is the Federalist that finally determines my position.")

[3] "The assertion of that principle, at that time, was the word, 'fitly spoken' which was proved an 'apple of gold' to us. The Union, and the Constitution, are the picture of silver, subsequently framed around it. The picture was made, not to conceal, or destroy the apple; but to adorn, and preserve it. The picture was made for the apple — not the apple for the picture." Basler 1953: 168.

[4] We thank Gary Jacobsohn for pointing out that Lincoln's commitment to the Declaration had been established long before he had any reason to invoke it.

easily than can a constitution. This idea of entrenchment is important to the status of the constitution as higher law. We see constitutions as not only being higher law (a characteristic that they may share with organic acts and other rules), but as *highest* law.

Nontextual Instruments

Modifications in the constitutional order, which are not encoded anywhere, may arise either in ordinary or constitutional law. In any constitutional system, the language of constitutional text is modified and interpreted by political actors and these modifications can utterly transform the original, and even explicit, textual understandings. In the United States, for example, justices of the Supreme Court have filled in the details of the vague eighteenth century document to make it suitable for modern life. They have done so notwithstanding the lack of an explicit textual basis for constitutional review. In other countries, such as Great Britain, political practices may evolve and be accepted as *constitutional* even if never written into law. These norms are sometimes called constitutional conventions or unwritten constitutional rules (Elster, forthcoming; Grey 1975; Horwill 1925: 21; Krishnamurthy 2009; Llewellyn 1934; Munro 1930; Tiedeman 1890; Young 2007). Practices as central to the British government as the requirement of a monarch to sign bills that pass both houses of parliament remain unwritten, yet, there has been no transgression of this particular norm since 1708.

Sometimes, unwritten constitutional norms serve to supplement the written text, helping to effectuate its provisions. The existence of judicial review in the United States is itself not captured in the constitutional document, although most scholars believe that the founders intended it (Marcus 1992; Treanor 2006). Similarly, the right to privacy is not written, but found only in the so-called penumbra of the text.[5] Other constitutional norms explicitly conflict with the written text. For example, in Australia, the governor general has the nominal power to dismiss the prime minister, but this power has not been used for the most part. However, in 1975, the governor general dismissed the Labor prime minister and called new elections because the Senate, controlled by the opposition, refused to vote the budget. This modified the constitutional understanding, even though it was perfectly consistent with the written text.[6] Another example occurred in France in 1962, when President Charles DeGaulle proposed and achieved a successful amendment of the constitution

---

[5] Griswold v. Connecticut, 381 U.S. 479 (1965).
[6] The Labor Party was also punished in the polls, confirming for some the modification of the constitutional convention. Elster, forthcoming, at 17.

by referendum, even though the Constitution of 1958 does not explicitly allow for amendment in this fashion. This amendment thus changed the constitution in a formal sense (by shifting to direct election of the President) and in an informal sense (by setting a precedent for amendment through referendum). These types of unwritten rules modify and supplement the formal text, often rendering the original text a very poor guide to present understandings. In such situations, the written constitution may stand in an ambiguous semiotic relationship with the unwritten constitution.

The unwritten constitution poses a significant challenge to comparative research. Efforts to examine the unwritten constitution are bedeviled by evidentiary and definitional problems. To take the American example, it seems clear that the founders had a set of understandings that underpinned the written text, even if not contained in it. But, the precise bounds of these understandings are subject to endless debate. For some, they include the moral sentiments of the founders (Ryn 1992; Levinson 1988: 33–36). For others, they include ideas and institutions that are not based in clear textual instruction, but are treated as constitutional for practical purposes, such as the establishment of judicial review. This rule of recognition problem is significant: even if a behavioral regularity is clear, it is not certain whether it represents the existence of a norm or simply a contingent practice that is subject to change. Given the scope of our inquiry, these problems are multiplied many times. It is difficult to determine exactly what norms ought to be included in the constitutional order in only *one* country; doing the same for multiple countries across time and space, while maintaining comparability, would be nothing short of Herculean.

To illustrate the difficulties involved, consider, for example, the longstanding practice in the United States of limiting the president to two terms.[7] There is no such provision in the original constitution. Indeed, the founders had worried that constraining presidents in such a way would encourage disempowered executives to make mischief. In Federalist #72, Publius worries about danger to the "peace . . . to have half a dozen men who had credit enough to be raised to the seat of the supreme magistracy wandering among the people like discontented ghosts, and sighing for a place which they were destined never more to possess." Nevertheless, George Washington, who declined to run for a third term, set a clear precedent followed by each of his successors, even those like Jefferson and Andrew Jackson, who clearly enjoyed sufficient popularity to win a third time. By the time that President Ulysses Grant was encouraged by a friend to run for a third term, a popular outcry ensued with some insisting

---

7 One might alternatively consider the norm against packing the Supreme Court, which was assumed by some to have a constitutional quality during and after the New Deal, even though it had been utilized by President Grant earlier in American history. Ackerman 2005: 1796–1797.

that Washington's precedent amounted to an unwritten law (Horwill 1925: 22). Incumbent President Grover Cleveland's own Democratic Party, to ensure intraparty rotation of candidates, even attempted to move the norm into written form, by adopting in its party platform in 1896 a statement recognizing the two-term limit as "law." One might assume, then, that the unwritten constitutional norm had been established, for it had led a major political party to set aside its own best candidate in an election it proceeded to lose.

The scope and limits of the norm, however, were tested by Theodore Roosevelt. Having already served a full term as well as most of the term vacated by the death of James McKinley, Theodore Roosevelt sought to win another term in 1912, by running on his independent Bull Moose ticket. While campaigning, Roosevelt was shot by a man who justified his actions "as a warning that men must not try to have more than two terms as President" (Horwill 1925: 95). Roosevelt was ultimately defeated. But, the whole discussion raises questions: does Roosevelt's defeat establish the existence of the convention? Or, is the fact that he gathered millions of votes evidence that the convention did not exist? If the convention was extant, when was it established? By George Washington, whose refusal of a third term was later used by others to justify its existence? By Grant? By the shooter of Roosevelt? Even if one believes that such a convention existed (and many authors did before Franklin Delano Roosevelt's election to a third term in 1940), did it include a nonconsecutive third term? And did FDR violate it or simply run under an implied wartime exception? The only thing that is clear is that the norm was constitutional once Alabama ratified the Twenty-second Amendment on May 14, 1951. And, this clarity helps justify our focus on written documents and formal processes.

ANALYTIC CHALLENGES IN THE CROSS-NATIONAL STUDY OF WRITTEN CONSTITUTIONS

In this section, we move from conceptualization to measurement. We begin by sketching some analytic challenges in comparing the empirical manifestations of alternative constitutional concepts across contexts. We then present a set of operational rules for identifying constitutions and report details of our census of constitutions since 1789.

Comparability and the Problem of Conceptual Stretching

Our endeavor is wide-ranging, both historically and geographically. Given this scope, issues of comparability necessarily arise. Some might wonder about the wisdom of comparing the longevity of documents written two hundred years or 10,000 miles apart. The relevant concern is essentially one of excessive heterogeneity in the sample. To wit, can we reliably compare twentieth century constitutions to those that existed in the nineteenth century? Do constitutions in democracies operate the same way as they do in authoritarian settings? Is what we call a constitution in Nigeria the same as what we call by that name in Brazil?

Surely, the contents of constitutional documents, their place in society, and their impact will differ across context. For example, scholars often dismiss some Latin American constitutions of the nineteenth century and those of the Soviet Union as not "mattering" (but see Brown 2008). This may be so in some sense, but the status of these constitutions as mere parchment does not condemn our enterprise. Rather, as we shall see, the *bite* of any individual constitution will have quite a bit to do with how long it will last. As such, these conceptual differences among constitutions are not threats to comparability, but, rather, explanatory factors in the analysis. To put this another way, consider Giovanni Sartori's (1970, 1984) discussion of *conceptual stretching*, the problem in which a concept that is highly relevant in one context may not be easily adapted to another. In our case, it might be argued that written constitutions are meaningful in some countries, but not in others. The solution, following Sartori, would be to ascend the *ladder of abstraction* (or *ladder of generality*, as some prefer) by comparing a more encompassing concept – in this case, the constitutional order – across contexts. In that way, cases that make use of different instruments or forms of lawmaking (say, written charters versus institutional acts) can be compared. However, we are focused on a particular form *whether or not it takes on the same meaning across cultures.* Indeed, to put the point more emphatically, we welcome significant variation in the meaning of constitutions across contexts, as we suspect that such factors will in part explain their survival.

Moreover, on a practical level, the conceptual difficulty of determining the precise scope of the small-c constitution across cases, as well as the empirical challenge of identifying and locating the various elements that compose it, argue against treating it as an analytic unit for large-n studies. In contrast, the deliberate, public, and discrete character of the big-C constitution yields an objective historical record of activity across a wide set of cases, which is invaluable to the analyst of institutional reform. Finally, we are confident that even those scholars who think that the broader constitutional order is the proper analytic unit would acknowledge that the big-C constitution provides a starting point for identifying the scope of the small-c constitution.

Identifying Constitutions

We identify written constitutions by invoking a set of three conditions. The first is sufficient to qualify the document(s) as a constitution, whereas the others are applied as supplementary tests if the first is not met. Constitutions consist of those documents that either: (1) are identified explicitly as the *Constitution, Fundamental Law,* or *Basic Law* of a country[8]; OR (2) contain explicit provisions that establish the documents as *highest* law, either through entrenchment or limits on future law; OR (3) define the basic pattern of authority by establishing or suspending an executive or legislative branch of government.[9]

Thus, our criteria are principally nominal, but, admittedly, include *some* broadly functional elements as secondary and tertiary considerations. In the Israeli case, for example, we define the constitution as the series of Basic Laws (as per condition 1), even though not all are superior to ordinary legislation and thus do not meet condition 2, and few of them meet condition 3. The functional criteria of highest law and establishing basic authorities help us to resolve problematic cases such as Canada, New Zealand, and Saudi Arabia.[10] In the case of Saudi Arabia, the holy Qur'an is the highest law and there is no formal constitution; however, we treat the three 1992 Royal Decrees establishing the basic system of government, provinces, and the consultative majlis (assembly) as constituting the government (Aba-Namay 1993). This is a case that meets condition 3, but not 1 or 2. Fortunately, at least for analytic purposes, formal constitutions are the norm and defining a state's constitution is largely straightforward.[11]

We exclude the United Kingdom from our sample entirely. Although it is sometimes said that the United Kingdom's constitution is unwritten because of the operation of many constitutional conventions governing important questions, it is more accurate to describe the constitution as uncodified (King 2007: 5). Many of the rules that can be described as constitutional in the United Kingdom are written down, and this is increasingly true after rounds of European-influenced constitutional reform in recent years. Nevertheless, the lack of entrenchment or a clear rule of recognition distinguishing constitutional from ordinary regulation of governing institutions leads us to treat the United Kingdom as a somewhat special, sui generis case, a category

---

8 One could quibble about whether the terms "fundamental law" and "basic law" are even nominally equivalent to "constitution." Certainly, some founders, such as those in Israel and Germany, adopted these names precisely to differentiate them from constitutions and signal the temporary nature of the laws. However, there are very few of these cases and most of them satisfy conditions two and three.

9 This set of conditions is similar to criteria used by Elster (1995: 364; forthcoming) and Negretto (2008) in his parallel study of recent Latin American constitutions.

10 Elster's forthcoming draft, *Unwritten Constitutional Norms,* adds several other criteria one might use, including the idea that a constitution regulates fundamental aspects of life (which we might call a functional view); a constitution is adopted by a specially convened assembly; and a constitution regulates statutes (this is the key criterion for Elster).

11 Roughly, 90 percent of constitutional materials in the sample qualify based on condition 1. The other ten percent qualify based on conditions two or three.

whose exclusive membership is unlikely to expand or contract in the near future (King 2007: 363).

Using our criteria, we have collected data on the constitutional history of every independent state (again, save Britain) from 1789 to 2006.[12] The year 1789, of course, marks the effective year of the United States' Constitution, the widely reputed "first" document of its kind. Certainly, other documents of quasi-constitutional status predate the U.S. document (e.g., the Magna Carta). Nevertheless, such documents are sufficiently rare and ambiguously constitutional that 1789 makes for an appropriate and practical beginning for our study.

Within this period, we include all independent states that existed for at least five years during the sampled time frame, for a cumulative total of 220 states. We recognize that defining states and their existence across time is not a simple matter. In our estimation, Gleditsch and Ward's (2006) list is the most authoritative and careful accounting of state births and deaths. As such, we base our sample of states on their list of states (including microstates), except where otherwise noted. We exclude jurisdictions such as subnational states and provinces for both practical and theoretical reasons.[13]

For each country, we record the promulgation year of *new, interim,* and *reinstated* constitutions, the year of *suspension,* and the year of any *amendments* (defined shortly). The promulgation of new, interim, and reinstated constitutions marks the beginning of *constitutional systems.* Constitutional death occurs when these systems are replaced by other new, interim, or reinstated documents or when they are formally suspended. In cases of state dissolution, we mark the constitution as having exited the analysis as opposed to having died, as the constitution's destiny is simply unknowable without a state to host it. The re-entry of the dissolved state, as in the case of some reconstituted pre-Soviet republics like Estonia, of course often coincides with a new constitution. However, even if such states reinstate their previous constitution, we start the clock anew. Our definition of constitutional life span has the virtue of clarity, although it may err on the side of formalism in cases in which a constitution ceases to be effective as a practical if not legal matter; we think of

---

[12] Gleditsch and Ward (2006) catalogue the existence of states from 1816–2006. For the years between 1789 and 1816, we use data about the birth of states from the Issue Correlates of War Project, or ICOW (Hensel 2006).

[13] Endurance of such constitutions is likely to reflect a different logic because of the relationship with the broader national constitutional structure. In the United States, for example, the federal constitution guarantees to each state a republican form of government. This guarantee reduces the costs of rewriting the constitution, as fundamental stability is assured by external forces. In such circumstances, we would expect less endurance for state documents generally. See Berkowitz and Clay (2005) for a test of state constitutional endurance in the United States.

these constitutions as persisting on life support.[14] Our census reveals a universe of 935 new constitutional systems, of which 746 have been replaced or suspended, and 189 are still in force.[15] The Appendix (Table A.1) identifies each of these 935 constitutions. We have located almost all the founding constitutional texts for these systems and many of the texts describing their amendments, and have recorded a wide array of characteristics about their content.

WRITTEN CHARTERS IN WIDER PERSPECTIVE

We now turn to an assessment of three thorny issues regarding the role of written constitutions in the larger institutional landscape. In particular, we consider the degree to which written charters dovetail with the larger constitutional order and constitutional practice, the impact of constitutional replacements versus amendments, and the relationship between constitutional change and regime change (that is, transitions to and from democracy).

Issues of Completeness and Representativeness of the Written Charter

We are now in a position to say something about the relationship of the written constitution to the larger constitutional order. In theory, it could be that the written charter and the functional constitution are effectively one and the same. However, because the content of written constitutions can vary significantly, it is possible that many written constitutions fail to specify functions that might be deemed crucial to the constitutional order. Some glaring omissions from most texts are readily apparent. For example, in a general sense, we might expect constitutions to regulate relations between citizen and state and provide some intertemporal limits on government action. With this expectation, surely written constitutions would frequently include such crucial issues as election laws, which generate great incentives for temporal majorities to manipulate the rules. We noted earlier that only 19 percent of constitutions specify, in any detail, the electoral system for the lower house of the

---

[14] An interesting example of this phenomenon comes from the People's Republic of China during the cultural revolution. A conventional understanding of Marxist constitutions is that they matter primarily as a descriptive template for the formal government machinery and not as a device to protect rights or citizens. During the cultural revolution, most government organizations and even party local committees were shut down. The National People's Congress did not meet for a decade and the president of the country was purged, jailed, and left to die in prison (in 1969). The office of the presidency went unfilled, until the Constitution of 1975 abolished it; the office was revived with the 1982 Constitution.

[15] As of this writing, we have collected the constitutional text for 720 new constitutions and the text or summary information for 1,687 out of roughly 2,200 amendments. A small number of countries had suspended constitutions as of 2005, and this is one reason the number of constitutions in force is somewhat less than the number of extant countries.

legislature. Instead, most constitutions either explicitly leave to ordinary law the design of electoral systems for the legislature (approximately 30 percent of constitutional texts since 1789) and the drawing of districts (approximately 10 percent since 1789), or do not mention election law issues of either kind at all (approximately 30 percent and 60 percent, respectively, since 1789).[16] Also, 47 percent of constitutions in our study do not even mention political parties, which are surely central to constitutional governance in both democracies *and* many autocracies.[17] Only 21 percent of constitutions in our study mention central banks, whose constitutionally protected independence is increasingly considered essential to macroeconomic stability.[18]

On the other hand, constitutions frequently include provisions for relatively minor matters, such as excruciating detail on national symbols such as anthems and flags. Afghanistan's 1977 document, for example, provides that the flag "consists of black, red and green colors arranged horizontally in fixed proportions from top downwards with the national emblem of the state affixed in its upper left hand corner."[19] The Constitution of Bangladesh states that "the national emblem of the Republic is the national flower Shapla (nymphaeanouchali) resting on water, having on each side an ear of paddy and being surmounted by three connected leaves of jute with two stars on each side of the leaves."[20] Normative theories founded in constitutional entrenchment or precommitment theory have a hard time explaining this: surely no drafter believed that future seamstresses might willfully fail to connect the three leaves of jute.

If not trivial, some constitutional provisions seem to be almost instantly anachronistic. For example, drafters sometimes specify dollar amounts in apparent ignorance of the forces of inflation. The American drafters of the Seventh Amendment famously allowed for a jury trial in all suits for more than twenty dollars. The British North America Act of 1867, rechristened the Constitutional Act of 1867 in 1982, provided for precise dollar figures for the amount of federal transfers to each province, and many constitutions have specified minimum values for claims to be eligible for appeal. Surely, these details could be better handled by ordinary law, which can be adjusted as the value of currency fluctuates.

In sum, many features that have become conventional to include in a written constitution hardly qualify as candidates for entrenchment and do not seem

---

[16] Data from the LHELSYS and DISTRICT variables from the CCP.
[17] Data from the PART variable from the CCP.
[18] Data from the BANK variable from the CCP.
[19] Constitution of Afghanistan (1977), Art. 23. The Article goes on to state the "the Definition and the Proportions with the National Anthem shall be regulated by law" implying that the specified details were of sufficient importance to necessitate constitutional entrenchment.
[20] Constitution of Bangladesh, Art. 4.

to play any plausible constitutionalist function. Nor do terms such as dollar amounts seem to help define the state: indeed, given modern understanding of the forces of inflation, they can make the constitution seem silly. If our understanding of the constitution is one of defining core institutions and setting out key principles, it is clear that not all terms in written constitutions are always constitutional (Strauss 2001).

Whatever one's view of the relative importance of textual versus nontextual sources of higher law, we think that it is extremely unlikely that *change* in one is completely independent of change in the other. We are not asserting that formal institutional change always, or even generally, precedes informal change; it may be more likely that informal changes are ratified by formal changes adopted only later (Strauss 2001). We do think, however, that ruptures in the formal system represented by constitutional births and deaths are likely to correspond with changes in informal constitutional understandings. Formal constitutional replacement may *reflect* underlying ruptures that have already occurred or may *cause* changes in informal understandings, but either way we expect that there will be *some* change in the underlying intersubjective view of the constitution when formal change occurs. This assumption is not critical to our enterprise, but it is useful to assess the relationship between the written charter and behavioral aspects of the constitutional order.

A complete evaluation of the relationship between formal constitutional provisions and constitutional practice is an enormous enterprise best left for another volume. However, we provide some suggestive evidence here. We assess the *bite* of the formal charter in two substantive domains: the power of the legislature and the protection of rights.

Figure 3.3 plots de jure constitutional provisions of parliamentary power and civil liberties against the de facto practice for the countries in our sample in 2006. We use the measures developed in Chapter Two. The de facto measures are Fish and Kroenig's parliamentary powers index and the Freedom House civil liberties index, which capture experts' perceptions of the two constructs. The de jure measures are conceptually equivalent to these two, except that the source information comes from our data on the content of constitutions.[21]

Although there is a fair amount of variation in both graphs in Figure 3.3, it is clear that the constitutional provisions regarding parliamentary power describe the reality in these countries much better than do the constitutional provisions about civil liberties. The correlation between the de jure and de facto measures of parliamentary power is a moderately strong 0.38, whereas the de jure and de facto measures of civil liberties correlate at only 0.07. The de jure/de facto relationship in Figure 3.3 demonstrates the more general finding

21 See the online appendix to this book at comparativeconstitutionsproject.org for more detail.

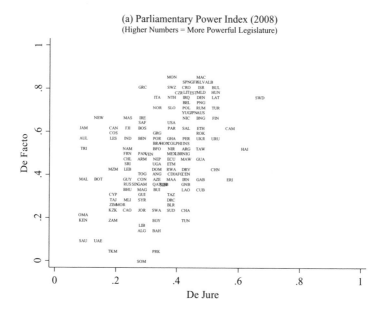

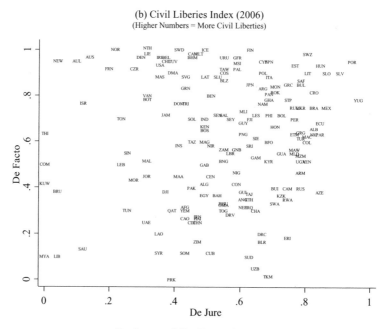

FIGURE 3.3. De Jure and De Facto Constitutional Law.

in our data that the functioning of important political institutions is described fairly accurately in constitutions, but the extent to which rights provisions are implemented in practice varies dramatically across countries, with some countries promising more than they deliver and others delivering more than they promise.

The Sometimes Fuzzy Line between Amendment and Replacement

In our formulation, the distinction between an amendment and a replacement is important. Amendments, as we shall see, forestall constitutional death and, thus, mistaking one for the other is literally fatal. We call a constitutional change an amendment when the actors claim to follow the amending procedure of the existing constitution and a replacement when they undertake revision without claiming to follow such procedure.[22] Thus, the U.S. constitution is a replacement and not an amendment of the Articles of Confederation, as initially envisioned, precisely because the founders ignored their original charge and its accompanying procedures. Of course, we should note that replacements and amendments are sometimes only nominal distinctions. In some cases, drafters have thoroughly revised a constitution with a set of amendments. For example, South Korea's six republics have each involved complete constitutional overhauls adopted through the formal process of amendment of the previous constitution. Other countries make minor changes to a document and yet christen a new constitution. Trujillo's constitutions in the Dominican Republic followed this pattern, as did Afghanistan's 1990 constitution, which is almost identical to the previous constitution adopted in 1987.

Ackerman's (1993) magisterial account of constitutional evolution in the United States case raises the issue quite evocatively. Ackerman describes two noticeable shifts (post–civil war and post-Depression) in the character and provisions of the U.S. constitution, which were affected via amendment and interpretation, respectively. One reading of Ackerman is that the United States has experienced not *one* constitution, but *three* (or two and four, respectively, if one counts the Articles). The claim very nicely emphasizes some surprisingly sizable shifts in the understanding and implementation of what is widely seen as a preternaturally stable document. However, if we compare the changes of

---

[22] For events whose exact process is unclear, we rely upon the nominal classification as it appears in historical texts, a classification that likely matches our criteria. For example, some scholars claim the 2006 constitutional amendments in the Ukraine, which helped complete the Orange Revolution were unconstitutional for procedural reasons. We do not enter this debate and follow the nominal classification of these as amendments rather than as constitutional replacements.

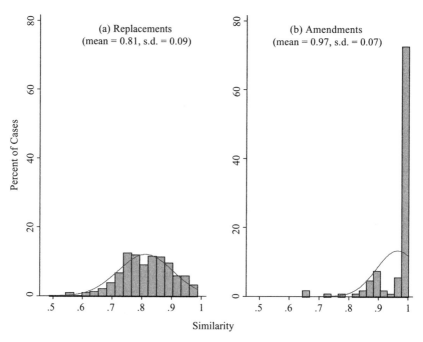

FIGURE 3.4. Distribution of Similarity Scores Pre- and Post-revision.

the 1860s and the 1930s in the United States to constitutional replacements in other, less stable, countries, the U.S. story – even during these tumultuous moments – is inescapably one much more of continuity than of change. As with many other topics, the U.S. experience looks very different when viewed in comparative perspective than it does in isolation.

We can explore the distinction between amendment and replacement systematically with the help of our data on the content of constitutions across time. We utilize the similarity index developed in the last chapter to compare the similarity of constitutions pre- and post-amendment with that of constitutions pre- and post-replacement.[23] If the change in content associated with amendments is substantial, or at least close to that of replacements, then it may behoove us to rethink the distinction between amendments and replacements. On the other hand, if replacements typically involve greater changes than amendments, our approach seems more promising.

Our sample for purposes of this analysis includes 349 replacements and 106 amendments that we can compare to the prerevision document. Figure 3.4 presents the distribution of these two sets of cases. The difference between

[23] The contents of the similarity index are found in the appendix.

the two distributions is as expected. On average, the replacements match their predecessor in 81 percent of topics, whereas amendments do so in 97 percent. The distributions of the two sets do overlap, however, and it is worthwhile to inspect the cases more carefully.

Consider a few prominent constitutions, often seen as pioneering documents. We find that the celebrated Mexican Constitution of 1917 does not appear especially pioneering, at least with respect to scope; it matches the coverage of its predecessor, the 1857 Constitution, in 87 percent of the topics. A powerful legacy is one reason, apart from its striking beauty, that we celebrate Monroy's paean to the 1857 Mexican Constitution on our cover. More typical of replacements are the Brazilian Constitution of 1988 and Germany's Weimar Constitution of 1919, which match the previous constitutions from these countries at 77 and 79 percent of topics, respectively (just below the sample average for replacements). The case with the most radical departure from the status quo is Libya's 1969 replacement of its 1951 document; the two constitutions address (or mutually omit) only 49 percent of the same provisions. At the other end of the distribution, there appear to be a fair number of cases that, at least by topic, do not cover new ground. The vast majority of these are Latin American constitutions from the nineteenth and early twentieth centuries. In this light, it is interesting to review the serial constitution makers from the Caribbean (the Dominican Republic, Haiti, and Venezuela), which together account for roughly 10 percent of the world's constitutions. Should we think of these long series of documents as a set of revisions of the same basic structure or do they represent more fundamental changes?[24] Most of Venezuela's early constitutions are in fact remarkably similar to their predecessors. The average similarity score is 0.94, and the only two constitutions whose similarity-with-predecessor score comes close to or even below the sample average for replacements are the 1961 and 1999 constitutions at 0.84 and 0.80, respectively. Figure 3.5 provides a graphical sense of these and other country patterns. Peru, Bolivia, and the Dominican Republic – all generous contributors to the worldwide total number of constitutions – exhibit a pattern similar to that of the Venezuela, with what appear to be a series of highly similar constitutions in the nineteenth century followed by some mild departures from the status quo after WWII. It could be, of course, that these constitutional pairs differ not in their agenda (the point of comparison that our measure of similarity captures), but in their institutional choices within topics. Such a comparison deserves further analysis.

If we turn now to amended constitutions, we again see variation in their similarity-to-predecessor, although at a significantly higher mean than that

---

[24] Our sample does not yet include the full set of constitutions from the Dominican Republic (33) or Haiti (27), but we do have 24 of Venezuela's 26 constitutions in the data.

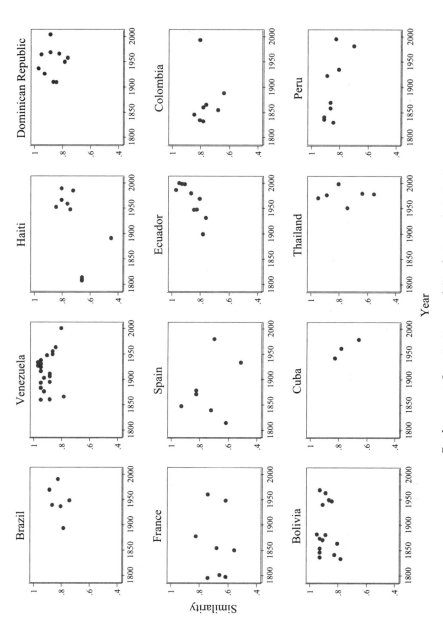

FIGURE 3.5. Replacement Constitutions and Similarity to their Predecessors.

58

of replacements. The average amended constitution covers 97 percent of the same topics as the previous document, prior to amendment. This is necessarily a noisier estimate as our sample of amendments is smaller.

For most countries, then, replacement results in a more dramatic change in the·scope and coverage of a constitution than does constitutional amendment. Two cases – the cumulative amendments to the Mexican Constitution of 1917 and the 1987 amendments to the South Korean Constitution of 1948 – appear to change the scope of the previous constitution dramatically. We should emphasize that these scores represent the *cumulative* effects of multiple amendments, some of which were more incremental than others. That comparison is relevant, however, if one is concerned about the drift of constitutions following a series of amendments and not just the effect of a single amendment. It also calls our attention to the fact that change need not be abrupt. In these cases, secular change has resulted in a constitution much different from the original. Indeed, the accumulated change in scope of the nonreplaced Mexican constitution between 1917 and 2003 (similarity $= 0.69$) is more substantial than the change reflected by promulgation of the celebrated 1917 Constitution itself (again, whose similarity score with the 1857 document is 0.87).

Constitutional Change versus Regime Change

Constitutional change and regime change would seem to be so closely related that a word of distinction seems warranted. From a rather broad perspective, we should expect that countries with a high degree of constitutional instability would also display a high degree of regime instability. In fact, a history of volatility in democracy scores (in this case, the standard deviation of a country's historical Polity score) is moderately correlated with a country's frequency of constitutional replacement ($r = 0.54$). The strength of this simple relationship invites the question of whether regime change and constitutional change are one and the same. If so, then our analysis reduces to one of explaining regime durability, for which theory and evidence are legion. In fact, the two constructs are closely related, but not synonymous. Constitutional replacements occur within one year on either side of a regime transition in roughly 19% of cases of democratic transition and 27% of cases of authoritarian transition.[25] Regime change, then, is not a sufficient condition for constitutional change, nor is it a necessary one. Looking at the relationship from the other side, of the total number of constitutional replacements, about 19% come into force within one year of a regime transition. Taking these two statements together, we can say that a small, but significant, minority of regime transitions

[25] Transitions are defined as a move from three or more points on the 20-point Polity scale.

are accompanied by constitutional replacement and, likewise, a small minority of constitutional replacements coincide with regime transition. We will investigate any causal link between the two phenomena in later chapters. Suffice it to say here that the two phenomena are clearly linked, but not one and the same.

One can understand these dynamics more concretely by observing trends in the level of democracy and the incidence of new constitutions within individual countries. Figure 3.6 presents such data for six countries, Brazil, Chile, Japan, France, the Dominican Republic, and Colombia. Democracy (Polity) scores are plotted across time and vertical lines mark the promulgation of new constitutions.

For three of the six countries, new constitutions in these countries correspond with major shifts in the structure of authority. The dates of each of Brazil's constitutions, for example, mark the milestones of its democratic history almost perfectly. Japan's overall history has been one of punctuated equilibrium with jump-shifts in a democratic direction marked by constitutional change. French history also shows significant shifts in levels of democracy around the time of constitutional change, with new constitutions corresponding to the oscillation between republic and empire. As one would imagine, however, some countries exhibit exceptions to this rule. Chile's 1980 Constitution, commissioned by Pinochet, dutifully institutionalized the authoritarian practices initiated by the coup in 1973. However, the Pinochet document has endured through the transition to democratic rule, albeit with significant amendments. Colombia is exceptional in the other direction, in that its multiple regime transitions have occurred under a single constitutional regime and 1991's constitutional change was not coincident with regime transition. These phenomena are fairly uncommon in Latin America, where most major shifts are celebrated with new constitutions. As the case of the Dominican Republic makes clear rather emphatically, however, regime change is not a necessary condition for constitutional change. The thirty-three Dominican constitutions since 1844 (the most of any country) have covered a period that has remained consistently authoritarian, and twentieth-century dictator Trujillo was responsible for four of them during his rule alone.

Figure 3.6 also provides clues as to what is at stake in our inquiry. We have a number of examples like the Dominican Republic, in which regime change is rare, but constitutional change is frequent. There are also countries in which regime change is as frequent as constitutional change, such as Greece, which has had roughly twelve of each, or Uruguay, which has had roughly six of each. What we do *not* observe, however, is a country with a stable democracy and frequent constitutional turnover. Even the French have had a number of enduring

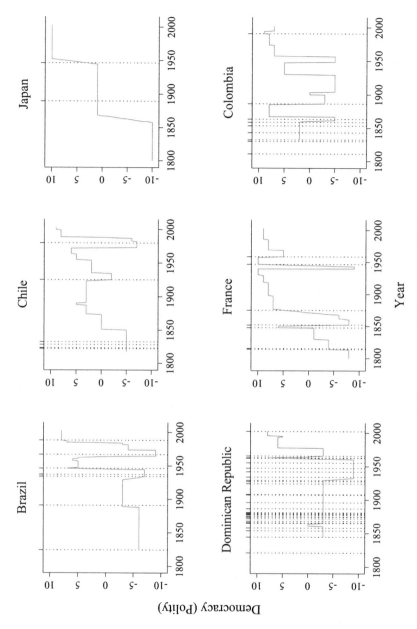

FIGURE 3.6. Democracy and Constitutional Replacement.

61

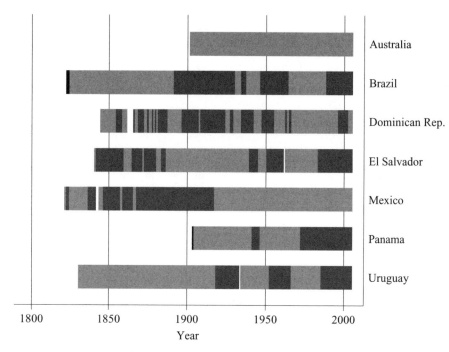

FIGURE 3.7. National Historical Patterns of Constitutional Life Span.
Note: The alternating shades of gray represent the duration of constitutions. The white space in some states' bars indicates periods when a constitution was suspended and a new constitution had not yet been put into force, and the black sections on the left side of some states' bars indicates the period between state formation and promulgation of the first constitution.

constitutions, and the current 1958 document is now the world's twenty-ninth oldest. Following on the previous chapter, this pattern suggests that finding the keys to constitutional stability is a worthwhile endeavor to the extent that democratic consolidation and constitutional stability reinforce one another.

One might think that the patterns we have described thus far are driven by country characteristics, with some places being particularly inhospitable to constitutional longevity. But, there is sufficient intranational variation to suggest that this is not the case. Whereas the Dominican Republic and the United States represent the extremes of the stability spectrum, many other patterns occur, as demonstrated in Figure 3.7. In some countries, such as Mexico, the early years of statehood are accompanied by great constitutional instability, but eventually institutions stabilize and more enduring patterns take hold. Uruguay represents the opposite pattern, with an early stable constitution followed by breakdown and a struggle to find enduring institutions. Panama represents another pattern that we might label Jeffersonian: periodic renewal of the constitution, every generation or so.

CONCLUSION

It is very likely that the concept of a *constitution* is inherently contested and a degree of heterogeneity in the use of the term will persist. We are by no means dogmatic on this point, and have no desire to convert those who are accustomed to use the term in an expansive fashion. In the end, we view the large-C, small-c distinction as mostly semantic and for the sake of intelligibility we will add the modifier "written," "formal," or "textual" as much as our publisher's demands for brevity permit. As should be obvious, the distinction marks for us an analytic focus, not a normative position. We make this stipulation in part to insulate our study from the parallel conceptual debate that rages from time to time with respect to judicial philosophy in the United States. In that arena, textualists such as Justice Black and loose constructionists such as Justice Brennan debate the boundaries of the *constitution* with much more in the balance and, at times, a healthy dose of politics. Our focus is on how and why national charters survive as the de jure law of the land, not how they should be interpreted in real disputes.

With this objective in mind, this chapter has tried to anticipate and address questions that arise when one chooses to study any single component of the constitutional order, no matter how central it may be – or *should* be, according to partisans. For example, how can we compare written texts that play vastly different roles across contexts? To what degree are these texts actually meaningful to the political actors the documents purportedly govern? How do we identify the *death* of any particular constitution and can we draw a bright line between that sort of change and amendment? Finally, to what degree is constitutional change epiphenomenal, in that it merely reflects a prior and more fundamental reform such as regime change? These are all important questions and we grapple with each of them directly in this chapter, appealing to evidence to inform our understanding whenever possible.

The question of comparability has a straightforward answer. Because we are focused on a particular form, or mode, of constitution making, we are not at all put off that written constitutions would look and perform differently across contexts. As we emphasize, these differences represent explanatory factors, not comparability problems. Moreover, in many ways, a focus on written constitutions is analytically attractive in that these documents represent an observable and discrete unit by which to track institutional change. What then can we say about the degree to which constitutions *matter*, in the sense of matching actual practice? As our evidence shows quite clearly, the association between the provisions of the written constitutions and the de facto rules in play will differ across countries and across substantive domains. Rules about executive-legislative relations, for example, seem to have much more bite than do rights provisions. This conditional answer may not satisfy the reader who wants evidence that written constitutions are always meaningful before reading a book about risks to their life. Fortunately or unfortunately, we cannot assert that they always matter. Sometimes they most assuredly do not, which in our opinion is part of their allure. Moreover, to reiterate our contention about comparability, the fidelity between de jure and de facto law is *part* of our explanatory framework, not a threat to it.

And, what of the issue of defining constitutional death? Our evidence on that matter suggests that, in general, constitutional replacements (as we define them) are notably different from constitutional amendments and represent sharper changes in the content of the governing document. We do see, however, cases for which the formal definition of change is misleading: some replacement constitutions are not meaningfully different from their predecessors whereas some amended constitutions are markedly so. These cases, however, are the exception. Finally, we turn to the issue of constitutions as epiphenomena, especially the connection between constitutional and regime change. A close look at the correspondence between the two transitions suggests that constitutions often seem to mark fundamental change. Just as often, however, the two sets of reforms do not coincide. Even when they do coincide, it is likely that constitutions contribute to regime change as much as they reflect it.

4

What Makes Constitutions Endure?

Jeanne Calment was 122 when she died in her lifelong hometown of Arles, France in 1997. No one has ever lived longer, or at least no records can verify anyone having done so. At 117, Calment gave up smoking only after her increasingly poor eyesight prevented her from lighting her own cigarettes. A year later, she took up the habit again, apparently undeterred by any vision problems. Until her death her diet consisted, in part, of chocolate (reportedly two pounds of a week, mostly Swiss) and generous shares of olive oil (eaten directly) and port wine.[1] In any predictive model of human life span, the case of Jeannne Calment lies considerably above the regression line.

The U.S. Constitution is, in our view, something of the Jeanne Calment of higher law. Like Calment, the U.S. Constitution defies expectations, at least according to our model of longevity. The U.S. document embodies many of the elements that we predict should lead to increased mortality rates. Our theory, as described below, focuses on the importance for constitutional longevity of higher than average levels of *flexibility, inclusion,* and *specificity* – none of which are in abundance in the Philadelphia creation. There may be good reasons to adopt the Philadelphia model – the constitutional equivalent of cigarettes, chocolate, and wine – but constitutional endurance is not one of them.

A THEORY OF CONSTITUTIONAL RENEGOTIATION

Our theory – call it a *theory of renegotiation* – involves notions of constitutional formation, adjustment, and endurance. It is a general theory. Like human

---

[1] Craig R. Whitney, "Jeanne Calment, World's Elder, Dies at 122." *The New York Times,* August 5, 1997.

beings, constitutions can expire for any number of reasons, and we certainly do not purport to account for each and every death. However, a general logic underlies the course of most, if not all, constitutional lives. It is rooted in the idea that all constitutions are, to one degree or another, bargains that embody agreement among the relevant parties. Whether the parties sustain these bargains depends, in basic terms, on (a) whether the parties feel that they would be better off under different terms; (b) the expected sanctions for breaching the agreement; and (c) whether the existing agreement can be amended easily or otherwise accommodate changes.

Our theory recognizes that national and global crises will likely have some effect on the persistence of these bargains. Nevertheless, we see our contribution as a correction to the conventional wisdom regarding the power of such events. A general theme of the literature on institutional change is that many social arrangements are stable until some external event – a shock – changes the players' calculus of costs and benefits and so induces pressure for new arrangements. We accept this basic framework, but suggest that certain structural features of constitutions promote stability in the face of external pressures.

Our account of the constitutional life cycle begins appropriately at birth – the constitutional negotiation process – and draws on insights from the study of incomplete contracts (Williamson 1985). Our particular focus is on the moment of potential *renegotiation* (or, less euphemistically, constitutional crisis). We identify aspects of constitutions or their environments that induce constitutional crisis, and thus the prospect of constitutional replacement. As we shall see, survival of the constitution turns very centrally on the degree to which it is enforced and accommodates change. Constitutions vary along a set of dimensions that affect this process. We focus on three features of the constitution itself that should prolong its existence – inclusion, flexibility, and specificity. Although constitutions exist in a world of constant change, these design features lower the risks of replacement.

NEGOTIATING THE CONSTITUTIONAL BARGAIN: TWO TYPES OF INCOMPLETE INFORMATION

Our theory of bargaining begins with a specification of the parties seated at the table. In the real world, constitutions are political bargains that vary widely in their level of inclusion of members of the political community. Many constitutions, particularly those in authoritarian regimes, are crafted by a small set of leaders in the proverbial back room without popular involvement. The Japanese Constitution of 1889 fit this category, as it was drafted by a small group and announced as a gift from the Emperor to his people. Other constitutions are inclusively generated and endorsed by the public in a referendum or other consensus-building strategies. Of course, the drafting process can differ along other dimensions that may be consequential with respect to particular choices (Elster 1995), but we leave that aside at present (but see Ginsburg, Elkins, and Blount 2009). However the process is conducted, it will include parties who invest in the negotiation process and seek to secure advantage in the set of institutions that result.

Suppose we have three groups – which we will not so abstractly call Sunni, Shiites, and Kurds – which share a geographic region and intend to form a single state. The groups may differ with respect to resources, geography, ideology, or along other dimensions – the content of their disagreement is not material for present purposes. But, presume that the Shiites are a numerical majority. They would like a constitutional arrangement in which they dominate the other groups – an arrangement that would require either: (a) going it alone (if geographic boundaries permit); (b) crude force; or (c) inducing the others to join in a constitutional agreement. The last is preferable for a variety of reasons: among them, international legitimacy, economic stability, and security (as the smaller groups may have the capacity to engage in some level of violence if their demands are not met).

Each group comes to the negotiating table to bargain. The bargaining process is costly, requiring the expenditure of time and political capital during both the negotiation and approval phases. (Furthermore, each bargainer must be concerned with ensuring that his supporters can be delivered, a problem we set aside here). The parties at the table will conclude a bargain, or not, based on an expected stream of benefits to particular groups net the transaction costs of negotiation. Parties will also consider alternative arrangements depending upon their feasibility. The concept of a *reservation price* from contract theory is relevant here. A reservation price refers to the least favorable point at which a party will accept a negotiated agreement, and depends in part on the value of alternative arrangements. In the example above, the Kurds or Sunni might consider the possibility of secession as a realistic alternative to concluding a deal and, consequently, their reservation price may be quite high if that alternative is sufficiently attractive. In any bargain that emerges, it is likely that the Shiites will get the lion's share of the spoils, but will also have to provide enough benefits to their smaller counterparts to induce them to choose to abide by the constitution.

Should the groups conclude a bargain, it will of necessity be incomplete, in that the parties will be unable to specify every future contingency (Persson et al. 1997: 1165; Maskin and Tirole 1999).[2] One reason it will be incomplete

---

[2] Persson et al. argue that the separation of powers scheme provides a mechanism to create default rules to fill gaps. See also Gillette (1997: 1355) and de Figueiredo and Weingast 2005

concerns the transaction costs of negotiating terms.[3] Parties that seek to specify every contingency will never conclude a deal. Beyond the costs of negotiation, we focus on two types of obstacles to specifying complete constitutional arrangements.

The Problem of Uncertain Payoffs

First, there is uncertainty about future payoffs, which may vary with exogenous factors not foreseeable at the time of drafting. Call this the problem of *uncertain payoffs*.[4] Conditions will change at a far greater pace than will the terms to a constitutional bargain. Every country is embedded in an international environment over which it lacks complete control. The international environment is particularly fickle; the one enduring feature of international relations is "persistent uncertainty" (Koremenos 2005). New technologies are invented, new threats emerge, and new powers arise, which affect the costs and benefits of cooperation. These factors can influence the relative payoffs to parties to the constitutional bargain.

Suppose, extending the earlier example, that the Shiites are the majority, but the Kurds are geographically concentrated in an oil-producing area. In bargaining, the Kurds are concerned that the Shiites will dominate the country's politics and so negotiate a provision that oil taxes will be locally administered and retained. The Shiites agree and the bargain is concluded. However, a year after the adoption of the constitution, world oil prices plummet as a result of the perfection of hydrogen technology. Kurdish revenues decline precipitously and the relative wealth of the two groups diverge, with the Shiites becoming richer and Kurds poorer in relative terms. The Kurds now face pressure to renegotiate for a share of revenues from the Shiite area. Exogenous change means that even otherwise stable constitutions may come under pressure for renegotiation.

Much constitution making is based on just such a miscalculation of the probabilities of downstream contingencies (Brown 2008). Consider the bargaining between northern and southern states in the U.S. constitutional convention. The sides disagreed over the most profound moral question of the

on incomplete agreements in the federalism context. For more on assumptions of institutional self-interest in constitutional design, see Ginsburg, Elkins, and Blount 2009.

[3] James Madison seems to have recognized this factor. Letter to Samuel Johnston, June 21, 1789 (describing the need for practice to settle points on which the constitution was vague).

[4] As a technical matter, it is uncertainty about payoffs rather than uncertainty about future states of the world that renders contracts incomplete. If parties could commit not to renegotiate, it might be possible to draft a contract that would overcome the variance in states of the world (Maskin and Tirole 1999). As we shall see this condition does not apply to constitutions, which have no external enforcer.

day, yet came together in a compromise that clearly contemplated the continued existence of slavery (Graber 2006). Both sides based their negotiating positions on the perceived likelihood that population expansion would proceed in the South and West. For southern states, the provision that no bill be passed banning slave importation until 1808 was seen as an acceptable compromise, given the expectations that the South would be in the majority by that time and the slave population would be self-sustaining. Even as the negotiations in Philadelphia were taking place, however, Congress passed the Northwest Ordinance, which led to great expansion in Ohio and other Western regions. By 1808, when Congress passed a bill banning the slave trade, the South's assumptions from 1787 appeared invalid and, yet, the South did not exit the Union (at least not immediately). Rather, it sought renegotiation in the series of pacts beginning with the Missouri Compromise, which embodied an unwritten constitutional commitment to bisectionalism (Weingast 2005). Had it not done so, the South's nullification may well have come earlier.[5]

The Problem of Hidden Information

Another source of incompleteness involves awareness of one's negotiating partner's true capabilities and intentions. This is the problem of *hidden information*, in which information is distributed asymmetrically across parties. A party to a negotiation may misrepresent her own endowments and intentions for strategic reasons. Suppose, in the example above, the Shiite ethnic group does not have accurate information on the extent of oil deposits in the territory of Kurdistan. It negotiates the revenue deal expecting to obtain sufficient funds for its needs from customs and other revenue sources. After the constitution is adopted, the Kurds gradually reveal that the amount of oil was in fact much higher than anticipated and, as a result, Kurdish oil revenues will be greater than those obtained by the national government from all other sources combined. In this example, hidden information led to a miscalculation of

---

[5] It is also noteworthy that it was the dispute about slavery itself, rather than the slave trade discussed in the constitutional text, which led to the constitutional collapse and the Civil War (Brown 2008: 683). We can draw a second example of unanticipated change from the much-maligned system that the U.S. founders concocted to elect presidents. The founders anticipated a multi-candidate system in which most elections (19 of 20, according to George Mason) would be thrown into the House of Representatives where state delegations, each with one vote, would choose from the top vote getters (Elliot 1784–1846). The advantage for small states in that second round was meant to balance the advantage that large states had in the first round, in which the electoral votes of each state were roughly proportional to their population. Of course, the founders did not anticipate the rise of the two-party system, which would render the second round almost inoperable.

relative costs and benefits. One can imagine that if the miscalculation is severe enough, the Shiites will seek to renegotiate the deal.[6] Constitutional bargaining involves attempts to induce counterparties to reveal private information. The Spanish transition to democracy, marked by the Constitution of 1978, was negotiated through an elite pact among political parties brokered by President Suarez (Linz and Stepan 1996). The context was one in which memories of the bloody civil war of the 1930s were quite raw, resulting in significant mistrust between the left and right. The left was seen as divisive and republican, whereas the right was seen as favoring military intervention in politics. The negotiation process of the so-called Moncloa pact facilitated the left's acceptance of the monarchy, with the right's agreement to dismantle the institutions of Franco's dictatorship. The bargain held during both the constitutional transition and the long period of socialist rule from 1982–1996.[7]

In general, time has different, and probably offsetting, effects on the problems of uncertain payoffs and hidden information. Almost by definition, time exacerbates the problem of uncertain payoffs. As the date of the initial bargain becomes more and more distant, future contingencies grow more difficult to predict, as more and more exogenous factors arise and interact with each other in complex ways. By contrast, the problem of hidden information becomes less pronounced with time. As parties interact in performing the terms of the constitutional bargain, they are likely to reveal information to each other more fully than can be done in the bargaining phase. They may even develop the constitutional equivalent of a *course of dealing*, a set of informal norms that supplement their formal arrangements. As time goes on, information on the type of partner that each faces is likely to increase. The problem of hidden

---

[6] A related source of incompleteness, which we do not address in detail here, is bounded rationality. There is a fear that the heat of the moment could lead the drafters to make poor choices or be unable to accurately calculate costs and benefits (Williamson 1985; Sunstein 2000). If cognitive biases lead parties to underestimate future benefits and overestimate costs, a deal will not be struck at all. But, in the reverse situation, parties will conclude a bargain they are then disappointed in, and seek to renegotiate.

[7] In the U.S. context, hidden information about intentions was a key factor in negotiations. The intense negotiation over the majority required to pass navigation acts reflected not just different views on morality, but hidden information. The South believed that the North was likely to tax the South on exports, which would both subsidize northern shipping interests and harm the South (Goldstone 2005: 161–63). The South thus demanded that any such acts require a two-thirds supermajority. The North, however, was able to resist this demand, in part because it had conceded so much to the South already. The point is that the constitutional negotiation was one in which the South distrusted the true intentions of its negotiating partner and sought to specify further detail and veto power as a way of preventing harm to its interests.

information is likely to be particularly severe in the first period of constitutional performance, and to be ameliorated over time. Such a growing sense of comfort seems evident in the case of the 1978 bargain in Spain, where the left and right appeared to gain a better understanding of the other's motives and resources only after the first several years of the agreement.

Thus, we should see that problems of uncertain payoffs increase over time, whereas those of hidden information decrease. In the case of Iraq, the major groups seem to be tentatively moving toward using constitutional processes to resolve their differences, although the process has been very slow. This suggests that the problem of hidden information is slowly being resolved. On the other hand, external actors (e.g., the United States and Iran) are changing their strategies in ways that might not have been anticipated in 2005. These changes represent shocks that may require adjustment of the original bargains. Time and the aging process of the constitution is an important element of our theory, and one we return to in more depth shortly.

Standard Contractual Solutions to Problems of Incomplete Information

It is worth considering solutions to each of the information problems. One standard answer to the problem of uncertain payoffs is to write loosely defined contracts that allow flexible adjustment over time as new information is revealed. This is the basic logic of the so-called framework constitution, one written in mostly general terms. The parties will be able to specify their commitments within general parameters that abstract from specific circumstances. There is, however, a well-known risk of moral hazard from such loosely specified contracts. If one party's commitments are not precisely specified, it might seek to claim that circumstances have changed to take a greater share of the constitutional surplus. Indeed, knowing that this is a possibility down the road, a general agreement may encourage a party to conceal its intentions and endowments from its constitutional partners. Trying to address the problem of uncertain payoffs through drafting flexible framework constitutions, then, may exacerbate problems of hidden information.

The reverse might also be true. A reasonable response to the problem of hidden information is to write a more complete agreement specifying contingencies. By forcing the other party to reveal information, one can minimize strategically generated surprises down the road. But, this solution to the problem of hidden information might create a risk of constraining adaptations to exogenous change. We explain later why we do not think, on balance, that this effect is fatal to constitutions, but we acknowledge that at extremes, too much detail can exacerbate the problem of uncertain payoffs.

Another common solution to problems of hidden information and uncertain payoffs is to rely on third parties. Analogizing to contract law, one might imagine a theory of constitutional review in which the courts resolve problems of uncertainty in the bargaining process. In such an arrangement, the role of the court would be to provide default rules that reflect its understanding of what the bargain would have been in the presence of complete information (Ayres and Gertner 1989). In contract theory, courts that play this role can provide a disincentive for parties to hide information from each other.

There are significant problems, however, with expecting courts to be able to play this function in the constitutional context. First, there are capacity issues such that the courts may be unable to determine what the appropriate rule is. Second, no matter what decision the court makes, the relevant parties *still* face the decision of whether to comply with the court decision. That is, there is no guarantee that the decision will be followed, because there is no external enforcer of the court decision. Indeed, this lack of external enforcement is one of the defining characteristics of constitutional bargains. Finally, it is important to remember that the existence of a constitutional court is itself the product of the constitutional negotiation, a term over which parties will bargain. Not all drafters are equally situated with regard to this question. One of us has argued previously that those who are prospective losers in the post-constitutional political process have a greater incentive to empower a constitutional court than those who are prospective winners (Ginsburg 2003). It seems odd, then, to treat an institution that is a product of constitutional negotiation as an essential guarantor of the bargain. In short, one should not expect judicially prescribed default rules to solve the problem of incomplete information (even though, as we argue later, judicial review might perform other important functions for constitutional endurance).

In summary, the two sources of incompleteness – rooted in the unpredictability of exogenous shocks and strategic incentives to hide information – mean that parties are unable to produce a complete contract. Revelation of new information, whether in the form of exogenous events that change payoffs or the release of hidden information, may affect the parties' perceptions of the bargain. In turn, these altered perceptions may lead to moments of potential adjustment – or breakdown – of the constitutional arrangement.

CONSTITUTIONAL RENEGOTIATION

For every period after the initial negotiation, the parties thus face a decision as to whether to remain in the current bargain or renegotiate (by, as we shall see, either revising or replacing the agreement). In the classic formulation of

Hirschman (1970), these options amount to exit, voice, or loyalty (in reverse order). In this section, we consider the renegotiation process and demonstrate that three structural factors within the constitution – inclusion, flexibility, and specificity – are critical to the maintenance of the existing bargain.

Deciding to Renegotiate

Renegotiation occurs when one party believes the anticipated future costs of remaining in the bargain exceed future benefits plus the cost of renegotiation. The proponents for renegotiation can be the relative winners or the relative losers in the initial constitutional bargain. Winners and losers are those for whom political advantages accrue or decay, respectively, following the initial bargain. The relative winners are in position to demand a larger share of the constitutional surplus during renegotiation. On the other hand, it may be a relative loser who seeks to regain standing, despite a weaker bargaining position. Even if losers do not have the power to win in ordinary politics, they may be able to impose sufficient costs on the winners so as to force renegotiation.

Consider as an example the case of an executive who is unhappy with term limitations in the constitutional text. Our review of constitutional chronologies reveals a historical landscape – especially in Latin America – which is littered with constitutions that stood in the way of executive ambition. A case in point is the short, unhappy life of Brazil's 1934 Constitution. Modeled after the Weimar Constitution, the 1934 document extended political rights to most Brazilians, established a strong judiciary, and strengthened the legislature. President Getulio Vargas chafed under the charter's restrictions, including one that would have prevented his re-election in 1938. Not to be so curtailed, Vargas declared the constitution null and void in 1937 and replaced it with new document, one that gave his administration considerably more room (and time!) to operate.[8] Sometimes, executives are induced to seek more power because of external shocks that render it prohibitively costly to work within constitutional limits conceived under more stable conditions. The most obvious example is military crisis, which often tempts the executive to pursue security and

---

[8] More recently, Alberto Fujimori in Peru and Hugo Chavez in Venezuela, unable to utilize the normal amendment process because of legislative opposition, oversaw the replacement of their countries' constitutions in 1993 and 1999, respectively. The new documents extended the presidential term. Chavez, and the Presidents of Bolivia, Ecuador, and Turkmenistan secured amendments in early 2009 to allow them to potentially extend their terms. Vladimir Putin oversaw amendments to the Russian Constitution to empower the Prime Minister's office, which he then occupied, in order to avoid limits on his term as president.

stability at the expense of individual rights or limits on executive power, such as scheduled elections. One can think of Lincoln's suspension of *habeas corpus* during the civil war, the relaxing of privacy constraints on law enforcement investigations in the post–9/11 environment, or Indira Gandhi's suspension of elections in India during her period of emergency rule in 1975–1977. Such circumstances can induce a proposal for renegotiation.

Depending on the number and size of the parties seeking renegotiation, three scenarios could evolve. The most interesting, and the one we focus on in the remainder of this section, is when some parties seek renegotiation and some parties oppose renegotiation. In this scenario, the main cleavage is between the proponents and opponents of change, but there could also be intra-coalition divisions over the type and magnitude of change sought or how best to oppose the proponents. The other two scenarios occur when all parties either oppose or seek renegotiation. These scenarios are less interesting, because renegotiation is either impossible or guaranteed.

Intra- versus Extra-Constitutional Change

Once the parties have chosen sides, the proponents must choose the means by which to approach renegotiation. Here, the constitution itself comes into play, for it will typically include provisions to amend its terms. More than ninety percent of constitutions written since 1789 have included provisions that specify the procedure by which to amend the document. Within the existing bargain, there are two primary mechanisms by which constitutional change occurs: formal amendments to the text and informal amendments that result from interpretive changes (typically, but not exclusively, facilitated by courts). Much debate in the literature concerns the extent to which informal devices can be considered perfect substitutes for constitutional text (Lutz 2006). If the methods of securing formal amendment are difficult (as in the United States, where ratification by three-fourths of the state legislatures presents a high hurdle), there will be pressure to adapt the constitution through judicial or other reinterpretation. Ackerman's well-known account of constitutional change in the 1930s in the United States draws on such logic (1993). If, on the other hand, formal constitutional amendment is relatively simple, as in contemporary Brazil where the legislature does not have to pass its amendments to the subnational units for approval, there may be less need for judicial or other institutional reinterpretations of the constitution.

Even more costly than amendment or reinterpretation is constitutional *replacement*, which in our terms is equvialent to a new bargain. Replacements are more costly because: (1) there may be more issues over which to

bargain, requiring more time and energy for negotiation; (2) previously settled issues may be raised again, rendering bargaining results less predictable;
and, (3) the costs of failure may be much more severe because in a strict
sense, replacement may be illegal.[9] Thus, replacement introduces some risk
that major shifts will work to the detriment of the group(s) that called for a
renegotiation. Imagine, for example, a particular country with two groups,
Majority and Minority, in which Minority is a consistent loser in the policy
process and seeks to overturn the constitutional bargain. It demands a constitutional guarantee of equality and a new mechanism for appointing the
Supreme Court that will interpret the constitution, so as to provide a Minority
veto over new appointments. Suppose further that Minority is overconfident,
and in the negotiation process is able to win on only one of these issues, so
that the guarantee of equality is adopted, but the Supreme Court appointment
mechanism continues to favor Majority. Under the new constitution, the new
Supreme Court interprets the guarantee of equality to prohibit affirmative
action, leading to even greater dominance by Majority. The Minority is now
worse off because it was unable to bundle multiple reforms in the negotiation
process. Multi-dimensionality means that a risk-averse party may have a high
threshold before calling for a total constitutional renegotiation. Even dominant groups who feel fully in control of a new negotiation process – and, therefore, potentially amenable to new issues surfacing – will have some concern
about the legitimacy of the new product and its resilience, should conditions
change again.

Even proposed amendments can run the risk of re-opening other issues,
often to the dismay of the proposer. In the aftermath of the South African
Constitutional Court's 1995 decision in *State v. Makwanyane,* in which the
court found the death penalty unconstitutional, some elements of the National
Party (the Afrikaans) sought a constitutional amendment to overrule the case.
The African National Congress, however, responded by calling for amendment of the property rights provisions that had been central to the country's
negotiated transition and were seen as slowing down popular land reform.
Rather than risk losing property rights protection, the National Party quickly
quieted calls for amendment of the death penalty provision. Ten years later,
a Constitutional Review Committee recommended that neither provision be
amended (Parliamentary Monitoring Group 2005).

In short, parties will consider their position in the current bargain, comparing it with expected outcomes of constitutional renegotiation, net the costs of

---

9 Consider the April 2009 repeal of the Constitution of Fiji by President Ilioilo in the face of
a court decision suggesting the 2006 coup d'etat was illegal. Fiji suffered severe international
sanctions in the wake of the President's move.

adjustment to, or replacement of, the new bargain. If the expected outcome of the alternative arrangement (conceived of as the set of all possible alternatives multiplied by the probabilities of obtaining them), less negotiation and switching costs, exceeds the current stream of benefits, parties will opt for renegotiation either through intra- or extra-constitutional change. We conceive of the choice between the two modes of change to be mostly a function of relative costs and benefits, with intra-constitutional change typically being the preferred choice of actors. The internal *flexibility* of the constitution potentially allows adjustment through amendment or interpretation without the potentially significant transition and reputational costs of ending the current bargain. Sometimes, however, the intra-constitutional means of adjustment may be unavailable. This may be because the party lacks sufficient political strength to accomplish change unilaterally or to bargain with other elites. It may also be the case because the constitution lacks internal flexibility that facilitates adjustment to changing conditions. In such circumstances, the party may simply breach the constitution through replacement or suspension, and see if other parties acquiesce.

The Problem of Enforcement

Suppose the proponent of constitutional renegotiation decides to use extra-constitutional means to accomplish change. That is, the proponent suggests suspending and/or replacing the constitutional bargain. We follow Ordeshook (1992), Weingast (1997, 2005), and others, in arguing that a key factor in the calculus of such a breach is the ability of other parties to the bargain to enforce the terms of the agreement. Specifically, the proponent's decision to breach or not is at least partially determined by the opposition's ability to organize and thwart such an action. There is rarely an external enforcer of constitutional bargains, so enforcement depends on the opposition (or the citizenry, more generally), but, these potential enforcers face a quintessential collective action problem. Potential enforcers, be they citizens or a subgroup of the elite, have disparate interests and will be unlikely to reach agreement on their own as to what constitutes a violation of the constitutional bargain, and on when and how to enforce it. A willingness to stand against the government to enforce the constitution requires common expectations that others will join in enforcement; otherwise, opposition members will fear ending up in jail and the constitutional breach will be allowed to stand – the worst of all outcomes for the opposition (or citizenry). When all potential enforcers can coordinate by generating common expectations that others will join in the confrontation, however, the threat of defection is minimized. When those who would breach recognize that their breach will be met with coordinated resistance, they restrain themselves from acting in the first place. This is what Ordeshook (1992), Weingast (1997) and others call the self-enforcing constitution. What factors increase the probability of such enforcement? Enforcement requires three conditions. The first has to do with clarity regarding the rules of the constitution and the factual predicate of any alleged violation; enforcers must understand when and how the constitution has been violated. In this sense, violations that take place in secret can hardly trigger enforcement action, and an independent media, a vigorous civil society, and free flows of information facilitate awareness of potential violations of the constitutional bargain. But, even if everyone is aware of the facts, many potential violations may be ambiguous because the boundaries of the constitution are unclear. Second, parties must be sufficiently attached to the Constitution as the rightful law of the land. Clearly, if there is consensus that the presiding document is fundamentally flawed, knowledge of its limits will not facilitate coordinated enforcement. Third, potential enforcers must believe that others share their understanding of, and devotion to, the constitution *and* are willing to take action to enforce the violation. Thus, the shared expectations and common knowledge are central to constitutional enforcement (Chwe 2003). These conditions affect the probability that dominant actors will breach particular provisions of the bargain, but they also affect the probability that actors will seek to replace the bargain – the ultimate breach. This dynamic is why we emphasize repeatedly in this book that fealty to the dictates of the constitution – constitutionalism, as it were – and endurance are inextricably linked.

The need for enforcement helps us understand why *written* constitutions may be important components of constitutional democracy, providing further insight into the points developed in Chapter Three. Written constitutions can assist potential enforcers in overcoming the coordination problem by providing a definition of what constitutes a violation by government and thus providing a focal point for enforcement activity (Carey 2000: 757; Strauss 2003: 1731–35). By stipulating the rules and defining violations, they increase everyone's perceived likelihood that others will join them in enforcing against violations. Hence "parchment barriers" may matter, not because of any magical power contained in their words, but because their role in facilitating coordination on the part of potential enforcers, who may otherwise be unable to agree. Written constitutions may also matter by creating authoritative institutions, such as constitutional courts, which can resolve ambiguities down the road and thus facilitate downstream enforcement (Ginsburg and McAdams 2004).

In the next section, we identify those aspects of constitutions that affect the likelihood of renegotiation, the mode of renegotiation (that is, intra-or extra-constitutional), and the probability that opposition groups and the citizens will enforce the standing bargain.

PREDICTIONS FROM THE MODEL

The contractual logic that we described allows us to generate some expectations about the factors that affect the risk of constitutional demise. Our focus in particular is on three elements of the design of constitutions: inclusion, flexibility, and specificity. Our theory regarding these characteristics leads us to generate specific hypotheses about the institutions that facilitate constitutional endurance: participatory processes, which facilitate inclusion; constitutional review, which facilitates all three mechanisms; ease of amendment, which facilitates flexibility, but also contributes to inclusion and specificity; and, the scope and detail of constitutions, which concerns specificity. We also make explicit our expectations regarding the effect of time itself (that is, whether aging will have a stabilizing or destabilizing effect on constitutional life).

Inclusion

Inclusion refers to the breadth of participation in formulating the constitutional agreement and in the ongoing enforcement of it. It is very clear that, throughout the world, constitutions are treated with varying amounts of respect by citizens and elites alike. Successful constitutions generate allegiance from those among later generations who do not initially consent to them, much less participate in the drafting of the texts. For some countries (e.g., the United States), the document is an important symbol of sovereignty and statehood; for others (e.g., many in Latin America during the nineteenth century), the constitution is of considerably lesser stature. In part, the connection between attachment to the bargain and survival is reciprocal: framers and citizens will protect a document to which they are attached and documents that survive will in turn engender norms of attachment. (This relationship is relevant to our discussion of aging below.) Our theory suggests a further reason: constitutions whose provisions are publicly formulated and debated will more likely be able to generate the common knowledge and attachment essential for self-enforcement. The passage of the constitution is important, independently of its content. When constitutions are passed in secret, with little fanfare, they would seem to be unlikely to generate enforcement action. When they are passed with great public involvement, there is likely to be more common knowledge about the content of the constitution. Because common knowledge is essential for enforcement, publicity may be a crucial condition for extending constitutional life. This suggests that inclusion in the process of producing the constitution will help ensure enforcement by the public or other relevant actors (Carey 2009b; Ginsburg, Elkins, and Blount 2009).

Inclusion matters both during the initial process of producing a constitution as well as later on when potential breaches might occur. With respect to the initial process, there are two critical stages – the drafting/deliberation and the approval – in which the degree of inclusion is manifest. An extreme case of secrecy in drafting/deliberation might be Myanmar's Constitution of 2008. There, the military government commissioned a constitution from a group of loyal authors (excluding members of an opposition party that won 80% of legislative seats in the prior election) and cloistered the assembly in a remote location outside the capital. Admittedly, a degree of privacy can be quite useful under some circumstances (as scholars have noted of the Philadelphia convention in 1787), and documents arising from private settings may be indirectly open as long as the group assembled is selected by the public or adequately representative (Elster 2000). In cases in which important factions are excluded (or, as is sometimes the case, exclude *themselves* as Sunni leaders did during the drafting of Iraq's 2005 document), citizen attachment is severely compromised. The case at the other end of the spectrum from Myanmar may well be that of Brazil in 1987–1988. The Brazilian constitutional convention was characterized by extraordinary public involvement, including the submission of citizen proposals, the result of which was one of the longest constitutions in the world. The Brazilian charter is an unwieldy document to be sure, but a highly public one in its origin and provisions. Already, it has endured significantly longer than has the typical Latin American constitution.

The approval process can be just as important as the drafting and deliberative stage. Ratification by a non–rubber-stamping public or by an elected body that is inclusive or representative of the public likely breeds attachment and common knowledge. Moehler (2007) reports survey evidence from a set of African cases that suggests that constitutions that are ratified by public referendum enjoy higher levels of support. Two specific hypotheses follow from this understanding of the implications of the drafting and ratification processes: Constitutional durability should increase with the level of public inclusion during both stages of constitutional design.

Inclusion is also an ongoing characteristic of constitutional life. The constitution is enforced not only by the founding generation, but also by those who subsequently live under its dictates. Even a constitution that is adopted with wide public participation can fall by the wayside if living citizens do not have a perceived stake in the enforcement of their ancestors' contract. Thus, we expect that constitutions that generate much debate and discussion among citizens will be those that are likely to be enforced and maintained when pressures for breach arise. Constitutional politics must be participatory and inclusive, even as citizens disagree over some aspects of the constitutional text. This broad notion of inclusion provides some role for interest groups. Much of the writing in constitutional political economy in recent years has been wary of interest groups, with the fear that they will hijack processes of public governance for private ends. The normative task of constitutional design, according to some writing in this vein, is to minimize rent-seeking, which occurs when groups expend resources to acquire poorly specified assets (Buchanan and Tullock 1961; Macey 1988). At the same time, other scholars have emphasized the necessary function of intermediate associations in helping citizens to overcome collective action problems (Putnam 1993).

In our view, it is important that interest groups have a stake in constitutional endurance, even if this involves distributing rents to groups in the constitution itself. Constitutions that have established increasing streams of political benefits to groups may be better able to withstand pressures that arise. As actors invest resources in utilizing these political institutions, they may find that the investments pay off and return political goods to the investor. Over time, actors may develop an increasing stake in constitutional viability.[10] This stake further increases the public's familiarity with and attachment to the founding document over time, making it more likely that they will enforce the bargain.[11]

Even if groups are not invested in the constitution through receiving ongoing benefits, they may choose to remain loyal to the constitutional order so long as they see some chance of being in the winning coalition in the future. Inclusive provisions render this hope more realistic. The key is that groups have enough at stake to support enforcement efforts against those who would breach current arrangements. So long as enough groups believe they are better off in the current bargain than in taking a chance on another round of constitutional negotiation, the constitution will endure.

What about the losers of the initial bargaining process? Because they lack the political strength to win in ordinary politics, losers are unlikely to be able to effectuate constitutional change, even if they desire it. They might,

---

[10] Note that this analysis deviates from one point emphasized in the current literature on self-enforcement. Weingast (2005) emphasizes that self-enforcement requires reducing the stakes of politics so as not to trigger actors' rational fears, which might cause a constitutional breakdown. We agree with this point, but also note that self-*reinforcement* requires raising the stakes of politics so as to give actors an incentive to participate and produce increasing levels of collective goods.

[11] Widner (2007a) provides the example of new multiparty constitutions in Africa. When leaders sought to amend these constitutions to extend their terms beyond the original bargain, popular resistance has been effective in countries where drafting was consultative, but not so when drafting was highly elite driven.

alternatively, seek to impose costs on the winners so as to expand the circle of dissatisfaction with current arrangements, even if they cannot overturn the bargain. Or, they might seek to align with other losers. The key question is whether a coalition of groups can form a plurality of power so as to be able to overturn the current bargain. If even a small number of losing interest groups believe in constitutional maintenance as an independent value, perhaps because they anticipate some benefits in the future, they can tip coalitions away from violation and toward constitutional maintenance. The larger point is that inclusion, by bringing in a larger number of groups, will help to extend the life of the constitution because more groups will have a stake in its endurance. And, as the distribution of costs and benefits changes over time, convincing interest groups representing a plurality of power to support the constitution will help it to endure. This will both prevent some crises from occurring because groups will not attempt to bring down the constitution, and may also render the document more likely to be enforced when such attempts are made.

To summarize, inclusive drafting processes and inclusive constitutional provisions increase the possibility of enforcement in two ways: (1) by increasing the visibility of the document and demonstrating societal consent; and (2) by increasing the stake that citizens have in the document and their attachment to it.

Flexibility

Having stressed the importance of proper enforcement of constitutional limits, we now turn to the equally important, if paradoxical, task of adapting these limits in response to changing conditions. Given the existence of exogenous shocks that change the costs and benefits to the parties to a constitutional bargain, constitutions require mechanisms for adjustment over time. As Jawaharlal Nehru remarked in the Indian Constitutional Assembly:

> [W]hile we want this Constitution to be as solid and as permanent a structure as we can make it, nevertheless there is no permanence in Constitutions. There should be a certain flexibility. If you make anything rigid and permanent, you stop a Nation's growth, the growth of a living vital organic people.... [W]e should not make a Constitution such as some other great countries have, which are so rigid that they do not and cannot be adapted easily to changing conditions. Today especially, when the world is in turmoil and we are passing through a very swift period of transition, what we may do today may not be wholly applicable tomorrow. Therefore, while we make a Constitution which is sound and as basic as we can, it should also be flexible and for a period we should be in a position to change it with relative facility (Indian Parliament 1948).

Nehru's successors have apparently taken his advice to heart, amending the constitution several dozen times as of this writing. As we describe later in Chapter Seven, we believe that this helps explain the endurance of the Indian Constitution and its remarkable success.

To be sure, if taken to an extreme, flexibility undermines the very notion of constitutionalism as a set of stable limits on ordinary politics. If a constitution is completely flexible, as in the model of parliamentary sovereignty, it may not be able to provide enduring rules that bind the polity together. Nevertheless, below some threshold, flexibility should clearly enhance constitutional endurance; beyond that threshold, increased flexibility will have unpredictable – perhaps even life-shortening – consequences. The optimal location of that threshold, however, is not obvious a priori.

Flexibility allows the constitution to adjust to the emergence of new social and political forces. It is thus related to the concept of inclusion. By facilitating the inclusion of new groups, frequent amendment generates a vital constitutional politics, in which groups have a stake in the maintenance of certain core elements of the constitutional bargain even as more peripheral elements change. In contrast, a rigid constitution may not allow the inclusion of new social forces or readjustment of the bargain between founding forces as time goes on.

Flexibility can ameliorate pressures for change, forestalling more radical overthrow of constitutional documents, which entail a loss of social surplus. Dicey's account of the failures of French constitutionalism is instructive:

> Nor ought the perils in which France was involved by the immutability with which the statesmen of 1848 invested the constitution to be looked upon as exceptional; they arose from a defect which is inherent in every rigid constitution. The Endeavour to create laws which cannot be changed is an attempt to hamper the exercise of sovereign power; it therefore tends to bring the letter of the law into conflict with the will of the really supreme power in the State. The majority of the French electors were under the constitution the true sovereign of France; but the rule which prevented the legal re-election of the President in effect brought the law of the land into conflict with the will of the majority of the electors and produced, therefore, as a rigid Constitution has a natural tendency to produce, an opposition between the letter of the law and the wishes of the sovereign. If the inflexibility of French constitutions has provoked revolution, the flexibility of English constitutions has, once at least, saved them from violent overthrow (Dicey 1960: 43).

Following Dicey, one might expect that formally rigid constitutions would die more frequently, and in fact, we provide some strong evidence for this in

Chapter Six. But, constitutions also have informal mechanisms of constitutional adjustment. The most obvious is constitutional review by constitutional courts, but there are other mechanisms, including unwritten understandings of the constitutional text (which sometimes differ quite radically from the words on the page), ordinary legislation, and the informal practices of government institutions. The key to adjustment is that common understandings among potential enforcers evolve over time in response to new pressures.[12]

The availability of informal procedures can sometimes offset the existence of rigid formal provisions. Consider, as an example, the United States between 1804 and 1865, a period in which there were no formal amendments to the U.S. Constitution, but a series of elite pacts to renegotiate the deal between North and South (Weingast 2006; Magliocca 2007).[13] These were necessitated by the westward expansion of the country and the threat that new entrants to the Union would upset the delicate sectional balance between slave and free states. Neither side wanted to allow the other to gain the upper hand, and both exercised a veto over admission of new states. In a series of agreements, they agreed to allow slavery in Missouri and states south of it, and to admit states in pairs so that sectional balance would be maintained. This series of renegotiations postponed, but did not eliminate, the possibility of violent conflict between the parties. For our purposes, it is of interest that the device of elite compromise induced parties to remain in the constitutional bargain. On some accounts, these compromises might be considered constitutional in character, but this is true in an informal sense only. The main point is that the existence of *some* method for adjustment to changing conditions over time forestalls pressure for more total revision.[14]

---

[12] This is similar to Ackerman's theory of constitutional change in the United States.

[13] By our reckoning, this is the second longest period for any *living* national constitution to remain formally unamended, having just been surpassed by the 1946 Constitution of Japan. Among all constitutions, the Italian Constitution of 1861 retains the record, having gone 82 years without any formal change.

[14] In addition, it should be acknowledged that constitutional amendment and subconstitutional legal change are closely related. David Strauss suggests that the difficult threshold of formal amendment in the U.S. constitution makes it irrelevant (2001: 1457). The higher threshold is only likely to be reached once society has already changed, affecting at most a small number of outliers who have not yet accepted the new norm. In contrast, lower thresholds of constitutional change may, in fact, be efficacious. As Strauss puts it "it may be that majoritarian acts (or judicial decisions) precisely because they do not require the ground to be prepared so thoroughly, can force the pace of change in a way that supermajoritarian acts cannot. A coalition sufficient to enact legislation might be assembled – or a judicial decision rendered – at a point when a society for the most part has not changed, but the legislation, once enacted (or the decision, once made) might be an important factor in bringing about more comprehensive change. The difference between majoritarian legislation and a supermajoritarian constitutional amendment

Specificity

Specificity refers to the level of detail in the constitution and the scope of topics that the document covers. There is a near-consensus among American constitutional scholars and advisors that a loosely drafted framework constitution is superior to a more specific one. The belief is that the U.S. constitution has endured precisely because it has not specified details, but left them instead to ordinary law and custom. This view internalizes Madison's stated preference for short, framework-oriented constitutions (Madison 1787; Elazar 1990; Hammons 1999). Other founders agreed: Edmund Randolph asserted that "[T]he draught of a fundamental constitution," should include "essential principles only; lest the operations of government should be clogged by rendering those provisions permanent and unalterable, which ought to be accommodated to times and events" (Hutson and Rapport 1987).[15] A.E. Dick Howard, the University of Virginia Professor who advised several East European governments on constitutional design, has criticized the husky Brazilian constitution, asserting that "Excessive length and detail in a constitution invites frequent amendment and early obsolescence" (1996: 393).

On the other hand, our theory of renegotiation suggests that the clarity and specificity of the constitutional contract may be helpful in providing an incentive for, and facilitating, enforcement. A clearer, more specified document will more easily generate shared understandings of what it entails. It will also solve issues related to hidden information at the time of bargaining. We thus have competing predictions about the optimal level of detail in a constitution. The somewhat counterintuitive view suggested by our theory starts from the assumption that negotiating textual detail and incorporating a large number of topics is costly. Specificity requires careful drafting and hard bargaining, both of which take time and political resources. Time is not

---

is that the latter is far more likely to occur only after the change has, for all practical purposes, already taken place" (Strauss 2001: 1468).

[15] As Chief Justice John Marshall wrote in 1819, "[a] constitution, to contain accurate detail of all the subdivisions of which its great powers will admit, and of all the means by which they may be carried into execution, would partake of the prolixity of a legal code, and could scarcely be embraced by the human mind. It would probably never be understood by the public. Its nature, therefore, requires that only its great outlines should be marked, its important objects designated, and the minor ingredients which compose those objects be deduced from the nature of the objects themselves." *McCulloch v. Maryland*, 4 Wheat, 316 (1819). Of course, even the U.S. Constitution is, in fact, quite detailed about certain matters, many of which do not seem to require constitutional entrenchment. Constitutional provisions on age limits seem to bear little justification in democratic theory. Article I, Section 8 enumerates the powers of the national Congress in some detail, and Article I Section 9 provides a precise date before which no law can be passed banning the importation of slaves, and also specifies the precise ceiling (of $10) on federal import duties for slaves. Perhaps most absurd, is the requirement in the Seventh Amendment for a jury trial for all suits at in common law over a stake of $20 or more.

something that constitutional designers have in abundance. Constitutional design often takes place in periods of crisis, in which there are great social and political pressures to produce a document in a discrete amount of time. Time pressure, of course, can be helpful for producing agreement. But, when combined with the costliness of negotiation, time pressure produces a scarcity of attention to detail.

Our contention that more specific documents are more costly than less specific ones is not indisputable. One could argue that time pressures might produce *longer* texts, as negotiators are prevented from reducing the text to a set of common principles and thus logroll a disparate set of priorities. Ultimately, whether time pressures produce more or less specific constitutions is an empirical question, on which we provide evidence in the next chapter, but to foreshadow that discussion, we find that the assumption that specificity is costly is supported by the evidence.

The costliness of constitutional bargaining means that designers must make hard choices as to what to include and what to leave out, and for any given issue area, how detailed to make the constitutional text. As with all legal language, we expect that decisions on specificity respond loosely to cost-benefit considerations. There is little need to specify detail for contingencies that are quite unlikely. Thus, a constitution need not specify, for example, the complete line of presidential succession, but may content itself with simply providing that a vice-president or deputy executive succeeds the president in the event of death. This, of course, leaves open the question of what happens if both the chief executive and deputy chief are killed in the same incident, but, if we think such an eventuality is sufficiently unlikely, the matter can be left to ordinary legal processes or ignored completely. The constitutional text is reserved, in principle if not always in practice, for matters whose combined probability and significance are such that the highest legal document ought to address them.

A related consideration is whether or not we think the polity can work out an ad hoc solution at the time a significant, but low-probability event materializes. Much of what constitutions do is to control behavior intertemporally (Sunstein 2001). Designers should thus restrict constitutional regulation to those issues in which they think ordinary processes are likely to produce poor outcomes. If we are confident in our ability to resolve contingencies in a flexible manner, we should simply leave the issue in question out of the constitution, and have a more general constitution that leaves detail to ordinary law.[16]

---

[16] Constitutional texts do not always seem to follow this rule of thumb. Article 8 of the Austrian Constitution provides that "The coat of arms of the Republic of Austria consists of an unfettered (*freischwebend*) single-headed black, red-tongued, gilt-armed eagle whose breast is covered by a red shield with a silver cross-piece. The eagle bears on its head a golden mural crown with

In some ways, the scope of the constitution will be very context dependent. Demand for constitutionalization of any given topic will depend on the partic- ular time and place in which the constitution is being written. Germany's 1871 Constitution, for example, spends eleven of its seventy-eight articles detailing aspects of the railroad and telegraph systems, hardly pressing concerns in the early twenty-first century. Sweden's constitution mentions reindeer herding, but we would not expect a similar provision in Singapore. Apart from qualita- tive differences in agendas across eras, there seem to be some secular trends in the quantity of topics under consideration in constitution drafting. As we describe in Chapter Two, the scope of constitutional rights has expanded from the eighteenth century conception of negative rights to include a panoply of positive rights and so-called third-generation rights that belong to groups. As these new rights have been invented and instantiated in international human rights instruments, they have also been extended to national constitutions. We thus observe an expansion in the scope of rights provisions over time. There are also new technologies of government that have emerged over time. One can hardly find a new constitution written in the last twenty years without dis- tinct commissions for judicial appointments, electoral oversight, human rights, and counter-corruption – bodies that were not considered by drafters in the nineteenth century.[17] New constitutional offices, such as an ombudsman or independent central bank, have similarly expanded the scope of constitutions. Finally, a host of new issues have arisen that are addressed in constitutions. Environmental protection, for example, did not warrant its first mention in a national constitution until the very end of the nineteenth century,[18] and of course is now regularly invoked as an important state function.

Specificity – whether in terms of detail or scope – helps constitutional endurance for three reasons. First, to the extent that specificity at the time of constitutional drafting anticipates and addresses relevant sources of

---

three visible merlons (*Zinnen*). The two talons are surrounded by a sundered iron chain. It carries in its right talon a golden sickle with the blade turned inward, in its left talon [it carries] a golden hammer." Constitution of Austria, Art. 8(2). The example comes from King (2007). All this excruciating detail is followed by a delegation to federal legislation of what might seem to be more important details about the protection of the coat of arms, presumably involving penalties for those who desecrate it. Id. Art. 8(3). Apparently, however, the symbolism of the broken iron chain was of some importance in Austrian constitutional history, capturing the country's emergence from oppression.

[17] At the same time, old institutions have faded away. Several nineteenth century constitutions, for example, featured tricameral legislatures. See, e.g., Constitution of Bolivia, 1825; Constitution of Sweden, 1808 (four houses.) Such innovations have died out. On balance, however, we believe the trend has been toward expansion in scope.

[18] Dominican Republic Constitution (1896), Art 25.10 mentions the preservation of national property.

downstream pressure on the constitutional text, it may be particularly helpful with regard to solving problems of hidden information among the bargainers. By forcing counterparties to consider various possible future shocks and scenarios, the drafters can minimize problems of strategic behavior and delays once the constitution comes into effect. We thus predict that these features will be associated with constitutional survival.

Second, specificity facilitates endurance precisely because it is costly. Interest groups may seek to embed their preferred policies in the constitution, making the document more specific. For these groups, specificity of a written constitution represents a certain amount of sunk-cost investment that cannot be recouped should the constitution fail. The greater the investment in a particular constitutional bargain, the less willing parties will be to deviate from it by switching to a new bargain. We expect that, *ceteris paribus*, it will take shocks of greater magnitude to trigger renegotiation.

Third, specificity provides an incentive for parties to invest resources in keeping the constitutional text current. A constitution of broader scope induces more interest groups, in more areas, to pay attention to the constitutional bargain and monitor its operation. Furthermore, once a certain level of detail has been achieved in spelling out the constitutional bargain, it will be in the interest of parties to ensure that it is up to date and reflects current political realities. Specificity incentivizes *ongoing* investments in the constitutional text, be they through formal amendment procedures or informal processes such as constitutional interpretation. In this way, the concept of specificity may be complementary with the notion of flexibility. As time goes on, the combination of specificity and flexibility will encourage ongoing constitutional politics.

To be sure, specificity and flexibility are in some tension with each other. Contract theory tends to consider specificity as constraining: more detailed agreements are seen as being more rigid in the face of future contingencies. Note that the dimension of flexibility in the constitutional context, however, is slightly different from the contract analogy. Flexibility in constitutions concerns the level of supermajority that will be required to amend the document, which is conceptually distinct from the parties' own recognition of particular contingencies that they anticipate. As a matter of both logic and practice, we can find detailed constitutions that are flexible (such as that of India), detailed constitutions that are rigid (that of the former Yugoslavia), general constitutions that are flexible (Luxembourg), and general constitutions that are rigid (the United States).

We recognize that specificity may in some circumstances be constraining, and do not want to overstate our claim. We also note that a constitution that is too detailed may sacrifice clarity and coherence and hence will undermine rather than facilitate coordination. However, in keeping with our emphasis on net effects, we believe that, up to some level, greater specificity will tend to enhance rather than hinder endurance. A constitution covering more topics will tend to incentivize more interest groups toward enforcement, whereas depth helps them develop shared understandings of what the constitution requires and allows. We also believe that, given that it is costly, specificity can serve as a proxy variable that evidences the extent to which parties have invested in the negotiation process. Parties that cannot come to agreement on details are likely to leave texts vague, rendering them less useful to downstream actors who wish to enforce them.

How the Mechanisms Interact

The three design elements – inclusion, flexibility, and specificity – are very likely to be mutually reinforcing. First, it seems likely that inclusive processes of constitutional design will increase pressure for specificity. The Brazilian process, so derided by many commentators, featured more than 500 legislators with full drafting rights and an extensive process of public comment. It generated an enormously detailed constitution, with many provisions that seemed oriented toward specific interest groups. It had broad scope in terms of topics and much detail that one might think was better left to the ordinary political processes. But all the detail facilitated an expanded number and range of potential enforcers of the constitution.

To be sure, inclusion also exacerbates the coordination problem among participants. *Ceteris paribus*, a larger number of groups with a wider range of interests will find it *more* difficult to coordinate and enforce. Their normative diversity may make it difficult to agree on what constitutes a violation and predict what other interest groups will join them in enforcing the constitution. But, this too means that *once agreement is reached*, the costs of leaving the bargain will be higher, for a prospective new negotiation will be more costly.

Specificity is important for generating ongoing interest in the constitution, as it tends to encourage more interest group activity. But, we note that specificity carries with it the danger of over-rigidity. We thus see specificity as helping produce demand for more flexibility in the bargain. More detailed provisions invite more refinement through formal amendment processes.[19] Longer constitutions are also likely to have a broader scope, constitutionalizing more issues and bringing more groups into the constitutional conversation.

[19] Indeed, there appears to be an empirical correlation between the initial length of the constitutional document and the number of times it is amended. See Lutz 2006; Berkowitz and Clay 2005.

Constitutional review processes also generate specificity, by articulating the bargain over time.

A more flexible document, in turn, induces further participation because of the lower threshold of constitutional change. When a constitution is flexibly amended, by definition, smaller coalitions will be able to effectuate change. This induces smaller groups to try to mobilize for constitutional amendment, giving them, too, a stake in the survival of the document.[20] The more vital constitutional politics are, the more likely the constitution is to be enforced.

To summarize the argument: three design choices help facilitate constitutional endurance. Flexibility, inclusion, and specificity result from the constitution-making process itself, but are also features of ongoing practice. All three mutually reinforce each other to produce a vigorous constitutional politics in which groups have a stake in the survival of the constitution. Without sufficient flexibility, exogenous shocks will induce constitutional violation and replacement. Without inclusion, few will stand ready to enforce the constitutional bargain in the face of demands for renegotiation. And, without specificity, enforcers will neither agree on the contents of the constitution nor care much when it dies.

The overall thrust of the argument can be stated simply: constitutions endure when they are most like ordinary statutes. Conventional wisdom postulates that constitutions are entrenched, whereas statutes are flexible; constitutions are general, whereas statutes are specific; and constitutional politics exist on a rarified plane in which interest groups will have less influence. We argue that constitutions are more likely to endure when they are flexible, detailed, and able to induce interest groups to invest in their processes.

We recognize that there is a certain degree of unavoidable endogeneity to our argument about these key mechanisms. Because many of the key design elements will be a product of choices of constitutional designers, they are likely to reflect underlying conditions that may themselves be conducive to constitutional endurance. To illustrate, elites bargaining over the constitution might choose an inclusive process only if their own level of agreement is

---

[20] Certain institutions might facilitate these factors. Constitutional review, for example, facilitates flexibility, but also plays a crucial role in making inclusion effective. Constitutional review helps to coordinate disparate groups in agreeing on constitutional violations, which might otherwise go unrecognized. Constitutional review can also serve to facilitate inclusion by allowing ongoing accommodation to new social and political forces that arise. In an oft-told story, the U.S. Supreme Court's response to African-American claims for civil rights inspired a similar set of rights claims by other groups in the United States and elsewhere (Scheiber 2006). The civil rights revolution largely occurred through the institution of constitutional review and involved accommodation of existing constitutional arrangements to new social forces (Epp 1998).

high, and so we would observe a positive association between inclusive processes and endurance that is not directly caused by inclusion itself. Specificity
helps overcome bargaining problems, but will also be easier to achieve when
elites are aligned. This is a missing variable problem that is, alas, unavoidable because the underlying level of agreement of constitutional bargainers is
hardly observable.

A Note on Time and Aging

Finally, we consider the important question of relative risks to a constitution
as it ages. Our theory suggests competing influences along these lines. On
the one hand, one might suspect that constitutions are more likely to wither
with age as their provisions and proclamations become increasingly out of step
with reality, thus increasing the probability of breach and the acquiescence to
such. Constitutions, after all, may be suited to the political environment at the
time of their adoption but, as we have emphasized, societies do not remain
constant. Exogenous technological changes occur; different international con-
figurations develop; and institutions alter the political makeup of the societies
they inhabit. Even a self-enforcing constitution can fall into disequilibrium
if the distributional benefits that it produces among groups change over time
(Ordeshook 1992).

Consider again the example of the United States and the bargain over
slavery. The series of pacts between North and South that began with the
Missouri compromise helped sustain the constitution for the first part of the
19th century. Over time, however, this arrangement broke down because of
the westward expansion of the population. By the time of the *Dred Scott* decision, the North could dominate the South and impose its will through the
original institutions designed in 1787 (Graber 2006; Weingast 2005). This possibility had not been anticipated by Madison, but formed the most profound
challenge to his work, and it took a civil war to resolve the constitutional questions. Many other constitutions have died as a result of political transformation
occurring over time.

On the other hand, a constitution may crystallize with time, as it grows
in stature and becomes enmeshed in the national culture and politics of the
country, thus increasing its consensual nature and enforceability. We might
imagine, for example, that citizens might be more likely to expect others to
join them in enforcing the constitution if there is already a track record of such
enforcement. Constitutions that have endured already for some time might
generate a belief among citizens that other citizens venerate the document,
and so are more likely to join in should enforcement become necessary.

And polities with a history of enduring constitutions might find it easier to coordinate expectations.

We might also imagine that some constitutions may generate increasing returns to their beneficiaries over time, "locking in" the current configuration (Arthur 1994; Hathaway 2001; Pierson 2004). Constitutions that have established increasing streams of political benefits may be better able to withstand external pressures, and parties will be less likely to overturn current arrangements. To illustrate, consider a constitution that provides for an internal free-trade zone among entities that might otherwise trade across borders, as the United States Constitution does in the Commerce Clause of Article I, Section 8. Such an arrangement solves a collective action problem among states by allowing them to capture the benefits of free trade (Shapiro 1992). As the United States expanded to the West, new states and territories joined the existing bargain. Each new state added to the overall population and market size of the country, so that existing states continuously saw their markets expand along with the country. This is an example of how a constitution can generate increasing returns: each new entrant served to enhance the welfare of existing members and the constitution as a whole generated increasing returns. Over time, this increased the incentive to remain in the constitutional bargain, while also raising the relative costs of going it alone outside the union.

Of course, the effect of time may be nonlinear. For example, the hazard rate may increase through the early years before reaching an age at which the constitution crystallizes and becomes relatively invulnerable. Another intriguing possibility is that there are certain ages or thresholds (corresponding to generational turnover, perhaps) that are particularly difficult for constitutions. This sort of periodicity undergirds the critical juncture approach to political and constitutional development (e.g., Burnham 1970; Ackerman 1993). Given the competing effects of age, we remain agnostic about its net effect on constitutional change. We explore this question, as well as issues of design choice, empirically in the next two chapters.

CONCLUSION

Our discussion has proceeded from the problems of coordination that lie at the heart of the modern theory of institutional stability and change. We have also seen how particular dynamics in constitutional negotiation can render documents more or less specific and lead to certain pathologies that will affect party incentives to maintain the constitution. We think more specific documents are more likely to survive, although they may be more difficult to achieve. Once a bargain is reached, however, it may remain stable and even generate reinforcing payoffs that encourage further endurance.

Exogenous shocks, however, are bound to occur. When internal mechanisms are sufficiently inflexible to accommodate constitutional change, there may be pressures for extra-constitutional change. In such instances, it is only the prospect of strong enforcement that will protect the constitution and allow it to survive. Enforcement implicates the well-known problem of coordination.

We believe that the key mechanisms of inclusion, flexibility, and specificity help constitutions to endure. Inclusively generated constitutions will be better known and more likely to become focal points among a public with disparate interests. Flexible documents allow for adjustment to changing circumstances. Specific documents are more likely to generate common knowledge and agreement on when a constitutional violation has occurred. The mechanisms are mutually reinforcing. Specific constitutions invite flexibility down the road; flexible constitutions facilitate inclusion; and inclusive processes create pressures for continuous articulation of the constitution, producing yet more specificity. The result is an ongoing constitutional politics in which parties are aware of the constitution, invested in it, and hence more willing to enforce it. The dilemmas of coordination and agreement can be overcome with a sufficiently vigorous constitutional politics.

5

Identifying Risks to Constitutional Life

INTRODUCTION

Officially, heart disease and cancer together accounted for roughly 50 percent of deaths in the United States in 2006.[1] These attributions are physiological explanations of death in that they focus on the most proximate set of causes, such as the failure of a crucial bodily organ. But, physiology alone does not provide much guidance to those seeking to live healthier lives. Doctors and patients would prefer additional information about what behaviors or characteristics led to the disease. Relevant questions about these more remote causes might include: are individuals genetically predisposed to the disease? Do certain activities or environments lead to increased incidence of disease? What can one do to treat the disease? These questions move us beyond physiology and into the realm of epidemiology, and to theory that connects the immediate cause of death with observable aspects of life. That too is our progression as we move from physiology (Chapter 4) to epidemiology (this chapter).

Chapter Four developed a theory of constitutional bargaining, which describes the mechanics by which constitutions enter periods of crisis in which they are under threat of renegotiation and, potentially, replacement. Here, we specify the empirical implications of the theory and identify the observable factors that affect the risk of constitutional death. The motive is the same as that of the epidemiologist who seeks to test assumptions about the physiology of disease by positing and then testing hypotheses about which *kinds* of individuals are more or less at risk. We thus review critical aspects of our theory of renegotiation and then, delving into the world that constitutions inhabit, generate hypotheses about which kinds of texts or environmental conditions will be predisposed to constitutional breakdown. Lest this account

---

[1] Heron et al. 2009. Stroke, respiratory disease, and accidents were the next three leading causes, accounting for another five percent of cases each.

remain exclusively at the level of the abstract (and, potentially, enable misunderstandings), we also take the opportunity to describe how, exactly, we will measure the concepts implied by our hypotheses. Our sense is that it is helpful to know what exactly counts as, for example, a "specific" or "inclusive" constitution, to understand more fully our theory and hypotheses. These measurement details are, of course, more obviously critical to the statistical analysis that follows in the next chapter. We introduce them here to begin our descent from the abstract and plant our feet on the ground in preparation for that analysis. Table 5.1 summarizes the hypotheses, concepts, and measures and serves as a schematic map of the model we propose to test in the following chapter.

DESIGN VERSUS ENVIRONMENT

At a basic level, one can understand the risks to constitutional life as pertaining to either constitutional *design* or the constitutional *environment*. As we describe in the introductory chapter, constitutions differ in an important way from human beings in that, among constitutions, design features are more subject to human manipulation than are environmental conditions. Thus, we have particular interest in the design factors of constitutional endurance. As it happens, conventional wisdom in the institutional change literature puts much more stock in the power of environmental shocks and pressures than it does on the design and structure of institutions. This emphasis in the literature places a heavy evidentiary burden on any claim regarding the impact of design factors. Analytically, the implication is that we should identify and estimate the effects of a rather inclusive set of environmental factors, both to evaluate the comparative impact of the two sets of factors and to control for any factors that might confound our assessment of the design factors. Happily, this is a welcome assignment, for we are decidedly curious about the effects of the environment, especially if they prove to be determinative of constitutional life span.

DESIGN FACTORS

The renegotiation theory in Chapter Four described the role of breach, enforcement, and adaptation in the process of constitutional crisis and replacement. We expect the specter of breach to continually threaten constitutional life, but the probability of breach will increase as a function of the incompleteness of the contract and the incidence of exogenous crises. The potential of constitutional enforcement will deter a breach, but enforcement of constitutions is difficult. A high probability of enforcement depends critically on

TABLE 5.1. *Concepts, measures, and their hypothesized effects*

Category	Concept	Measure	Effect	Source
Crises	Global Constitutional Events[1]	Percent of countries in the world with new constitutions in the prior year	−	COW; CCP
	Neighboring Constitutional Events[1]	Percent of immediate neighbors with new constitutions in the prior year	−	COW; CCP
	Territory Gain	Binary variable coded one if the state merged, annexed, or otherwise incorporated territory	−	COW
	Territory Loss	Binary variable coded one if the state ceded territory to another state	−	COW
	Defeat in War	Binary variable coded one if state was defeated in war	−	COW
	Domestic Crisis	Binary variable coded one if Banks' conflict index is greater than or equal to 10,000	−	Banks
	Economic Crisis	Binary variable coded one if per capita GDP decreased more than 10% annually	−	Barro, Penn, World Bank
	Democratic Transition	Binary variable coded one if a democratic transition occurred	−	Polity
	Authoritarian Transition	Binary variable coded one if an authoritarian transition occurred	−	Polity
	Extra-constitutional Leadership Change	Binary variable coded one if the executive lost power as a result of a process not prescribed either in the constitution or by convention	−	Goemans et al.
	Intra-constitutional Leadership Change	Binary variable coded one if the leader lost power as a result of the process prescribed either in the constitution or by convention	−	Goemans et al.
Structure of the State	Democracy	Binary variable coded one if the country is a democracy	+	Polity
	Ethnic Heterogeneity	Ethnic fractionalization score	−	Fearon
	Economic Development[1]	Energy consumption per capita	+	COW
	State Age[1]	Years since state formation	+	ICOW
	Legacy of Endurance[1]	Average life span of previous constitutions	+	CCP
Structure of the Constitution	Interim Constitution	Binary variable coded one if constitution is interim	−	CCP
	Reinstated Constitution	Binary variable coded one if constitution is reinstated	+	CCP
	Inclusiveness[1]	Additive index indicating the inclusiveness of the constitution-making process and constitutional provisions	+	CCP

(continued)

95

TABLE 5.1 (continued)

Category	Concept	Measure	Effect	Source
	Democratic at Promulgation	Binary variable coded one if state was democratic when the constitution was promulgated	+	CCP
	Occupation Constitution	Binary variable coded one if constitution is written during or within two years of foreign military occupation	–	CCP
	Amendment Rate	Predicted probability of the promulgation of a constitutional amendment	+	CCP
	Judicial Review	Binary variable coded one if any court can review the constitutionality of laws	+	CCP
	Scope	Percent of selected issues covered in the constitution	+	CCP
	Detail[1]	Words per issue covered in the constitution	+	CCP
	Single Executive	Binary variable coded one if the constitution calls for a single executive	–	CCP
	Executive Term Limits	Binary variable coded one if there are term limits placed on the head of state	–	CCP
	Parliamentary Power	De jure measure of Fish and Kroenig's Parliamentary Power Index	–	CCP
Region (Western Europe, U.S., and Canada is the reference category)	Latin America	Binary variable coded one if country in Latin America	–	CCP
	Eastern Europe	Binary variable coded one if country in Eastern Europe	–	CCP
	Middle East	Binary variable coded one if country in the Middle East or North Africa	–	CCP
	Sub-Saharan Africa	Binary variable coded one if country in Sub-Saharan Africa	–	CCP
	South Asia	Binary variable coded one if country in South Asia	–	CCP
	East Asia	Binary variable coded one if country in East Asia	–	CCP
	Oceania	Binary variable coded one if country in Oceania	–	CCP
Era (prior to 1914 is reference category)	1914–1945	Binary variable coded one if year is between 1914 and 1945	–	CCP
	1946 to Present	Binary variable coded one if year is between 1946 and 2006	+	CCP

[1] Rescaled in the analysis to range from 0 to 1.

96

the ability of citizens to coordinate, which in turn depends on the degree of citizen attachment to and investment in the constitution. Finally, actors will avoid pursuing a breach if the constitution can be adapted easily through intra-constitutional means and, thus, secure a non-lethal modification of the constitution. The theory implies a set of observable design factors that should be closely associated with one or more of these overarching concepts of breach, enforcement, and adaptation: (1) the degree of inclusion; (2) the flexibility of amendment and other adaptive procedures; and (3) the specificity of the document. In this chapter, we describe how these concepts are manifest in written constitutions and specify their expected effects. As we stressed earlier and in the introductory chapter, these factors may affect constitutional life span through multiple channels, some of which may be complementary, some contradictory. As such, we focus our discussion on the net effect of these factors, but in so doing, we also identify the particular causal channels that underlie the overall effect.

Inclusion

Actors are more likely to enforce the constitution if there is consensus about what the law of the land is, and what it should be. That is, the constitution must be widely understood and widely respected. In part, this sort of consensus is a function of the charter's fit with societal needs and norms. Rules that are consistent with underlying unwritten norms and expectations in the society are more likely to be enforced. Indeed, as we have emphasized, time alone might enhance this congruence. As a document survives, potential enforcers are more likely to have a shared understanding of constitutional norms and identify them with the written document, helping to coordinate expectations (even if the expectations do not perfectly match the text). Mechanisms other than aging can facilitate coordination, however. Our theory predicts that constitution-making processes that are highly open and inclusionary (or at least appear to be so) increase citizens' awareness and regard for the document as well as their confidence that *other* citizens have developed the same awareness and respect. Such consensus not only increases the expectation that others will join in enforcement, it also provides incentives for enforcement through a wider distribution of stakes. But, it is not just the processes at the origin of constitutions that matter. Constitutional provisions that involve the public directly in ongoing governance, through referenda and other such mechanisms, will also generate ongoing interest in the functioning and maintenance of the constitutional order, which may at crucial junctures allow it to survive.

Thus, our concept of constitutional inclusion denotes the process of constitution-making as well as the constitutional provisions that result from that process. Taking the mode of constitutional formation first, we note several discernible stages, including writing, deliberation, and approval, which can be more or less inclusive (Ginsburg et al. 2009). We can focus on the deliberation and approval stages, under the assumption that the drafting and other stages may be unproblematically exclusionary (we do not suggest that the public look over the shoulder of writers as they pen an initial draft). In particular, given the relatively limited variation in constitutional process, inclusion in these two stages of the process reduces to whether or not a publicly elected body deliberates and whether the ratification procedure involves a public referendum. Both of these methods, we reason, are strong consensus building procedures. Information on these aspects of process is not easily come by. For deliberative procedures, we consulted a variety of historical sources (see Ginsburg et al. 2009) and for evidence of public ratification, we rely primarily on the ratification instruction in constitutional documents.[2]

In terms of inclusion in ongoing governance, we examine whether the public is involved in the election of the head of state and first chamber of the legislature. We also examine whether the constitution includes mechanisms of direct democracy, such as referendum, initiative, or recall of executives and legislators. Finally, we examine whether the public can challenge the constitutionality of legislation. Because we view these elements as capturing the same basic concept, albeit across different substantive arenas, we combine them into a single index of inclusion to reduce complexity in a multivariate model that is already fairly comprehensive. We thus produce an index that averages across eight binary features of inclusion in both constitution-making

---

[2] With respect to the drafting stage, we would ideally have some information on the level of inclusion in the group of constitution writers. Such a measure is difficult to construct in systematic form (but see Widner 2005 for a promising approach to recent cases), so in our analysis we utilize two proxy variables that should be broadly indicative of inclusion. The first is whether or not the state was occupied by a foreign power during or within the two years prior to a constitutional replacement (e.g., Japan in 1946 or Iraq in 2005), a variable we construct from historical sources. In all, we identify 89 episodes of occupation, 42 of which are associated with a new constitution. The second variable is the extent to which the context of constitution making could be characterized as democratizing. We reason that those constitutions written under circumstances in which the state is moving (or has recently moved) toward democracy are more likely to utilize – or at least be perceived to have utilized – inclusive processes. We measure this by calculating the total change in Polity democracy scores (positive values meaning increased levels of democracy) within one year of the constitution's promulgation.

and ongoing governance.[3] In separate analyses, we follow a more disaggregated approach in which we examine the items individually, especially those tapping inclusion in constitution-making as opposed to ongoing governance.

The index, however, seems to differentiate constitutions with respect to inclusion fairly well, at least by face-validity standards. For example, one of the most inclusive constitutions is Colombia's 1991 document, which includes six of the eight items in the scale. The constitution, sometimes known in Colombia as the "Constitution of Rights," replaced the historic 1886 constitution – one of the oldest in history, but one of the least inclusive by our measure. The somewhat unceremonious replacement came only after several unsuccessful attempts to reform the 1886 document by adding a set of more participatory rights and, as Nielson and Shugart (1999) describe, expanding the power of the urban median voter. Remarkably, in a plebiscite used to justify a constituent assembly, a whopping 88 percent of Colombians – in part frustrated by the fruitless attempts to render the 1886 constitution more inclusive – voted to replace the age-old document.

Ease of Amendment

Our renegotiation theory suggests that, *ceteris paribus*, constitutions with lower thresholds for amendment will be more flexible and likely to survive in the face of constitutional crisis. Formal amendment allows adaptation to inevitable, but unanticipated, circumstances such as shifts in the balance of power among groups. In this sense, amendment operates as a substitute for constitutional replacement, and often a more desirable substitute given the higher costs of replacement. We have already noted, in the context of executive efforts to extend their terms, how amendment flexibility can save the life of a constitution. An elaboration of this phenomenon may be instructive here. In the cases of Brazil in 1996 and Colombia in 2005, for example, the constitution was potentially threatened by presidents who were intent on, but constitutionally denied, reelection. In those cases, a flexible amendment procedure allowed the executive to preserve the constitution, but still pursue reelection. The Mexican constitution, whose hard term limits would seem to have doomed the document long ago, may also have benefitted from amendment flexibility, albeit not as a mechanism to relax term limits. In Chapters Three and Eight

---

[3] The eight scale items are: public referendum or publicly elective deliberated body; elected head of state; elected legislature; public can challenge constitutionality of legislation; citizen initiatives; citizen referenda; recall of legislators; and recall of the executive. The resulting scale has a reasonably high measure of reliability (alpha = 0.81), suggesting that the eight items are tapping *something* systematically.

we show how dramatically the Mexican constitution has changed over the years through amendment – more so even than many other constitutions that have undergone full replacement. These adaptations, which have been facilitated in part by a flexible amendment process, quite possibly have sustained a constitutional bargain that was otherwise subject to rather high risks.

Amendment can also be seen as enhancing the specificity of the constitution. Most amendments will be adopted either to (1) clarify or correct a lacuna in the original drafting process; or (2) extend the constitution to cover a new issue that had not been anticipated. The former motive enhances detail, whereas the latter extends the scope of the constitution. Thus, the accumulation of changes through amendment can have downstream effects on the life span of constitutions through specificity, quite apart from their more immediate adaptive effects.[4]

Through these various channels, we expect that low thresholds for amendment will generally be associated with endurance. We add the qualifier "generally" because of our uncertainty about the effects of extreme flexibility. When amendment constraints are no more difficult than those of ordinary legislation, the healthful aspects of flexibility would seem to give way. Indeed, we might even think of excessive flexibility as compromising incentives to enforce the constitution. Whether or not we think in terms of such a trade-off, it seems reasonable to expect that extreme flexibility will yield unpredictable results with respect to life span. Our measurement strategy (discussed later) anticipates this possibility of non-linearity.

We measure ease of amendment using information on both the observed amendment rate and the formal amendment procedures of each constitution. Amendment rate alone is unsuitable, as it will be a function of many of the same factors that explain constitutional replacement. Instead, our preference is for a measure of amendment ease based on amendment procedures themselves. However, the comparative flexibility of the hybrid set of procedural arrangements in constitutions is not obvious *ex ante*. For example, it is difficult to evaluate whether a constitution that requires a two-thirds vote of the legislature to amend the constitution is more or less flexible than one that requires an ordinary legislative majority with a subsequent referendum by the public. In a pioneering and careful article on the subject, Donald Lutz (1994) assigns weights to various different amendment gates and arrives at a measure of amendment ease for a set of modern constitutions.

---

[4] We do recognize that informal substitutes are available for formal procedures, and so do not expect the strength of the relationship to be too great. Still, we do have strong predictions about the direction of the relationship, if not its magnitude.

We are less certain about the relative constraints imposed by these various gates. Our approach is to model the amendment rate and estimate the effects of particular amendment rules, net of other predictors. Thus, we regress the amendment rate on a set of amendment procedure variables as well as on a host of factors that should predict political reform more generally, including those factors in our model of constitutional duration.[5] The unit of analysis in this model is the constitutional system, and the dependent variable is binary, capturing whether or not the constitution was amended in a given year. We estimate the model using logistic regression and include all of the independent variables from our principal model as well as several variables that capture the amendment procedure: the number of actors involved in various stages of the amendment process, the margin necessary to pass amendments through the legislature, and dummy variables to indicate the role of different bodies in the process. After estimating the model, we predict the probability of amendment for each constitutional system by constraining all variables except the amendment procedures to their mean.[6] The predicted amendment rate varies from 0 amendments per year to 1.0 amendments per year (with a mean of 0.38 and a standard deviation of 0.38).[7] To test the possibility of non-linearity, we include in our model the square of the amendment difficulty variable, whose effect should be negative if flexibility at the extreme represents a high risk to constitutions.

How well does our measure of amendment ease capture differences across constitutions? Consider, for example, two historic constitutions from the Americas: that of the United States and the Colombian constitution of 1886. The U.S. Constitution is scored as one of the most inflexible (at 0.04) and the Colombian one of the most flexible (at 0.99). The provisions themselves read as follows:

Colombian Constitution of 1886, Article 209

This Constitution may be amended by a legislative act, discussed and passed after three separate readings in the usual manner by Congress, submitted by the Government to the following Congress for its definite action, and discussed and finally passed in the latter by two-thirds of the members of both houses.

---

[5] Lutz (1994) and Lorenz (2005) recommend roughly similar measures in another context.

[6] Our approach is akin to 2SLS, albeit 2SLS "by hand," which implies that we should adjust the standard errors of our estimates in the second stage equation. Such adjustment, however, is not straightforward in the event-history framework that we use (see Achen 1987 and Chapter 6).

[7] For a more thorough description of this procedure and the resulting predicted amendment rate, see the online Appendix at www.comparativeconstitutionsproject.org.

United States Constitution, 1789, Article 5

The Congress, whenever two thirds of both Houses shall deem it necessary, shall propose Amendments to this Constitution, or, on the Application of the Legislatures of two thirds of the several States, shall call a Convention for proposing Amendments, which, in either Case, shall be valid to all Intents and Purposes, as Part of this Constitution, when ratified by the Legislatures of three fourths of the several States or by Conventions in three fourths thereof, as the one or the other Mode of Ratification may be proposed by the Congress; Provided that no Amendment which may be made prior to the Year One thousand eight hundred and eight shall in any Manner affect the first and fourth Clauses in the Ninth Section of the first Article; and that no State, without its Consent, shall be deprived of its equal Suffrage in the Senate.

The Colombian system is relatively simple. The legislature – and *only* the legislature – passes constitutional amendments, albeit with a two-thirds supermajority and the approval of successive sessions in both houses. The U.S. system provides for two procedures, but each one requires approval by a three-fourths supermajority of states in addition to *either* a supermajority of congress *or* a convention proposed by two-thirds of the states. As Americans who have followed the plight of seemingly consensual, but ill-fated, amendments like the Equal Rights Amendment know, securing approval by three quarters of the states is a herculean task. The U.S. provision also protects two aspects of the document from any amendment under these procedures (the slave trade, until 1808, and the manner in which the Senate is apportioned). On its face, then, the U.S. document does seem more restrictive than the Colombian and, certainly, the comparative output of amendments in their tenure provides some predictive validation of this. In its hundred years in force, the Colombian constitution was amended in seventeen of those years, whereas the U.S. document has been revised in only sixteen of its 220 years of existence.[8] Nevertheless, one of the lessons of the demise of the Colombian constitution is that amendment procedures that are the exclusive preserve of one body – even a theoretically representative body like the legislature – can be quite rigid in practice. To return to the saga of the fall of the Colombian document, we recall that it came about because of a failure to pass a set of amendments in the late 1980s. One reason for their failure is that they would have chipped away at the disproportionately rural base of the presiding legislative delegation – revisions that were not going to pass through one session of the legislature,

---

[8] Years, as opposed to number, of amendments is probably the best way to validate amendment flexibility, because amendments (such as the first ten in the United States) are often passed in clusters with similar levels of support across items in the cluster.

much less two in succession (Nielson and Shugart, 1999). In comparison, the two amendment procedures in the U.S. document allow, quite crucially, citizens to bypass Congress entirely to amend. Granted, this alternative method has never been attempted, but one could argue that simply the threat of going down that path, and toward an open-ended convention, would be enough to coax a reluctant Congress into giving more consideration to an amendment. Thus, the Colombian provision may not be nearly as flexible, nor the U.S. provision as rigid, as they appear in our scoring. Nevertheless, our examination of our measure of flexibility suggests that the magnitude of any error across cases is not substantial.

Specificity: Scope and Detail

Chapter Four also emphasized the importance of textual specificity for constitutional endurance. We conceive of specificity as having two dimensions: *scope* and *detail*. Scope refers to the breadth of coverage of the constitution, or the number of issues that it chooses to regulate. *Detail* refers to the precision and elaboration of the provisions of the constitution in any given topic area. Conceptually, we might think of these two dimensions as representing a trade-off: given scarce time, designers can deal with fewer issue areas in greater detail or a greater number of issues in less detail. In practice, however, designers are more likely to add both scope and detail, or neither (but more on that is forthcoming).

However they relate, detail and scope result from careful bargaining at the time of constitutional design and so can ameliorate problems of hidden information. They also reflect the sunk investments of constitutional bargainers and interest groups, who then subsequently may play a role in constitutional enforcement. More detailed constitutions provide evidence that bargainers spent time in working out conflicts, rather than relying on general language that will be open to interpretation. Furthermore, we believe that constitutions that govern a wide scope of activity invite further investment in amending the text as conditions change. In summary, then, our expectation is that constitutions that are more detailed and have broader scope will be more enduring.[9]

To be sure, scholars have differing intuitions about the role of generality in constitutional endurance and our theory of specificity is somewhat nonconventional. As we discuss in some detail in Chapter 4, the "framework"

---

[9] As far as we know, no one has yet examined the relationship between specificity and endurance at the national level, but there is some relevant evidence. For example, Berkowitz and Clay (2005) show in the context of U.S. states that shorter constitutions are more durable. We do not believe that state level constitutions are equivalent to national documents. See Chapter Three, footnote 13.

constitution is a model that scholars (including ourselves) have long thought to be the source of longevity in the United States and elsewhere. Apart from the adaptive benefits of a vague, short document, one might argue that excessive detail reflects a *lack* of agreement in bargaining.[10] Analogizing to Pascal's famous quip that he wrote a long letter, only because he had not time to make it shorter, one might believe that long constitutions simply reflect an unwillingness of bargainers to resolve conflicts. In this view, short documents may be more costly to write than longer ones, a claim that most college students regularly and vigorously dispute. Nonetheless, it is plausible (contrary to our assumption) that failure to resolve issues might lead to a kind of low-cost, "kitchen-sink constitution." To evaluate this possibility, we gathered information on the time spent drafting 148 randomly-selected constitutions from our database, under the assumption that time spent is a reasonable, if imperfect, proxy for the cost of the drafting process. We compared the duration of those drafting processes to our measure of detail. The results of this analysis support our assumption. Constitutions with more than the mean level of detail took, on average, twice as long to draft as did constitutions with less than the mean level of detail.[11]

We measure the breadth of a constitution – its scope – by the number of topics covered in the document, as a percentage of some ninety-two possible topics. This measure is related to the one that we employ in the analysis of constitutional similarity in Chapter Two. In that chapter, we measure the proportion of issues that were either mutually included or excluded by any two constitutions, thus capturing the association between any given *pair* of constitutions. Here, the measure is simply the proportion of issues covered by any single constitution, but the raw ingredients of the two measures are identical.[12] On average, constitutions have included forty-five of the ninety-two topics on our list (for an average scope score of 49 percent). The Colombian Constitution of 1991 and the Thai Constitution of 1997 are the most wide ranging on this measure; both include 78 percent of topics. Libya's 1969 Constitution, by contrast, is the least so at 14 percent. The scope scores for the widely imitated constitutions of the United States (1789), France (1946), and Mexico (1917) range in the low 40s, and thus very close to average.

---

[10] Among others, John Carey raises this possibility (personal communication).

[11] More detailed constitutions had more variance in drafting time, so it is possible that some highly detailed constitutions could be of the "kitchen-sink" variety. We found no association between our measure of scope and drafting duration.

[12] It is worth reiterating our selection criteria for the ninety-two topics. We chose topics that were relatively independent of context (in terms of era, geography, and basic characteristics of the state) and that displayed sufficient variation (that is, they were not especially consensual or rare). See the appendix for the contents of our measure.

We construct a measure of detail by dividing the length (in words) of the constitutional text by the number of scope items (from our group of ninety-two) that are included in the document. The measure thus amounts to the number of words per topic in a given constitution, with the understanding that this is an overestimate of detail in that not all of a constitution's topics will be captured by our scope measure, the denominator. The average number of words per topic for constitutions since 1789 is 306, ranging from China's succinct 1982 document (26 words per topic) to Kenya's (1963) verbose inaugural charter (1690 words per topic).

These variables shed light on the structure of constitutions, past and present. Word length itself – the numerator of our detail measure – is illustrative. The average constitution since 1789 runs approximately 14,000 words. Brazil's current charter, 65,000 words at its birth in 1988, is famous for having constitutionalized nearly every aspect of public life; Thailand's recently deceased constitution of 1997 was almost as long, with 336 articles and more than 40,000 words in English translation, when it expired. India's constitution is the longest ever, having swelled to over 140,000 words after frequent amendments and adoption of an extensive set of schedules. Some constitutions are surprisingly verbose, such as that of tiny Tuvalu, whose 34,801 words outnumber the island-nation's 11,992 inhabitants.[13] By contrast, the U.S. constitution, at a mere 4,600 words at birth, is seen as providing a framework for politics rather than a repository of policies.[14] Mauritania's 1985 document may be the shortest national constitution yet produced, a scarce 865 words in length, providing virtually no detail on the operation of government.

One might wonder about the relationship between scope and detail given the potential trade-off between the two. Although the *word length* of constitutions and scope are understandably highly correlated (r = 0.46), detail (words per topic) and scope are also positively related, albeit less so (r = 0.21). That is, not only do constitutions that cover a large number of topics tend to be longer, but those that cover a larger number of topics also tend to include more words per topic. In fact, constitutions that cover fewer than 40 topics include 260 words per topic, whereas those with over 40 topics use 320 words per topic. Figure 5.1, which plots the length of constitutions in words by the proportion of topics covered, provides some sense of this relationship between constitutional length, scope, and detail. Whereas it may be true that, on average, higher scope constitutions also include more detail, there appears to be significant variation across those cases. Once again, China

---

[13] As does the country of Nauru (13,000 words for a population of 10,000).
[14] Even with its small number of amendments, the length of the U.S. Constitution has almost doubled since 1789, counting 7,762 words in 1992, when last amended.

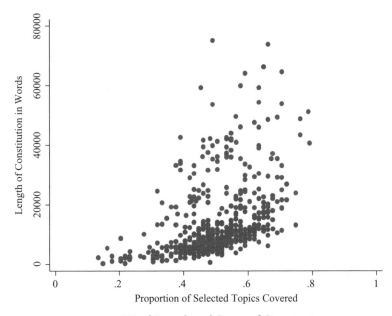

FIGURE 5.1. Word Length and Scope of Constitutions.

(1982) and Kenya (1963) provide a vivid contrast here. Both constitutions include 46 percent of topics (nearly the sample average), but China does so in about 1,200 words, whereas Kenya's document runs nearly 75,000 words. This variation suggests that scope and detail, although related, are clearly distinct dimensions.

Constitutional Review

Our renegotiation theory suggests that the practice of constitutional review can play a key role in easing the constitution through shocks and other pressures. Its role is three-fold in that it assists inclusion, specificity, and adaptation. In this sense, the net effect of constitutional review is like that of exercise on human health – the sum of multiple positive mechanisms.

Most importantly, constitutional courts play an important role in helping parties to a constitutional crisis coordinate their behavior, and thus enforce the bargain (Ginsburg and McAdams 2004). Suppose two parties to a constitutional bargain disagree over the scope of legislative power. They are of equal strength and each has an incentive to demonstrate resolve in the bargaining process and threaten constitutional renegotiation should their position not be adopted. However, they may have more to lose from constitutional renegotiation than from simply losing on the particular issue of legislative power. This strategic situation corresponds to the dynamic in game theory scenario of *Hawk/Dove* or *Chicken*.[15] Both parties would prefer to cooperate rather than pursue a costly conflict, but they disagree over the terms or manner of cooperation. Such situations are extremely common in politics, and particularly so with regard to constitutional renegotiation.

A natural solution to this problem is to defer to a neutral third party: someone exogenous to the parties' interaction can assist by providing a focal point for coordination (Schelling 1980). Consider a stylized scenario: two cars come to an intersection at exactly the same time and are unsure which car should go first. Other things equal, they each prefer to go first rather than be delayed, but their overriding priority is to avoid a costly accident. If a pedestrian were to go out to the middle of the street and wave one car forward while indicating stop to the other car, both cars would probably follow the pedestrian's signals, even though the pedestrian's judgment is not formally binding as a matter of law and is unlikely to be enforced by an *official* third party (Ginsburg and McAdams 2004). The reason is that both parties believe that the other one will play by the rule suggested by the pedestrian. Expecting the other car to go ahead, the car told to stop will indeed do so, even in the absence of external enforcement. Recent analysis has emphasized this coordinating role of courts in explaining compliance with court decisions and, consequently, the rise of judicial power.[16]

---

[15] "Chicken" refers to the dangerous American pastime in which two cars drive headfirst at each other to see who will be the first to swerve. Each party would prefer to play the aggressive strategy and refuse to swerve so as to appear more fearless, but if both follow this first best strategy, they will wind up in the collectively worst outcome of a head-on collision. The task for each party is to convincingly demonstrate that he will not swerve, thereby inducing the other party to swerve.

[16] Take, for example, the celebrated case of *Bush v. Gore*. In facts recounted extensively elsewhere, the U.S. Supreme Court intervened in a partisan election that had produced a statistical tie. The court's decision has been widely criticized as poorly reasoned, legally flawed, and unnecessary (Dershowitz 2001; Gillman 2001; cf. Posner 2001). Arguably, however, it made functional sense. The game in election disputes like *Bush v. Gore* is akin to that of chicken. In election disputes, there is only one presidency with two claimants. Each party prefers that she be the one to occupy the office. Ultimately, however, the most important thing is that some sort of resolution occurs. The costs to the constitutional order of continuing to fight exceed the costs of being the "loser." The trick is to figure out who will play the role of loser and back down from the confrontation. Left to their own devices, the parties will not be able to coordinate their roles. Each will try to express resolve to induce the other party to back down. The role of a constitutional court here is to point to one or the other contender and identify her as the "winner." Once a court identifies one party as a winner, the decision may become a self-enforcing focal point. Gore's perception of the likelihood of Bush's backing down changed as soon as the Supreme Court announced its decision. Whereas before the decision, Gore seemed to have a legitimate claim on the presidency and might have expected Bush to accede, after the decision, Bush was unlikely to do so. Gore could have stayed on but the chances of Bush ever adopting the *swerve* strategy were greatly reduced.

Extending this coordinating function of courts to the context of constitutional enforcement describes one of the principal functions of judicial review. If the constitution is vague on a certain point, it may set up a competitive coordination game between the parties in which different parties prefer different interpretations of the text and yet would prefer to cooperate on the other's terms rather than negotiate the document from scratch. Highly specific documents eliminate some of these games simply by being clear, but even specific documents have some ambiguities. Constitutional review provides focal points for enforcement while it articulates a standard interpretation of the constitutional bargain.

This discussion of coordination illustrates how constitutional review can also facilitate adaptation and encourage investment. Constitutions that are expected to work over multiple generations as norms, technology, and demographics change will necessarily encounter situations that their original authors did not even contemplate. Constitutional review can provide the connective tissue that allows a nineteenth century document to adapt to a world with the internet and genetically modified food. This process of adaptation has the related effect of inclusion, in that reinterpretation has the potential of incorporating the rights of interest groups that materialize after the founding. The jurisprudence of the Warren court in many areas – criminal procedure, election rights, and civil liberties – was largely motivated by the need to overcome legal discrimination against African Americans (Powe 2002).

This sense of constitutional review as adaptive seems at odds with a vision of courts (or other bodies responsible for constitutional review) as erecting constraints to government action, not facilitating it. In a real sense, courts can certainly be obstructionist. Should an executive wish to thwart constitutional limits on individual rights, a body empowered with constitutional enforcement may be a potential nemesis. Our assertion, however, is that even executives appreciate the role of the pedestrian (the court) entering the crosswalk to direct traffic and, likewise, the pedestrian will appreciate the power of the executive (the pedestrian is, after all, standing in the middle of the street). Indeed, although sometimes the executive will be directed to swerve, more often, a very practical court or constitutional council, mindful of its precarious position in the middle of the street, will allow the big car of the executive to maintain its course (Epstein and Knight 1998). The court, in its interpretation, thus preserves the formal legality of the constitution as it adapts its provisions to an exigent situation.[17]

[17] Note that there may be greater demand for such an articulation function as the constitution grows in detail. Parties who become accustomed to using courts to provide focal points will continue to do so over time, particularly as the court develops a reputation for effective articulation (Shapiro and Stone Sweet 2002; Law 2008; Ginsburg and Garoupa 2009). A positive

Our hypothesis is, therefore, that an explicit provision or widely accepted norm of constitutional review will extend the life span of constitutions. This is a rather general claim. One might wonder, appropriately, whether the *kind* of judicial review matters (see Ginsburg 2003). That is, does it matter whether the review is performed by an ordinary court as opposed to a designated constitutional court? Or whether laws or decisions are reviewed before or after legislation? Or who has the right to initiate the review? These variations may very well be consequential, but we suspect that the most significant difference will be between constitutions that provide for some review (of whatever kind) and those that do not. We construct a binary variable from our own data as to whether there is any judicial body entitled to conduct constitutional review. We separately analyze constitutional review in democracies and autocracies, on the theory that the courts may have more bite, and hence more ability to promote endurance, in democratic regimes.

Executive and Legislative Power

One feature of constitutional design, which might be thought to have some impact on endurance concerns the balance of power between executive and legislature. The last chapter suggested that many constitutions die at the hands of executives frustrated by limits on their powers or terms, particularly in light of environmental shocks. Wars, for example, are associated with a grab for expanded of executive power (Posner and Vermeule 2007; Rehnquist 1998). Internal disturbances may also be accompanied by claims for more executive power. The empirical implication, normatively troubling as it may be, is that constitutions with fewer constraints on the executive may be better able to survive shocks because they require little adjustment during crises.

A well-known example is that of the French Fourth Republic. Intended to overcome the defects of the Third Republic, the Fourth Republic Constitution of 1946 in fact replicated many of the same institutional defects, including a powerful but divided parliament and recurrent cabinet crises. Meanwhile, a major national crisis ensued in the form of the Algerian War of Independence, as well as an inflationary economy. The right wing engineered a coup d'etat, and General De Gaulle returned to power on the condition that a new, more executive-focused constitution be adopted, with a period of six months of emergency governance. That constitution, adopted with nearly eighty percent support among those who voted in the referendum to adopt it, is now fifty

feedback cycle can ensue, in which constitutional review continuously provides specificity, inclusion, and flexible adjustment over time.

years old and has provided for flexible, but executive-centered, democratic governance for much of that period.

On the other hand, this expectation cuts against our view of the healthful effects of inclusion, to the extent that legislative power represents some degree of inclusion. As collegiate bodies, legislatures are by their nature more inclusive than executives. Furthermore, unlike executives who might control the armed forces, legislatures have few resources outside of constitutional structures, and hence are likely to invest in enforcement efforts of constitutional norms. One might then argue that legislative power would facilitate constitutional endurance. That is, executives may have incentives to move against the constitution because of its constraints, but legislatures may for the same reasons be more invested in the document and more likely to defend it.

In short, either legislative or executive power might be thought to better facilitate constitutional endurance, depending on such contextual factors as the propensity of crisis and the relative importance of inclusion. A third possibility is that it is not so much one locus of power or the other that is important, but a balance between the two. This recalls Madison's (1826) argument in Federalist 48 that, in constructing a separation of powers scheme, the powers "should not be so far separated as to have no constitutional control over each other." Balance is a consistent theme of Madison's efforts to protect liberty through government structure; if either the legislative or executive branch becomes too powerful, we would expect pressures for constitutional revision. We thus have three different possible conceptions of the relationship between governmental structure and constitutional endurance.

In our empirical analysis, we consider both legislative and executive power as possible facilitators of endurance. For purposes of this analysis, we treat executive power and legislative power as reciprocal. Increased legislative power should come at the expense of executive power in terms of decreased authority and decreased autonomy. We construct a measure of legislative power with items from the CCP data and based on Fish and Kroenig (2009)'s de facto measure. We also test the effect of individual constraints on executive power, such as term limits and the presence of a single executive.

One set of factors that we do not directly test in this volume concerns the distinction between presidential and parliamentary forms of government. A large debate in comparative politics has considered whether either of these systems is superior on a number of dimensions, including regime durability (Stepan and Skach 1993). Net of our general prediction about executive power, we do not have an a priori theory as to whether presidentialism or parliamentarism would be better for constitutional endurance, and the current state of theory is somewhat agnostic (Cheibub 2007).

Life Cycle and Period Effects

An important question concerns relative risks to the constitution as it ages. Our theory suggests competing influences along these lines. On balance, however, we expect the risks of replacement to decline with age. In particular, age should improve problems of hidden information, and it should facilitate enforcement by increasing the knowledge of, attachment to, and investment in, the constitution. The next chapter describes in some detail how we assess the effect of constitutional aging on mortality.

We also inquire into period effects. Some eras may be more or less risky for constitutions, independent of the age of the documents that inhabit them. We therefore assess the differences in life span among constitutions written before 1914, between 1914 and 1945, and after 1945.

THE ENVIRONMENT

We have rather strong intuitions about what sorts of crises would destabilize constitutional systems. They should be those that are likely to lead to unrest or a shift in the balance of power, either one of which can potentially cause elites to justify extra-constitutional action. It is not hard to assemble a list of such events, as they constitute the milestones of a state's political history. Because we are interested in testing the explanatory power of these events against that of more structural factors, we err on the side of inclusion in specifying them.

Territorial Change

Traditionally, one of the first acts of a new state is to write a new constitution. This moment – the "hour of the lawyers" in Dahrendorf's (1990: 3) vivid description of the stages of statehood – represents a strong signal of the state's sovereignty as well as a covenant for the disparate factions that come together to form the state. Both are critical needs for a new state, and constitutions serve these admirably. Take Kosovo, for instance, whose founders prepared a draft constitution after declaring independence from Serbia and promulgated the constitution only two months later. That timeline suggests that constitution making was a pressing concern. Of course, states that came of age long before the ritualistic practice of constitution making will have been deprived (mercifully?) of their "hour of the lawyers." Some of these older states (Britain) never call in the lawyers, whereas others do so only much later. Thailand's first constitution was in 1932, although the state had retained independence since its establishment in current form in the eighteenth century. As we describe in Chapter 3, our data suggest that most states that emerged after 1789 wrote a new constitution within the first year of their birth.

It follows from these patterns that major changes in the territory of the state (to the extent that they approximate rebirths) would require some reconsideration of the state's fundamental document. Examples range from mergers in Arab world (e.g., the United Arab Republic in the 1960s, Iraq and Jordan in 1958, or North and South Yemen in 1991) to breakups of federations such as Czechoslovakia or the Soviet Union. One can divide territorial changes into cases of loss and gain, two types of changes that conceivably have divergent effects on constitutional life. As we suggest in Chapter Four, crises that indicate some deficiency or even failure on the makeup of the state most likely represent a higher risk to the constitution than do those that indicate success. In this sense, it seems likely that a loss in territory reflects poorly on the state (and its institutions). We hypothesize that any territorial change (but especially territorial losses) will increase the probability of constitutional replacement. Our measure for the change in state boundaries (either by loss or gain) is from the Correlates of War (COW) dataset for Territorial Change (Tir et al. 1998). Our sample includes 274 cases of territorial loss and 445 cases of territorial gain.

Diffusion

Constitutions are highly symbolic and public documents. As such, it seems likely that the adoption of new constitutions in other countries (especially in geographically or culturally proximate countries) will increase the probability of a new constitution in a neighboring country. Diffusion in other arenas of policy reform is well established (see a review by Strang and Soule 1998), and it is unquestionably the case that the content of constitutions is produced by a highly interdependent process (Elkins 2009). It also seems likely that the decision to replace a constitution will itself be contagious. Elster (1995: 368) has observed that constitutions tend to be written in waves, typically following the end of great conflicts like World War II and the Cold War. Indeed, the distribution of new constitutions across time seems to conform to a nonrandom process (see Figure 5.2). The figure plots the probability of a new constitution across time with a smoothed line fitted to the distribution to detect and identify clusters. The pattern suggests some degree of temporal clustering in the replacement of constitutions. These clusters may well be countries responding simultaneously, but independently, to a similar set of conditions. However, it seems likely that some sort of contagion is at work, whether it takes a geographic, linguistic, or some other networked channel.

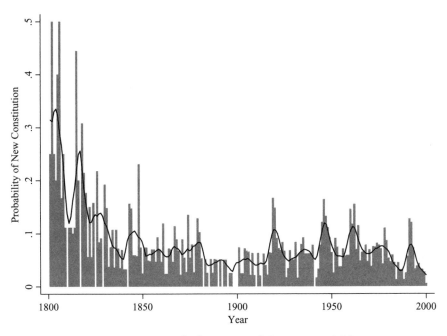

FIGURE 5.2. Temporal Clustering and Constitution Making

Indeed, the inspection of several recent cases suggests constitutional reform in one country inspires constitutional reform in another. For example, Colombia's 1990–1991 reform allegedly triggered the idea of reform (albeit with ideologically distinct designs) for Hugo Chavez, the architect of Venezuela's "Bolivarian" constitution in 1999, a constitution that has subsequently inspired rumblings of reform in Ecuador and Bolivia. In a recent interview, Chavez recalls:

We discussed how to break with the past, how to overcome this type of democracy that only responds to the interests of the oligarchical sectors; how to get rid of the corruption. We had always rejected the idea of a traditional military coup, of a military dictatorship, or of a military governing junta. We were very aware of what happened in Colombia, in the years of 1990–1991, when there was a constitutional assembly – of course! – it was very limited because in the end it was subordinated to the existing powers. It was the existing powers that designed Colombia's constitutional assembly and got it going and, therefore, it could not transform the situation because it was a prisoner of the existing powers.[18]

[18] Interview with Marta Harnecker (2002).

We also see what appear to be interdependent processes within alliance networks. Mongolia, for example, adopted constitutions in 1924, 1940, and 1959, following ideological developments in the Soviet Union, as did Vietnam in following China in 1989. The general hypothesis here is that increases in constitutional replacements in the prior year, both globally and locally, will increase the probability of constitutional replacement.

The *diffusion* variables are specified as spatial lags, which typically measure the central tendency of the dependent variable within a relevant group of cases in the prior year (see Simmons and Elkins 2004). We test two simple measures: one of new constitutions globally and one of those in the neighborhood, defined as a country's contiguous neighbors. The first computes the percent of countries in the world, other than the country in question, which replaced their constitutions in the prior year. This variable ranges from 0 percent of countries in the several years prior to World War II[19] to 18 percent of countries in 1960. The second measures the percent of the countries' neighbors that replaced their constitution in the prior year. This variable ranges from 0 percent of countries to 100 percent of countries; the variance in this variable is highly related to the number of neighbors a country has as well as the region of the world in which a country resides. We include controls for region in our analysis.

Regime Change

As we discuss in Chapter Three, constitutional change and regime change (that is, broadly speaking, shifts between democracy and authoritarianism) are closely related. However, the conceivable connections between political regime and constitutional reform are multiple. On the one hand, one may expect that abrupt shifts in political regime (either to or from democracy) will be associated with constitutional reform. Regime changes are about shifts in the institutional structure of politics and constitutions are the embodiment of these rules. In theory, the causal arrow in these coincidental events could go either way. Constitutions can lay the groundwork for a new regime, just as they can represent marching orders following a preconstitutional change in regime. In all likelihood, however, the impetus and source of the change is extra-constitutional, with the constitution made to fit the new regime rather than the reverse. One may wonder whether shifts in one direction (say, to democracy) are just as likely to lead to constitutional replacement as are shifts in the other direction (say, from democracy). We do not have a strong theory to suggest much of a difference, although one could speculate that

---

[19] There has not been a single year since World War II when no country in the world replaced a constitution.

new democrats would be more likely to repudiate the authoritarian past with a new constitution than would a new authoritarian. However, rewriting is not that costly for an authoritarian, so we remain agnostic on that basic question. On the other hand, it seems likely that the decision of the new democrat or authoritarian will depend on the origins of the constitution that he inherits. That is, if the new democrats are faced with a constitution drafted by an authoritarian government, they will be more likely to replace the constitution than if it were drafted by democrats. It is not clear whether the same reasoning would apply to authoritarians because, as we suggest above, they may not necessarily view a democratic creation negatively; to the contrary, it may offer them added legitimacy. Apart from these conditional hypotheses, then, it could also be that the origins (democratic or not) of constitutions bear a level of risk that is independent of the inheriting regime. That is, generally speaking, constitutions that are born in democratic settings will be more resilient than will those born in authoritarian settings.

Thus, we have three sets of expectations regarding political regimes. First, we expect that abrupt changes in regime, in the direction of either democracy or autocracy, will increase the probability of replacement. Second, we expect that constitutions that were written in democratic settings will be more stable than will those written in authoritarian settings. Third, we expect interactive effects between regime changes and origins in the following manner: shifts to democracy when authoritarian-born constitutions are in place will be more unstable than shift to autocracy when democratic constitutions are in place.

The bases of our regime measures are the Polity scores, a widely used measure of democracy that ranges from −10 (Authoritarian) to 10 (Democracy). We define a democratic or authoritarian transition as a three-point increase or decrease, respectively, in a country's Polity score. Based on this metric, we find 527 democratic transitions and 366 authoritarian transitions throughout the world from 1816 to 2003.

Leadership Transition

Constitutional change following regime change makes sense. A change in the basic institutions and philosophy of governance calls out for formal change in the charter. It also seems likely that smaller scale shifts in the leadership of governments will increase the probability of replacement. This may be so for a number of reasons. First, new executives may not see their administration as following so closely in the tradition of their predecessor. They may desire a change in the rules and structure of the government they now lead or they may simply desire a symbolic break from the old leadership and a new document that bears their own imprimatur. Our reading of the historical record suggests that new constitutions sometimes result from transitions in executive leadership, especially when the change reflects an ideological or programmatic shift. For example, the alternation of power between liberals and conservatives in many Latin American countries triggered frequent constitutional change in the nineteenth century. After the assassination of King Abdullah in Jordan in 1951, the passage of a new Jordanian constitution by his son and successor reflected a personnel shift. A constitutional change under these circumstances suggests a shift in the composition of the elite, at least compared to that of the group that reached the original constitutional bargain.

In other cases, a constitutional shift in concert with a leadership shift seems to be built into historical custom. The various Socialist constitutions, for example, seem to follow the installation of new leaders in the Soviet Union (1936, 1977) and China (1982), a practice that was often justified by the Marxist view of evolution in stages (see Go 2003). We should note that some of these leadership changes may be extra-constitutional (i.e., coups) whereas others may be constitutional transitions in power. In the case of coups, of course, the result may be regime change as well as simply a change in leadership (approximately 25% of coups occur the same year as a regime change). Our expectation, then, is that changes in leadership will increase the risk of constitutional change. However, we do not anticipate that this will be an unconditional effect. The reason is that in democracies, orderly leadership change is built into the system. New democratic leaders reflect constitutional stability and may have relatively little incentive to undermine it.

Leadership change comes in a number of varieties ranging in their legality and abruptness. One may suspect that the kind of leadership change would place different pressures on the constitution. We measure change, of whatever kind, with leadership data from the Archigos project (Goemans et al. 2009). We utilize the Archigos project's differentiation of regular and irregular leadership change to create variables indicating extra-constitutional and intra-constitutional leadership change. Based on these data, we observe more than 1,000 extra-constitutional leadership changes and nearly 2,500 intra-constitutional leadership changes between 1875 and 2004.

Intrastate Conflict and Consensus

Constitutions are meant to hold together disparate groups with different needs, preferences, and goals. We recognize that countries will vary with respect to this challenge: some countries will be more diverse, economically and culturally, than others, placing greater stress on the covenant that binds them.

Homogenous states will differ from those with a multiethnic population, in part because ethnicity provides an organizing basis to challenge existing power distributions and in part because it is more difficult to sustain consensus on unwritten constitutional norms in such environments. It is also no surprise that much constitutional infighting often takes place between those pushing for more or less centralization. The United States' case is instructive here. As is well known, the Articles of Confederation suffered from a number of defects that hastened their demise. These defects included the national government's inability to raise taxes to provide for the common defense and other public goods, the inability to overcome internal barriers to trade, and the inability to issue currency. Without a strong central government, the Articles did not provide for the generation of public goods and thus provoked the writing of a constitution to remedy these defects. Another example of an internal institutional reform was the demise of Indonesia's 1949 post-independence Constitution, federal in character, which was discarded in favor of a unitary constitution in 1955. The hypothesis that emerges from these insights is that ethnically diverse, or at least large, countries should have less stable constitutions. We test these two background conditions – state size and ethnic diversity – separately, but also test their consequences more directly by measuring domestic institutional crisis with an omnibus index in Banks (2001) that aggregates a set of events from assassinations to strikes to demonstrations. Following some validity analyses of Banks' measure, we opted to transform it into a simple binary variable that is coded 1 if the conflict index is over a certain threshold.[20] By this metric, there are 926 country-years of intrastate conflict in the data.

Interstate Conflict

War provides a major challenge to most political systems. War can lead to demands for recalibration of domestic political bargains as executives seek to expand their power to respond to exigent circumstances. Many believe that national security challenges require some shift toward greater executive power, given the natural advantages in speed, information, and accountability of a head of state (Nzelibe and Yoo 2006; Posner and Vermuele 2007). Wars can also lead to pressures on constitutional bargains among interest groups. If the war is going badly, absolute levels of benefits under the constitution are declining, but even a war that is successful can shift the relative benefits among

---

[20] Banks' (2001) index sums the following events with their respective weighting in parentheses: assassinations (24), strikes (43), guerrilla warfare (46), government crises (48), purges (86), riots (102), revolutions (148) and antigovernment demonstrations (200). Our threshold indicator is coded 1 if the conflict index is greater than 10,000 for that country-year.

interest groups. This also has the potential to put pressure on constitutional bargains. Of course, a constitution that is sufficiently flexible may be able to accommodate the necessary changes. But, many a constitution has died in the face of invasion and war.

Military defeat seems to be particularly risky for constitutions. The two world wars, for example, seem to have eliminated the existing constitutions for each country on the losing sides (e.g., for World War I, Austria-Hungary's constitution of 1876 and Germany's constitution of 1871; for World War II, Germany's constitution of 1919, Italy's constitution of 1861, and Japan's constitution of 1889). Notably, many of these constitutions were established documents, ranging in age from twenty-seven to eighty-two years, suggestive of the power of military defeat. Of course, defeat in war is often associated with other crises as well. For instance, the end of World War I coincided with the breakup of Austria-Hungary and the Ottoman Empire (state death and/or loss of territory), whereas World War II is associated with the foreign occupation of Germany, Italy, and Japan, the break-up of Germany, and regime change in Italy and Japan. Our multivariate analysis in Chapter Six, which controls for a host of risk factors, tells us something more definitive about the effect of war.

A related prediction concerns the fate of constitutions written in periods of state collapse. Defeat in war or takeover by an outside power can lead to *occupation-imposed constitutions*. Such incidents often compromise the state's sovereignty and imperil the ruling elite, thus implying a reconsideration of the original bargain. Well-known cases include Japan's 1946 Constitution and Iraq's 2005 Constitution. Others include Afghanistan 1979, Dominican Republic 1924, Haiti 1918 and 1932, and Cambodia 1981.[21] Afghanistan 2003 was not a formal occupation, but had elements of heavy foreign advice. A special case of crisis after a loss in war, but not direct occupation, would be Paraguay in 1940. Note that those constitutions written during an occupation may be less stable than those originating under other circumstances, for at least two reasons. First, they are likely to be drafted under heavy influence from abroad, and hence will not be inclusive of local actors. Further, because enforcement is secured by an outside power, these constitutions are not self-enforcing at their outset, although in some cases they may become so after the occupying authority withdraws.[22]

Our expectations here are that a defeat in war will increase the risk of constitutional replacement and that those constitutions written under occupation

---

[21] One might more broadly consider Cambodia's UNTAC-drafted Constitution of 1993 as a case of multilateral occupation, when the UN Transitional Government helped ease the country's end of the long civil war.

[22] Elkins et al. (2008) explore this hypothesis more formally.

will be less resilient. Defeat in war is scored 1 if, according to the COW project's data on militarized interstate disputes, the country lost a militarized interstate dispute which reached a hostility level of "use of force" or "war" (Reed Sarkees 2000). The data contain 585 such defeats between 1816 and 2001. To identify the set of occupation constitutions, we rely on our earlier work (Elkins et al. 2008), which also drew on the COW project's data as well as our own historical inquiry. We defined occupation constitutions as those written during the occupation period as well as those written within two years following the end of an occupation, to account for the possibility that the occupier's influence extends past the period of occupation. We found 42 such "occupation constitutions" in our data.

Economic Crisis and Development

"It's the economy, stupid."[23] James Carville's famous note resonates for constitutional demise as well. If bad economic times lead to reconsideration (and removal) of a government's leadership and even reconsideration of more fundamental political rules and structures, it makes sense that they may imperil formal constitutions. Economic development has a well-established empirical relationship with regime change, the mechanics of which have long been disputed (Lipset 1959; Acemoglu and Robinson 2005). Przeworski et al. (1999) make a compelling case that the relationship between economic development and regime change is a stabilizing one: the more development, the more stable the regime, whether it is democratic or authoritarian. We expect the same sort of stability effect with respect to constitutions, so that more developed countries will have more enduring documents. However, it is also probable that economic crisis – short-term negative shifts in the health of the economy – will have destabilizing effects on the constitution.

We measure *economic development* with a measure of energy consumption per capita (in 1000s of pounds of coal per capita per year). This indicator correlates highly with GDP per capita, which is only sparsely available prior to WWII. Following Barro and Ursúa (2008), our measure of economic crisis uses data on GDP per capita and GDP growth from Barro, the Penn World Tables, and the World Bank to identify which years GDP per capita shrinks by 10 percent or more from the previous year. These data suggest that of the 8,970 country-years with GDP data available between 1789 and 2005, 648 have been years of economic crisis.

---

[23] An excerpt from a sign that political strategist James Carville hung in Bill Clinton's campaign headquarters during the 1992 campaign.

Historical Legacies

Epidemiologists like to say that the best thing that children can do to ensure good health is to pick their parents. Family history, it would seem, is just as important to constitutions as it is to human beings – perhaps more so. Recall that our theory regarding constitutional enforcement revolves around coordination – in particular, the expectation among citizens that other citizens will assist them in defending the document. Nothing informs these expectations more than past experience. Consider the island of Hispaniola, where Haiti and the Dominican Republic have both produced constitutions every six or seven years. What should the average Haitian expect regarding constitutional enforcement having lived in this tradition of constitutional churn? Should he expect fellow Haitians to back him up if he steps outside to challenge a president who dares to trample on the constitution? Probably not. The constitutional culture, or tradition, in that milieu is one of nonenforcement.

Family history works in other ways as well. One important aspect of this history concerns the aging of the state. Simply put, we might expect that states that have existed for several generations will have greater clarity about the nature of the political contract and what the relevant political institutions should look like. By contrast, states that write their first constitution upon independence, or within a generation of independence, will be somewhat unsettled and any bargains reached at this early stage of state development will be less stable. This thinking echoes normative claims associated with Hegel and Rousseau that constitutions should develop organically. Hegel especially was skeptical of positivist notions that a rationalized constitution could be adopted without any strong ties to cultural or political conditions (see Ritchie 2005). The implication is that states with more experience (as a consolidated state) will have more stable constitutions than will younger states.

Thus, we posit two hypotheses. To capture the effect of legacies, we expect that the stability of constitutions will vary directly with the average longevity of its previous constitutions. Second, we expect that constitutions of states that have lasted at least thirty years (roughly one generation) will be more stable than those of younger states that have not. Our measure of the constitution's family history of longevity is the average duration of prior constitutions. (We call this *legacy of endurance* in the tables and in other parts of the book.)

Other Relevant Factors

We include a number of other variables in the model to control for systematic variation, which are not particularly relevant to our theory, but may be consequential and confounding. These factors include (1) a binary variable that indicates constitutions that were explicitly adopted as *interim documents* as well as one that indicates constitutions that are *reinstated*, having been in force at an earlier time in the country's history and (2) binary variables indicating geographic region.

CONCLUSION

This chapter connects the physiology of constitutional replacement with identifiable risk factors of constitutional life. Some of these risk factors have to do with the design and structure of constitutions – their genetic code. Another set of factors has to do with the environmental conditions under which constitutions live. Our theory suggests that, in addition to environmental shocks, several aspects of the design of constitutions themselves will affect constitutional mortality; namely, aspects of inclusion, flexibility, and specificity. We identify a rather extensive set of environmental factors to isolate the independent impact of design as well as to test some of the conventional wisdom regarding particular explanatory variables. We have a particular appreciation for measurement and, given the challenges of our rather comprehensive sample, we have endeavored to connect concepts with their empirical manifestations as early as possible. In the next chapter, we put these measures to work in tests of our hypotheses in a historical, cross-national analysis of constitutional mortality.

6

An Epidemiological Analysis of Constitutional Mortality

INTRODUCTION

The dwindling supply of organs for organ transplants is sometimes attributed to the use of motorcycle helmets, of all things. Head injuries to helmetless riders are often fatal, but leave the riders' otherwise healthy organs intact, thus making the riders perfect organ donation candidates. Helmets, which, by standard estimates, reduce motorcycle fatalities by a remarkable 39 percent (Norvell and Cummings 2002), have appeared to reduce the number of organ donors as a consequence. The estimates that we report later suggest that the elements of constitutional design have almost as dramatic an effect on constitutional mortality. It may be that, like its effect on organ donations, decreased mortality leads to similar downstream unintended consequences for constitutions (as our normative discussion in Chapter Two indicates). But, we do not concern ourselves with that matter here. Our goal in this chapter is to describe and report the findings from our analysis regarding the mortality of constitutions over the last 200 years. In particular, our purpose is to test the hypotheses specified in the previous chapter.

Our focus is on hypotheses having to do with the *design* of constitutions, as opposed to their *environment*. Because we are interested in understanding the impact of design *over and above* that of the environment, we are obliged to specify and measure the consequences of an inclusive set of environmental factors. Doing so pays the analytic dividends of controlling for such effects, but also can be enlightening in its own right. After all, one scholar's control variable may be another's life work. The analysis we present spans many decades and covers the globe. We remain cognizant of the limitations of this analysis, as we describe shortly. Nevertheless, as we shall see, the actuarial insights from this analysis allow us to rule out some explanations while directing more attention to others. In the case-oriented autopsies and family histories that we present in later chapters, we return to many of the findings that we uncover here.

ON THE ISSUE OF HETEROGENEOUS, REMOTE, AND MULTI-CHANNELED CAUSATION

In identifying risk factors, our epidemiological analysis has a deliberately aggregate character. Like a human life, a constitutional one takes many twists and turns and undergoes distinct phases of development. Like human beings, constitutions can die of many causes and, although we can assess the average effect of certain risk factors, we cannot make determinative estimates of constitutional life. There are, to employ the demographer's parlance, many competing risks. Not only can the causes of death be heterogeneous, but susceptibility to these causes can also vary across constitutions. Just as the "constitutions" of some individuals can seem impervious to the deleterious effects of high fat and smoking, so too can the constitutions of some states (e.g., Japan) seem immune to risky features such as amendment inflexibility. So, moving from the statistical results to particular constitutions will inevitably reveal cases that do not seem to fit. The United States is potentially one such case. Some of these puzzling outcomes can be resolved by identifying compensating therapeutic traits, which help to keep constitutions alive. That is, a constitution may possess an especially healthful factor that may offset a particularly risky one. These sorts of effects are easily accounted for in the social scientist's standard model of additive independent effects. But, some effects might be conditional on others. For example, some of the variation in a factor's lethality might have to do with the point in the constitutional life cycle at which they occur – factors that are risks in infancy may be innocuous in adolescence and still different in their virulence for the elderly. We can anticipate some of these interactions, but much of the heterogeneity of these effects will by necessity accumulate in the error term of the statistical model. This sort of heterogeneity reflects some of the inevitable indeterminacy that accompanies any estimate of life, constitutional or otherwise.

Second, the proximity of cause and effect will vary in our analysis and will necessarily complicate our testing of the causal process. We are connecting design and environmental traits with the most distant and final of outcomes – constitutional death. But, constitutions can come into crisis, founder, or lapse into the legal equivalent of a coma (as leaders temporarily ignore them) – all without actually being replaced (dying). These intermediate ailments may, in some cases, be of more analytic interest than death. To illustrate in the human context, it may be that red wine can be shown statistically to prolong human life. However useful it is to establish this overall impact on mortality – an outcome that has obvious intuitive appeal – it may be diagnostically more satisfying to connect wine consumption to more proximate effects, (such as cholesterol levels), which might, first, be more acute, and second, help corroborate the mechanism by which wine delivers its salutary result. In this book, we are not focused on the constitutional equivalent of cholesterol levels, mostly for the lack of data. To be sure, it would be extraordinarily helpful to have measures of the health of constitutions with respect to a variety of different risk factors *throughout* their life cycle. Alas, we do not have such information, except in some cases in the form of historical documentation of constitutional behavior. In the case of the United States, we can track many of the Constitution's vital signs because legions of scholars and lawyers, who might be thought of as constitutional care givers, review its health periodically and historically. We know very well, for example, that the U.S. Constitution teetered on the brink of collapse in the Civil War era. The close analysis of cases (Chapters Seven and Eight) – which we think of as *autopsies*, from the perspective of the constitutions themselves, and *family histories*, from the perspective of the constitutional trajectory of host states – is enormously helpful to us in tracing and elaborating more intermediate outcomes.

One of the problems associated with the distance between risk factor and outcome in our analysis is that factors can have multiple, sometimes contradictory, effects. The case of red wine most obviously invokes this notion. One of the reasons for the notoriety of the red-wine findings is that the effect of alcohol on health is widely expected to be negative. Certainly, whatever benefits result from red wine, they may be offset by any number of harmful effects. Constitutional specificity, as we note, is very much like red wine in this sense. As the preceding chapters make clear, although we believe that specificity forestalls the need for re-negotiation and creates incentives for enforcement, excessive detail might be in some tension with the need for adaptation. As such, one should regard the effects of specificity on life span as quite possibly the sum of two contradictory effects, much as red wine's total effect on human life span would represent a net effect of multiple, countervailing factors.

Other factors might work in multiple, but complementary, ways. For example, constitutional review is likely healthful for its effects on both coordination and adaptation. In this sense, constitutional review is analogous to physical exercise in the human context. Just as exercise may improve cardiovascular health, it may also have significant psychological effects and even reinforce good nutritional habits. Establishing the statistical connection between exercise and human life span or constitutional review and constitutional duration will allow us to say something important about the overall effect of that factor without necessarily allowing us to assess the validity of the specific causal paths.

On the other hand, some factors may not be like red wine or exercise at all in that they may operate through a channel that is perfectly direct and clear to the analyst. Consider for a moment the Kawasaki Ninja, an extremely powerful sport motorcycle. It has been rumoured, perhaps apocryphally, that the life expectancy of an owner of the Ninja following the date of purchase is six months! If the estimate is accurate, owning a Kawasaki Ninja is undoubtedly a strong predictor of mortality, but more to the point, it is not especially difficult to understand the causal mechanism that would lead to death. Suffice it to say that cholesterol levels would not be germane to the investigation of such fatalities, nor would an autopsy likely be necessary. In this sense, the collapse of a constitution following a state's subjugation by a foreign power may be similar to the Kawasaki Ninja effect in both its causal proximity and lethality.

The example of red wine (and even those of physical exercise and the Kawasaki Ninja) illustrates another complexity in the analysis. Some factors may, on the whole, be salutary, but *only* when present at certain levels. Academic studies on red wine routinely, and very soberly, counsel that any therapeutic effect comes with a dose of one or two glasses (not bottles!) a day. One may expect that this sort of Goldilocks problem will crop up in the constitutional risk factors under consideration here. There may be a delicate balance between, say, flexibility and commitment, between participant inclusion and design coherence, or between specificity and generality – a balance that must be "just right" to produce healthful results. We are not able to identify the precise balance of these things very easily. As we shall see, analytical tools allow us to test the degree of nonlinearity in some of these effects, but on the whole our hypotheses assume that factors are either good or bad, and that more of a good thing is even better (and vice versa). Again, our case studies can help us assess these issues of balance and, in cases of nonlinearity, the threshold at which effects tip this balance.

To this issue of *quantity*, we should add the related caveat with respect to *quality*. Not all exercise is healthful, nor is every wine (to the Chardonnay aficionado's dismay, it is reportedly only red wine that has any discernible positive effect on health). With respect to the factors under analysis here, the lesson is that conceptualization and measurement matter. Although we want to make claims about the healthful or harmful effects of constitutional factors without being overly nuanced, we should not lose sight of the possibility that the measurement of concepts across time and space will inevitably miss potentially important qualitative differences among cases. As always, the issue is finding the proper level of sensitivity with respect to measurement. This is not an easy task in any scientific discipline. Ultimately, the answer, however difficult, is to maintain constant communication between conceptualization, measurement, and theory, and to keep concerns for measurement validity front and center. It is, in part, for that reason that the previous chapter combines a discussion of hypotheses and their related concepts *with* a discussion of measurement strategies. We take up these and other concerns in the present chapter as we turn to the cross-national evidence.

SAMPLING AND THE DEMARCATION OF LIFE AND DEATH

Chapter Three runs through a set of conceptual issues regarding the identification of national constitutions and, in passing, describes our notion of constitutional mortality – the outcome of interest in this study. That section also defines our sample. We take a moment to clarify and elaborate these parameters. Constitutional life, for us, begins at promulgation. Certainly, the seeds of the new constitution are planted earlier and its gestation, as we report shortly, lasts on average a little over a year. Nevertheless, our interest is in when a constitution comes into force, not when it is conceived. Constitutions expire when they are formally suspended or replaced. A replacement is defined as a set of revisions that is formally designated as a "new" constitution or significant revisions that do not use the stated amendment procedure. Following the statistical model we introduce below, our dependent variable is the hazard rate (or mortality rate), which is the probability of death at a point in time conditional upon having survived until that point. The hazard rate is functionally equivalent to the survival rate, in that one is a function of the other, and, accordingly, in our results we discuss expected mortality rate and life expectancy more or less interchangeably. An increase in the hazard rate corresponds to a shorter life span.

Our sample includes the constitutions of all independent states that have existed between 1789 and 2005.[1] A number of issues arise with respect to timing as well as changes in the status of states – such as mergers, divisions, and deaths. We turn to these issues and others below.

ANALYTIC AND STATISTICAL ISSUES

Having specified the hypotheses, measures of the relevant concepts, and the sample under consideration, we are now in a position to estimate the effects of the risk factors on constitutional duration. We use an event history approach, a family of statistical models commonly used by biostatisticians to estimate time-to-event data, anything from the mortality of patients under treatment

---

[1] As we note earlier, we rely upon the list in Gleditsch and Ward (1999) for our historical census of states. They identify a separate list of micro-states, which we include as well.

to the expiration of machine parts. The principal advantage of these models is that they take time-dependence into account as a matter of course in their distributional assumptions, because the hazard, or failure, rate (constitutional death, in our case) rarely follows a normal distribution across time (Box-Steffensmeier and Jones 2004).

A variety of methodological decisions arise mostly regarding the treatment of time. The first issue concerns the temporal unit, which for us is the year. Admittedly, sometimes months, weeks, and even days matter, especially with respect to the timing of crises and the promulgation of constitutions. Nonetheless, the historical record rarely allows us to be this precise, at least across a broad set of cases. In rare cases, multiple constitutional replacements, suspensions, or births occur in the same calendar year (e.g., Haiti's two constitutions in 1946 or Venezuela's two constitutions in 1914). In these cases, we count the second event as being born half way through the year, meaning the first event is given a life span of 0.5 years.

A second issue concerns censoring, the idea that some constitutions might exist before (left-censoring) or after (right-censoring) our period of observation. All constitutions currently in force are right censored, because our observation period ends with all 189 constitutions still alive. It follows, then, that their fate (assuming they are mortal) is unknown, but we would lose valuable information were we to exclude them from an analysis of constitutional mortality. One of the principal benefits of event-history analysis is that it accounts for this sort of censoring naturally (see Box-Steffensmeier and Jones 2004). Left censoring affects fewer of our cases, because our observation period begins with the promulgation of the U.S. document and thus predates all modern constitutions as we define them. For several cases, though, the constitution's promulgation predates the state's official date of formation, which is also when states technically come under observation in our data. In these cases, the clock on any of the state's existent constitutions does not start until the state gains sovereignty. A related issue concerns the death of states that served as the host environment for the constitution. Twenty-four states, from Estonia's early incarnation (1918–1940) to East Germany (1949–1990), expired during the period under examination. Because we do not know how long the constitution of an expired state would have lasted had the state survived, we consider their constitutions right-censored.

A third issue concerns the effect of time on the baseline hazard. Specifically, do constitutions have an increased, decreased, or stable risk as they age? Recall that this is an important substantive concern for us, but it also has important methodological implications. Our theory suggests crosscutting influences, and we remain rather speculative about their combined effect.

Most statistical models are parametric, in that they are built on assumptions about the distribution of the dependent variable, in our case the distribution of the hazard rate over time. Because we have only a speculative a priori belief as to the shape of the hazard, we begin with the Cox Proportional Hazard model, which is semiparametric in that it is not premised upon a particular distribution of the hazard, although it does make some assumptions.[2]

A fourth methodological consideration concerns the problem of connecting events causally with one another across time. Many of the environmental crises that we describe occur, for the most part, within a single year, but the effects of these events can lag for some unknown amount of time. If an economic crisis hits and the constitution dies one, two, or even three years later, should the crisis receive the blame for downing the constitution? This question is, of course, as much of a substantive concern as it is methodological, and requires that we inspect the causal process closely. Consider regime change. In many cases, we find that constitution making, when it occurs, is one of the first acts following a shift to either democracy or authoritarianism. In Chile, however, Pinochet's constitution did not come into effect until seven years after his *coup d'etat*. But, how unusual is the Chilean case? A critical element in estimating the lag between crises and constitutional replacement concerns the duration of the drafting process. To gain a better sense of the timing, we randomly chose 148 constitutional systems and measured the duration of the drafting process, from the first proposal for replacement to promulgation. Although there were some cases of protracted drafting (e.g., Myanmar's recent seventeen-year process and the lengthy drafting of Russia's 1977 constitution), most constitutions take a little over a year from drafting to promulgation (the mean is 1.32 years with a standard deviation of 1.84). We therefore specify one-year lags for event variables to increase the probability that these variables receive proper credit for their effects, at the minimal risk of giving them *more* credit than they are due.[3]

A final issue concerns missing data. Because of the breadth of our study, very few of the independent variables are observed *everywhere* or throughout the entire sampled period. Therefore, in order to analyze the full sample,

---

[2] As the name implies, the Cox model assumes proportional hazards, or that different values of the covariates in the models will have a proportional impact on the baseline hazard (Box-Steffensmeier and Jones 2004). Violations of the proportional hazards assumption can lead to biased estimates of the hazard ratio. Several covariates from the models in the Appendix violate the proportional hazards assumption, including death of the state, domestic crisis, democratic transition, specificity, and parliamentary power. We have run the model with and without correcting for these violations and the results are neither substantively nor statistically very different. A Weibull model delivers substantially similar results. For ease of interpretation, the results displayed in the tables do *not* correct for the proportional hazard violations.

[3] Defeat in war, loss of territory, domestic conflict, economic crisis, democratic and autocratic transitions, and coups are all lagged, repeatedly, for one year. That is, an event occurring at time t is coded as occurring in t and $t + 1$.

we use multiple imputation to fill in the missing data. Provided that the data are missing at random (MAR), this approach will provide consistent, asymptotically efficient, and asymptotically normal estimates (Allison 2001), and is superior to either list-wise deletion or mean imputation, which both rely on the unlikely assumption that data are missing completely at random (MCAR) (King et al. 2001).

RESULTS

Baseline Estimates of Mortality

In general, constitutions do not last very long, at least if we consider the lofty ambitions of those who write them. Figure 6.1(a) plots the baseline survival curve, which indicates the expected proportion of constitutional deaths by age without any predictors in the model. The median survival time (the age at which one-half of constitutions are expected to have died) is nineteen years. This quantity is a reasonable estimate of life expectancy, at least its central tendency; the full distribution across ages of the proportion surviving can also be read directly from the graph. Recall that these survival estimates account for the censored observation of current constitutions, almost all of which will live longer than their age in 2005, the year our analysis stops. We note, again, that this estimate of nineteen years corresponds exactly, and almost miraculously, with the expiration date that Thomas Jefferson prescribed for constitutions.

Life cycle and Period Effects

These baseline estimates provide not only a sense of life expectancy, but also a sense of when in their life cycle constitutions are most vulnerable. Recall that our theory suggests crosscutting effects with respect to aging: we expect to see processes of both decay and crystallization. The data allow us to sort out these contradictory expectations. Figure 6.1(b) plots the hazard rate over time. The hazard rate, or mortality rate, is an estimate of the probability a constitution will die at a certain age conditional upon its survival to that point. Thus, it represents the slope of the survival curve (Figure 6.1(a)) and allows us to assess relative risk according to age. The hazard rate increases until about the age of seventeen years, when risk of death is at its highest, after which the rate decreases steadily over time. This does not mean that constitutions over seventeen years old are safe, of course. In fact, more than 30 percent of total deaths occur in constitutions older than seventeen years of age, including, at the extreme, the deaths of Sweden's 1809 constitution at the age of 165 years (Congleton 2003a) and the death of Liberia's 1847 constitution at the age of 133

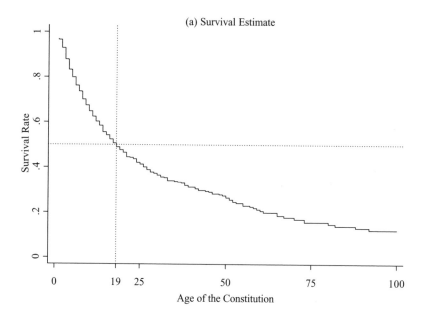

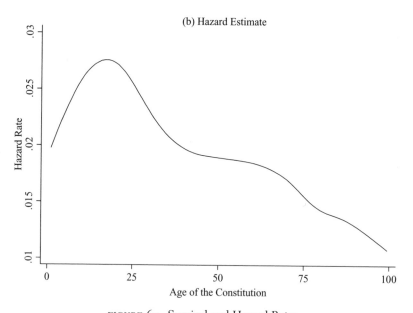

FIGURE 6.1. Survival and Hazard Rates.

years. However, it does seem that the age of seventeen years or so represents a threshold of sorts after which some degree of crystallization occurs with increasing degrees of rigidity.

As it happens, the shape of the hazard rate for constitutional dissolution seems to mirror that of marriage dissolution, at least in some cultures. With data on Norwegian couples, for example, Aalen and Gjessing (2001) show that the risk of divorce is low in the first one or two years of marriage (roughly 1 of 1,000 couples will divorce), but the divorce rate rises steadily until the age of six years, when it peaks (the peak rate differs by era, but for couples married in 1980 the rate was 22 in 1,000), and then decreases gradually with a trivially small uptick in the divorce rate after twenty years. In the case of constitutions, the hazard rate takes longer to reach its peak at the age of seventeen years (where it sits at roughly 27 deaths per 1,000) but then decreases steadily and substantially until by the age of fifty years, the rate is approximately .02, or 20 deaths per 1,000 constitutions.[4] Curiously, then, not only does the shape of the hazard rate match across the two domains, but the magnitude of the hazard rate itself is almost equivalent when both rates are at their peak. For the many scholars who have found the marriage covenant to be a useful analog to the constitutional one, these results provide more corroboration.

We turn now to period effects. In contrast to the general story of human mortality and ever increasing life expectancy, we find that there is a decline in constitutional life spans after World War II. Our intuition is that this finding results from a shift in norms regarding the bargains that bind groups within states. Essentially, groups that aspire to statehood have found it easier to dissolve bargains after World War II than before (Alesina and Spolaore 2003). Herbst (2000:104), however, points out that in Africa at least, national borders remained mostly fixed after independence. Recall that our theory of constitutional endurance centers on parties to an existing constitution bargain believing that they are better off in the current outcome rather than taking a chance on negotiating a new one. In bargain theory terms, this depends on the reservation price, the outcome obtained in the event that the bargain fails. A higher reservation price means that a party is less likely to conclude a bargain, and the scope of potential bargains narrows.

Our view is that the postwar international order has lowered the fixed costs of state building, and thus increased reservation prices. The post-World War II environment was characterized by the Cold War, in which the superpowers subsidized the costs of national defense for many nations, and minimized overt

---

4 It may seem strange to speak in terms of 1000s when no more than 200 constitutions have ever existed at a given time. We do so following convention and, especially here, to compare to the divorce rate, which is typically expressed per 1000 couples.

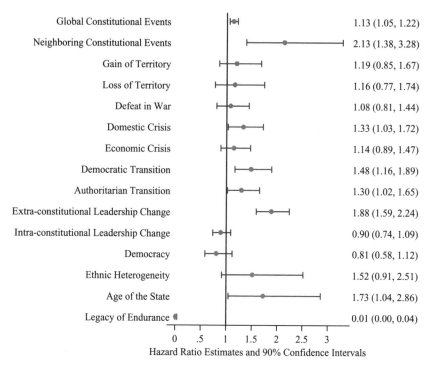

FIGURE 6.2. The Effect of Crises.
Note: Estimates are from a Cox Proportional Hazard Model. Only select variables are reported. The full model results are reported in Appendix A.5 (Model 1).

threats or use of force. Indeed, as a legal matter, the UN Charter prohibited taking over other countries. This relatively benign security environment meant that it was less risky for groups to secede from existing arrangements.[5] In addition, as Lake and O'Mahoney (2004) have pointed out, the value of territory has declined with economies of scale and increased economic openness. Economic liberalization has reduced the costs of small size, and reduced the benefits of large national markets. All these factors mean that the cost of

[5] Roeder (2007) considers the question of which secessionist projects succeed and which do not, and a key factor is whether the unit in question has a distinct administrative apparatus, be it as a subnational unit, autonomous entity, or colony. This provides useful insights into why secession was rampant in the former Soviet Union but less so in Africa, which lacked effective state apparatuses. Our bargain theory helps to illuminate Roeder's hypothesis. An administrative apparatus provides the ability to generate some public goods fairly quickly; a prospective nation with no state apparatus is unlikely to credibly convince its residents that it is viable, and hence may have trouble in constitutional bargaining. A substate apparatus increases the reservation price for new rounds of constitutional bargaining with the metropole, makes secession more viable, and hence should contribute to constitutional turnover.

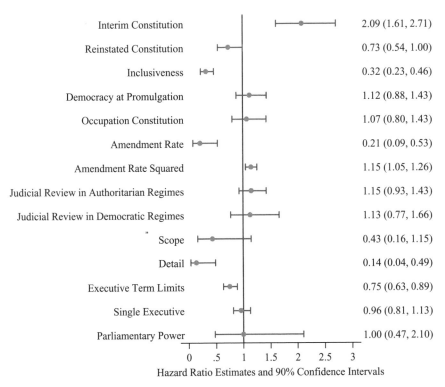

FIGURE 6.3. The Effect of Design Features.
Note: Estimates are from a Cox Proportional Hazard Model. Only select variables are reported. The full model results are reported in Appendix A.5 (Model 1).

secession is lower.[6] Just as divorce rates in many countries rise as women enter the labor force and have the option of providing for their own welfare, so too the costs of constitutional exit through secession have decreased after World War II. We thus observe more frequent constitutional death.

Estimates of Risk Factors

We are now in a position to estimate the effect of the risk factors identified in Chapter Five. The results that we report here are from a fully specified

---

[6] Strictly speaking, the literature on state size might be argued to be neutral about the probability of constitutional death for any given constitution. Whether the international environment encourages state expansion or contraction, there are pressures on the payoffs to parties to a constitutional bargain. When the environment favors expansion, we will see external conflict as a cause of constitutional death; when the environment favors contraction, we will see internal secession as a more frequent cause. Still, for the population of states as a whole, we should see secession as producing more deaths. This is because secession not only results from death, but also can produce new intra- and inter-state conflict, leading to yet further deaths.

model, run on the entire sample, and estimated with a Cox Proportional Hazard survival model. In a rather extensive set of sensitivity tests, we have also run the model with alternative specifications, samples, and statistical estimators. A table with estimates from the principal model and a selection of alternative models is printed in the Appendix. Figures 6.2 and 6.3 graph the estimates for the environmental and design factors, respectively. The estimates are reported as hazard ratios, in which values over 1.0 should be interpreted as *increased* odds of constitutional demise and values below 1.0 as *reduced* odds. An estimate of 2.00, for example, indicates that a one-unit change in the independent variable doubles the hazard rate, whereas an estimate of 0.50 implies that a one-unit change halves the hazard rate. For each variable in the analysis, we also calculate the life expectancy and the estimated mortality rate (hazard rate) when each variable is at its minimum and maximum, with all other variables held at their means. This is in Table 6.1, which we at times refer to as an "actuarial table," given its rather long list of risk factors and seeming utility for would-be insurers who would write policies and premiums based on these estimates. There are many potentially interesting results from these results, each of which could and should be explored in greater depth. We examine a selection of these below in varying degrees of depth based mostly upon the relevance to our theory.

Environmental Factors

The environment, both international and national, has demonstrable effects. As we might expect, the two spatial lags that we included in the model, *global events* and *neighboring events*, are associated with constitutional demise. Recall that these variables capture recent constitutional deaths in the world and neighboring countries, respectively. The hazard ratio for the neighbor lag of 2.13 reported in Figure 6.2 suggests that a shift in the regional death rate in the prior year from 0 to 100 percent would double the hazard rate of countries in the region (as Table 6.1 suggests, the mortality rate would go from 27 per 1000 to 56 per 1000). This presumed shift in neighborhood mortality, of course, is implausibly high (if not catastrophic!), but it implies that more moderate shifts in regional constitution-making activity would still be quite consequential. We should note again that these are catch-all variables, which simply indicate a high degree of temporal and geographic clustering in constitutional replacement. Whether these effects represent diffusion or simultaneous responses to similar conditions is unclear. However, the strong effects indicate that we cannot rule out the diffusion processes that we have inferred from our reading of constitutional histories.

The results suggest that traumatic events and crises are sometimes, but not always, lethal for constitutions. Nearly all of estimated effects are in the

TABLE 6.1. *An actuarial table of constitutional mortality*

		Life expectancy[1]			Hazard rate[2]		
		With risk factor at			With risk factor at		
Category	Variable	Min	Max	Δ	Min	Max	Δ
Crises	Global Constitutional Events*	23	6	−17	23	78	55
	Neighboring Constitutional Events*	19	8	−11	27	56	29
	Territory Gain	18	14	−4	28	33	5
	Territory Loss	18	15	−3	28	32	4
	Defeat in War	18	16	−2	28	30	2
	Domestic Crisis*	18	13	−5	27	36	9
	Economic Crisis	18	15	−3	28	32	4
	Democratic Transition*	18	12	−6	27	40	13
	Authoritarian Transition*	18	13	−5	27	35	8
	Extra-constitutional Leadership Change*	21	10	−11	25	47	22
	Intra-constitutional Leadership Change	17	20	3	29	26	−3
Structure of the State	Democracy	16	21	5	30	24	−6
	Ethnic Heterogeneity	23	13	−10	24	36	12
	Economic Development	17	>216	—	29	4	−25
	State Age*	20	10	−10	26	44	18
	Legacy of Endurance*	11	>216	—	41	1	−40
Structure of the Constitution	Interim Constitution*	18	8	−10	27	56	29
	Reinstated Constitution	17	27	10	28	21	−7
	Inclusiveness*	14	69	55	34	12	−22
	Democratic at Promulgation	18	16	−2	27	30	3
	Occupation Constitution	18	17	−1	28	30	2
	Amendment Rate*[3]	14	25	11	34	22	−12
	Judicial Review in Authoritarian Regimes	20	16	−4	26	30	4
	Judicial Review in Democratic Regimes	18	16	−2	27	31	4
	Scope	12	26	14	38	22	−16
	Detail*	14	83	69	34	11	−23
	Single Executive	17	18	1	28	27	−1
	Executive Term Limits*	15	22	7	32	24	−8
	Parliamentary Power	18	18	0	28	28	0
					0	0	0
Region (Western Europe, U.S., and Canada is the reference category)	Latin America*	26	8	−18	21	56	35
	Eastern Europe*	20	8	−12	26	53	27
	Middle East	18	15	−3	32	28	4
	Africa*	20	9	−11	50	25	25
	South Asia	18	10	−8	44	28	16
	East Asia*	19	9	−10	48	27	21
	Oceania*	17	131	114	9	29	−20
Era (prior to 1914 is reference category)	1914–1945*	19	13	−6	35	27	8
	After 1945	20	17	−3	29	26	3

Note: All values calculated from estimates in Model 1 (Appendix A.5), with specified values for each factor and all others set to their means.

* Statistically significant at 10%.

[1] Calculated as the median survival estimate at birth.

[2] Reported as deaths per 1000. The hazard rate varies by age; we report when it is at its maximum (age 17 years).

[3] Because the relationship between the amendment rate and life expectancy is curvilinear, we report estimates for the lowest- and highest-impact values rather than those for the the maximum and minimum of the variable.

expected direction. That is, in Figure 6.2 all of the point estimates, except for *intra-constitutional leadership change* (more on that shortly), are above 1 (which, again, represents even odds of death), suggesting that these crises increase the odds of death. Most of these effects, however, are statistically indistinguishable from 1, as the confidence intervals indicate. Thus, shocks such as the loss and gain of territory, defeat in war, and economic crisis – events that would seem highly traumatic and, consequently, lethal to the prevailing constitutional order – appear mostly innocuous. For example, the omnibus measure of intrastate conflict, domestic crisis, is only weakly predictive (hazard ratio = 1.33, meaning that constitutional replacement in years surrounding a crisis is one and a third times as likely as in non-crises years).

These mixed results with respect to the environment are somewhat surprising. Why is it that cataclysmic events like defeat in war and economic crisis do not put the constitution at risk? Certainly the bivariate relationship between military defeats, at least, and constitutional change is a strong one. Our data include 585 instances of defeat in war since 1789, and roughly 10 percent of these episodes are associated with constitutional replacement – a hazard rate that is twice that of non-war years, a significant difference statistically ($X^2 = 19.64$, p = 0.00). The multivariate analysis, however, suggests that other processes – whether environmental or design factors – are lurking behind these traumatic events and are consequential. For one thing, the diffusion variables, which would pick up clustered military defeats like those of the two world wars, might be robbing the war and other crisis variables of their explanatory power. Part of what looked like a strong war effect may in part result from contagion or other temporally clustered variables not included in the analysis.

Economic crises are puzzling in a different way, however. Even in the bivariate analysis, economic crises are not coincident with constitutional change. Consider the Great Depression, undoubtedly a time of great stress for most countries. Between 1929 and 1934, there were twenty-three constitutional deaths, which together represent a hazard rate of approximately six percent, only slightly larger than the worldwide historical hazard rate of five percent. That is, even during this historically dismal economic period, constitutions were not noticeably more unstable than they were at other points. The Great Depression is not unique. If we consider all 648 times in which a country's GDP dropped more than 10 percent (our definition of economic crisis), only seven percent resulted in constitutional death in that year or the next, still not appreciably higher than the baseline death rate of 5 percent. Of course, we can never rule out the possibility that this finding is an artifact of our analytic approach. Measurement error in our explanatory variables, for example, will depress the magnitude of regression coefficients. Given the challenge of assembling comparable economic data across the last two centuries, we can be confident that we have misidentified some number of crises and non-crises alike. Nonetheless, the cross-national analysis here – data error notwithstanding – certainly suggests that economic crisis does not uproot constitutions the way we thought it might.

Regime change – in both directions – does have a decided impact on constitutional change, as we would expect from the bivariate data we presented in Chapter Three. The bivariate hazard rate for constitutions in the years before and after a regime change was remarkably high – roughly five times as many deaths during years with of shifts to democracy as not and three times as many during shifts to authoritarianism. The estimates from the multivariate model suggest a much more modest but decided effect: hazard rates are 1.5 times as high after democratization and 1.3 times as high after authoritarianization, compared to stable years (Figure 6.2). As the difference in these effect sizes suggest, new democrats appear more likely to replace the constitution than do new authoritarians. Curiously, in other results (not shown) we found no evidence of any interaction between the direction of regime change and the regime origins of the constitution. That is, new democrats who inherit an authoritarian constitution were not especially likely to replace the constitution. Thus, the Chilean transition to democracy, in which leaders declined to replace the Pinochet constitution, was apparently not unusual, to our surprise. This finding leads us to believe that the accommodationist forces described in accounts of the Chilean transition may be prevalent in others as well.

Our model also allows us to say something about the stability of constitutions in democratic situations versus that in authoritarian situations; that is, the effect of persistent regime conditions versus that of changes in regime. Democracy, it appears, is measurably more hospitable to constitutions – roughly thirty percent more hospitable than the authoritarian situation is, in fact. The life expectancy of a constitution in democracy, on average, is twenty-one years, whereas that in an authoritarian situation is fifteen years. This effect, combined with our finding with respect to regime change, leads us to an interesting and rich perspective concerning regimes and constitutional change. Shifts to democracy increase the risk for the constitution even more than do shifts to authoritarianism. However, once in power, democrats are considerably less likely than are authoritarians to replace the constitution. This pair of findings accords with patterns such as that of France, in which we see periodic constitutional change only during major shifts in the regime. Stable democracies, it appears, do not replace their constitutions the way stable authoritarian states, such as the former Soviet Union, were accustomed to doing.

We can also report some related findings regarding leadership change. Extra-constitutional change, measured by the Archigos project's recording of irregular leadership changes, is almost twice as likely to precede a constitutional replacement as are years not preceded by extra-constitutional leadership change. Note that the predictive ability of this variable may come at the expense of that of authoritarian transitions because the two are moderately correlated. Parsing this relationship might be interesting, but we do not do so here because our primary interest in extra-constitutional leadership change is to help specify a full range of environmental variables to assess the independent effects of the design variables. Interestingly, intra-constitutional leadership change has no effect on constitutional stability. Generalizing from cases such as the Soviet Union, we had conjectured that the practice in authoritarian regimes of new leaders inaugurating their new administration with a new document may be widespread. It is not. If anything, these periods of leadership transition are more stable than otherwise, on average.

Several environmental factors from Table 6.1 concern structural features of the state. Somewhat surprisingly, the level of development does not seem to be a strong predictor of constitutional change. The coefficients from each of the models in which we included this variable suggest a moderate effect ($10 Billion of GDP in 1995 U.S. dollars yields an 8 percent decrease in the hazard rate), but the effect is not statistically different from zero in most specifications. This is somewhat startling given the stabilizing effect that development has in the context of regime change. But, of course, we should remember that economic development will have an indirect effect on constitutional change *through* the former's effect on regime change.

We also can point to an interesting finding regarding ethnic heterogeneity. Recall that we reasoned that this variable would help us describe particularly challenging conditions for constitution drafters, with more heterogeneous states presenting greater challenges. Sure enough, when this variable is included in the environment-only model, the direction of the effect suggests that heterogeneity is associated with constitutional instability, although we cannot be statistically certain that the effect is non-zero. The life expectancy for constitutions in maximally heterogenous states is thirteen versus twenty-three for those in maximally homogenous states. However, when we include this variable with the design factors, its effect reverses. That is, controlling for the way drafters design the constitution, heterogeneity seems to *reduce* the probability of constitutional change. We can certainly imagine that careful constitutional design might compensate for challenges like size and heterogeneity. However, that heterogeneity would be an *asset* to constitutional duration is intriguing and certainly begs for further analysis.

One possibility is that the variable we are using to measure heterogeneity is poorly suited and hence producing unstable results. Fearon's (2003) fractionalization measure is a continuous one that increases with the internal diversity of a country. But, it might be the case that extremely diverse environments, such as India, are actually beneficial for constitutional endurance because no single group is strong enough to dictate a new set of institutions to others. When a constitutional design configuration looks like contemporary Iraq, with one large group and two small ones, the largest group will have trouble credibly tying its hands and may provoke fear in smaller groups. This sort of unbalanced arrangement may thereby lead to the unwinding of constitutional bargaining.

A final environmental factor concerns the historical legacies of the state. Specifically, does a tradition of enduring constitutions increase the life expectancy of future constitutions? The answer appears to be yes. Every 10 years of average duration of a previous constitution appears to reduce the probability of constitutional replacement by 12 percent. The virtuous and vicious cycles that we see in certain country histories do seem to be pervasive. Just as children of divorce are themselves more likely to experience a failed marriage, constitutional bargainers whose inheritance includes prior instability find it more difficult to create an enduring bargain.

Design Factors

We turn now to our hypotheses regarding constitutional design. Three important and robust design factors emerge as strong predictors of constitutional survival, predictors that retain their strength even in the presence of the environmental covariates. First, constitutions written under inclusive conditions, and that also then incorporate inclusive provisions, are more likely to survive than those that do not. The effect is fairly dramatic. The life expectancy of the least inclusive constitution is fourteen, whereas that of the most inclusive is sixty-nine. Given that the inclusiveness measure combines constitution-making conditions along with aspects of ongoing governance, we tested the various component parts of the measure as well. Most of the separate elements yield results similar to, if more modest than, those of the overall measure. For example, constitutions that are subject to public ratification are eight percent more likely to survive than those that are not. We also tested another hypothesis implied by our theory of inclusion: the notion that constitutions written under occupation involve particularly low levels of inclusion and consensus and are likely to be unstable. The results suggest that, if anything, such constitutions do have higher levels of mortality (hazard ratios were around 1.20 in most models we tested), but these estimates were not statistically different from even odds. We suspect that the lack of a pronounced effect stems from the surprising longevity of constitutions like those of Japan and Germany, where initially the

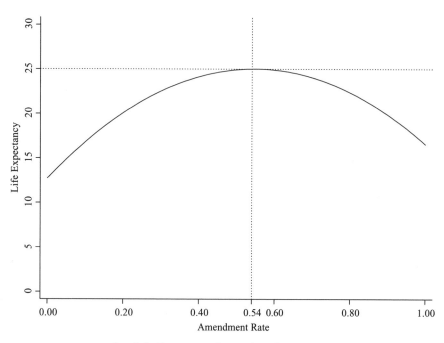

FIGURE 6.4. Life Expectancy by Predicted Amendment Rate.

security umbrella of the United States provided at least the possibility of an external guarantor of the constitution (see Elkins, Ginsburg and Melton 2008).

Another strong predictor of longevity is amendment ease. As we expected, the effect is non-linear. The predominant effect of the variable is to decrease the odds of replacement as flexibility increases (hazard ratio = 0.32). However, the squared term yields a hazard ratio that is significant and greater than one, suggesting that extremely high values on flexibility are associated with an increased risk of death. Figure 6.4 plots an estimate of life expectancy based on the combination of these two effects.[7] The graph suggests an inverted-U pattern in which high and low values of amendment ease are associated with shorter life spans. Amendment flexibility appears to be "just right" at about 0.54 on our flexibility scale, which corresponds exactly to India's score on the measure. India's amendment procedure depends upon the topic. For most matters the procedure is comparatively easy – amendments are passed by a two-thirds majority in Congress and then signed by the President (a mostly symbolic office in India). However, the amendment of certain topics requires, in addition to a supermajority in Congress, the assent of one-half of the states,

[7] The figure plots a smoothed estimate of the predicted scores based on the two variables in question (with others set at their means).

which adds considerably tighter restrictions. Nonetheless, it appears that any procedure that tends away from India's in either the more or less restrictive direction will increase the mortality rate of its constitution.

We turn now to the two subdimensions of specificity, scope and detail. Our findings suggest that increased scope, as we suspected, is associated with increased duration. Constitutions at the high extreme have life expectancies more than twice as high as those at the lower extreme (26 years versus 12 years). This is a strong effect indeed, although it is statistically indistinguishable from zero (or one, if we are thinking in terms of hazard ratios). As we suggested earlier, this larger confidence interval may be the product of competing causal processes at work. Although broad ranging constitutions may be helpful in encouraging investment in the document and facilitating enforcement, it may also have some destabilizing effects with respect to flexibility. The net result, like that of red wine on human life span, may then be zero after we account for effects in both directions. Detail, however – the other element of specificity – exhibits unequivocally stabilizing effects on the constitution. Constitutions at one extreme of detail (such as those of India, South Africa, and Brazil) have life expectancies in the eighties, whereas those on the other extreme (such as recent constitutions from China or even the French constitution of 1852) have life expectancies in the low teens.

Constitutional review is more puzzling. We had reasoned that constitutional review would increase constitutional endurance through multiple complementary processes. If anything, however, the practice seems to have a destabilizing effect, albeit one statistically indistinguishable from a null effect. A number of methodological explanations for this result come to mind. The first has to do with measurement error. We know that our binary measure of constitutional review is simplifying and, in some cases, misleading. Ours is a formal measure of constitutional review and we know – most notably from the U.S. case – that formal provisions for constitutional review are not always reliable. Although a measure of the extent of de facto judicial review might be helpful, such a measure does not yet exist cross-nationally. Another possibility is that different variants of constitutional review have different effects, so that, for example, public access to the constitutional court is crucial. We review this problem again when we turn to the family histories and autopsies in Chapters Seven and Eight.

Finally, we see little corroboration for our competing hypotheses regarding executive and legislative power. Recall that many new constitutions seem to coincide with executive grabs for more power, and so we speculated that executive dominance might correlate with constitutional endurance. However, it does not appear that increases in legislative power (presumably at the expense of executive power) increase the hazard rate significantly. This non-result holds

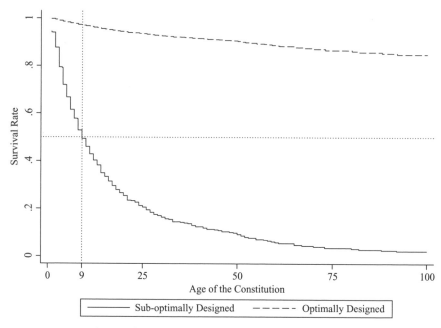

FIGURE 6.5. *Predicted Survival Rate for Two Constitutional Designs.*

even after we modified the functional form by substituting a logged version
of the variable and, in another specification, adding a squared term to pick
up nonlinearity. We reasoned that the effect of constraining an executive may
be particularly intense regarding certain modes of constraining executives;
namely, by term limits. However, a binary variable for executive term limits
was *not* associated with constitutional replacement, and was even associated
with a slight decrease in the mortality rate. Constraining executives does not
appear to trigger constitutional replacement in the cross-national data, no
matter how prevalent the cause in eyewitness reports of constitutional death.
Conversely, however, enhanced legislative power does not seem to have an
effect either. Perhaps this provides support for Madison's argument about
the virtue of balanced powers in the constitutional order, though we do not
systematically test this conjecture.

Some Projections

We can take these three principal design elements – inclusion, specificity,
and flexibility – and imagine optimal and suboptimal package of provisions
from the perspective of framers bent on preserving their creation. In doing
so, we assume that the provisions are not mutually exclusive and do not interact in any way. The solid line in Figure 6.5 illustrates the survival rate of a

suboptimal constitution (amendment rate = 0, detail = 0.01, and inclusiveness = 0) and the dashed line represents that of an optimally drafted constitution (amendment rate = 0.54, detail = 1,690, and inclusiveness = 7). Note that these packages reflect, respectively, the least and most optimal values from the data of each of these variables. The suboptimally designed constitution has a life expectancy of nine years, whereas that of the optimally designed constitution has one of well over 200 years (literally off the charts in Figure 6.5). Constitutional design, it appears, can potentially make a profound difference in mortality.

These hypothetical packages might strike some readers as fanciful. Let us consider, instead, two recently promulgated constitutions, those of Afghanistan and Iraq. Many hope that these two constitutions can help to provide some stability to two countries that are, to put it delicately, rebuilding. The circumstances of constitutional drafting in these two cases are broadly similar. Most obviously, both have undergone an extended period of occupation by the United States, which oversaw the drafting process. Nonetheless, the provisions of the two constitutions diverge on several critical points, and the national environment of the two also differs. If we plug in the values of these variables for these two cases, and keep any unknowns (such as the probability of crisis) at their means, we can project their life expectancy based on the estimates from our model.

Panels (a) and (b) of Figure 6.6 plot the predicted survival rates for each constitution. The differences are striking. Iraq's constitution is projected to survive fifty-nine years from birth, and Afghanistan's only fourteen years. Of course, one may think that, given the current instability in both of these countries, both of these life expectancies are high. Or, one might assume that under U.S. occupation, events like regime transition and domestic crisis – two of the more lethal crises for constitutions – will be less likely. Certainly, one could adjust some of the crisis variables to account for these varying expectations, adjustments that would acknowledge the real power of the environment – power that we decidedly do not deny. As we stress, constitutions can die for various reasons, and mortality rates may indeed spike or plummet because of exogenous events. Nevertheless, the non-crisis features suggest stark differences in mortality expectations for the two cases.

Robustness of the Estimates

Our analysis has involved a series of decisions regarding sample, measurement, model specification, and estimation. How sensitive are our results to variations in the analytic approach? Overall, the effect estimates were fairly constant across models. Here we summarize the results of some of a series of alternative

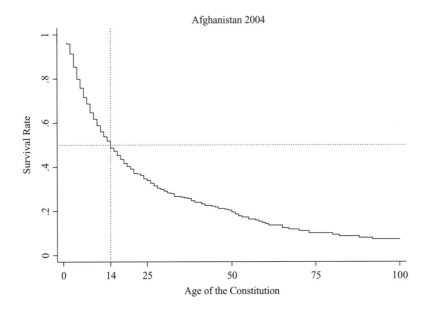

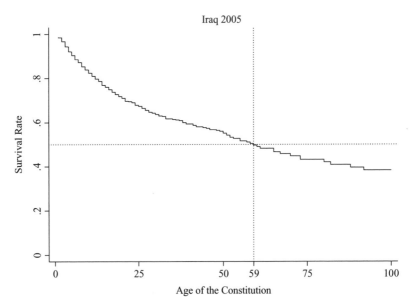

FIGURE 6.6. Predicted Survival Rate for the Constitutions of Iraq and Afghanistan.

analyses that we have run to evaluate the robustness of our results. Some of these results we report in the Appendix.

To test the sensitivity of the results to outliers, we ran the full model on a sample that excludes the ten countries whose constitutions exhibit the longest average life span and the ten countries whose constitutions have the shortest average life span, with similar results. Also, it seems reasonable to think that constitutions with a democratic origin would function differently from those with an authoritarian one. We thus ran separate models for sub-samples of constitutions promulgated during democratic and authoritarian country-years. We note several interesting differences for effects between these two populations. Starting with the environment variables, loss of territory seems to affect authoritarian constitutions, but not those with democratic origins. All of the other environment variables have the same effects across the different samples. In terms of constitutional structure, some specifications suggest that constitutional review may extend the life span for authoritarian constitutions, a finding quite consistent with work on courts in authoritarian politics (Ginsburg and Moustafa 2008). When run on the partial samples, the effect of ethnic heterogeneity seems to increase the hazard. Perhaps unsurprisingly, economic development decreases the hazard rate for constitutions written in democratic regimes but has no effect in authoritarian written constitutions, in which a small elite may take the bulk of the wealth.

In various specifications, we examined the effects of state age and birth order of constitutions. One might think that older states would have more enduring constitutions because norms of cooperation are more established. Another conjecture was that later-born constitutions would endure longer than earlier-born ones in a country's history, as designers learn from experience. We found no support for either of these hypotheses, independent of the strongly beneficial effect of having a legacy of enduring constitutions. In other words, the survival of later-born constitutions is best predicted by the longevity of earlier ones, regardless of the age of the state.

In looking at period effects, we find that some crises seem to have different effects in different time periods. For instance, loss of territory, domestic crises, and democratic transitions have a statistically significant effect on the hazard only in those constitutions written since 1945, but neighboring events and authoritarian transitions have a statistically significant effect on the hazard only in those constitutions written prior to 1945. Moreover, the two crisis variables that affect the hazard during both time periods – global events and coups – have a much stronger effect in constitutions written since 1945.

The constitutional design variables had little effect on life span prior to 1945. In fact, the only variables that are significant during that period are amendment rate and whether the constitution was explicitly a temporary document. This changes after 1945. Easy amendment procedures and scope decrease the hazard, whereas interim constitutions and a strong parliament seem to increase the hazard in that period.

CONCLUSION

In this chapter, we have analyzed an original set of cross-national historical data to test the theory elaborated in previous chapters. In general, the theory holds up fairly well. Environmental factors do play a role, as suggested by both our theories and those of other scholars, but, most notably, the design features that we expected to be consequential are indeed so. In particular, the amendment procedure, detail of the constitution, and a level of inclusiveness all seem to have a decided impact on constitutional endurance. Our illustrative examples suggest that an optimal design can reduce the mortality rate of constitutions significantly. These findings have important implications for drafters, whose pens may be more powerful than scholars had previously thought. Given the strength of these findings, and their divergence from conventional wisdom, closer inspection of the causal processes seems warranted. In the next two chapters, we explore the causal processes behind life and death of constitutions through a study of family histories and autopsies.

7

Cases of Constitutional Mortality, Part I: Similar Contexts, Contrasting Outcomes

"All happy families are alike," began Leo Tolstoy in *Anna Karenina* (1877), "but every unhappy family is unhappy in its own way." Certainly, the last three chapters remind us of the multiple sources of unhappiness in constitutions. Perhaps, however, our focus on failure has obscured the qualities of stable constitutions. Is it that elderly constitutions have simply avoided all of the crises and disabilities that afflict the more fleeting systems? Is there something about them that defies epidemiological analysis? A biographical account of these longer lives seems in order. Even among the unhappy cases, we still have large gaps in our knowledge. How exactly do certain crises destabilize constitutions? How, if at all, do the design features whose therapeutic effects we praise actually work in practice? Case-level material can be insightful for a host of reasons. The next two chapters explore constitutional reform (and non-reform) in two groups of case-oriented analyses. As we describe in the following section, we have adopted a case-study design that, in our view, illustrates the concepts and processes under consideration and maximizes analytic leverage on the challenge of causal inference.

A STRUCTURED CASE-STUDY APPROACH

A close inspection of cases provides a number of distinct analytic advantages.[1] Most obviously, such analysis can illuminate the causal process, something that is sometimes lost in large-n statistical analysis that follows a less sequential evaluation of the association of cause and effect. In this sense, Brady and

---

[1] We draw here from the literature on the comparative method; in particular, Collier (1993), Brady and Collier (2004), Lijphart (1971); Przeworski and Teune (1970), and Ragin (1987).

Collier's (2004) distinction between "causal process observations" and "dataset observations" captures the evidence employed in micro and macro-research quite usefully. This focus on process also yields valuable illustrative benefits. Narratives that include the proper names of people, places, and events come alive in a way that clarifies the causal process more vividly, or at least more concretely, than statistical parameters usually do (although statistical findings can be eye-poppingly resonant). This is true not just for processes, but for concepts. For example, the cook who spits in the soup in James Scott's (1985) *Weapons of the Weak* evokes a poignant and memorable understanding of the concept in the book's title. In our case, inclusion, flexibility, and specificity could all use further elaboration. These sort of illustrative benefits lighten the burden for case studies in that the analysis need not serve strictly as evidence for hypothesis testing. Something akin to what Skocpol and Somers (1980) describe as a "parallel demonstration of theory" may be justification enough. Certainly, part of our objective in these two chapters is to illuminate the constitutional reform process in this way.

Nonetheless, a structured analysis of cases can potentially carry a heavier burden and engage in hypothesis testing, or at least identify "theory-confirming" and "theory-infirming" cases (Lijphart 1971). Toward this end, two classic designs of case-oriented comparative research offer promise. In the first, which Przeworski and Teune (1970) term the "most similar systems" approach, analysts select cases that differ with respect to the outcome, but match across a host of potentially explanatory variables.[2] Differences in outcome can thus be explained by any differences between the otherwise very similar cases. The design, something Stinchcombe (1978) refers to as "deep analogy," has a highly intuitive logic that mirrors the notion of statistical control. Przeworski and Teune, however, argue that the method often leads to an analysis of outcomes that are largely "overdetermined" and suggest that a "most different systems" design yields greater leverage for causal inference. A most different systems design compares cases that differ across a host of explanatory factors, but share similar outcomes. No one pretends, of course, that either one of these approaches provides for an airtight test of rival hypotheses. However, both methods are widely used in the field of comparative politics and have yielded insights that form the core of knowledge in the discipline.

---

[2] Mill (1843), more classically, refers to this as the "method of difference," and constrasts it with the "method of agreement," which Przeworski and Teune call the "most different systems" design. To sidestep this rather confusing and contrasting combination of labels, we use the terminology of Przeworski and Teune, whose labels have the advantage of identifying what, exactly, is the same or different.

One obvious limitation to these methods has to do with the sample of cases, which is always small in number, rarely randomly drawn, and, as Geddes (1990) points out, nearly always involves selecting on the dependent variable. Some degree of bias and inefficiency seem unavoidable. Given these limitations, one effective strategy – emphasized by Lieberson (1991), Collier (1993), and others – is to look *within* sampled cases in order to analyze multiple instances of the phenomenon of interest. In such a way, analysts can generate an expanded case set and increase their analytic leverage, while they preserve an understanding of the context and control for a large set of rival explanations. This idea has rightly renewed enthusiasm for the study of subnational and historical analysis in comparative politics (see Snyder 2001).

Our analytical approach borrows elements from each of the designs described above. We adopt a sampling plan that draws two samples – one with a "most different systems" design and another with a "most similar systems" design – and we explore within-case variation in each sample. Recall that the unit of analysis in our study is the constitutional system (for example, the French constitution of 1875–1940). Recall, also, that many of our explanatory variables are characteristics of the country (not the constitutional system) and that even characteristics of the constitution itself, including its duration, are often highly correlated with those of other constitutions from the same country. These family affinities and inheritances suggest a country-based sampling design, as opposed to a constitution-based design. Accordingly, our approach is to select pairs of *countries* according to most-similar and most-different system criteria, and analyze the historical series of constitutions within each country. We compare constitutions within each country to each other, but also compare, as appropriate, a country's constitutional history to that of its matched country. To summarize our strategy in more technical terms, our sampling unit is the country and our unit of analysis is both the constitutional system (within countries) and the country (within matched pairs).

We begin in this chapter with a sample of most-similar system country pairs: specifically, (1) India and Pakistan, (2) the United States and France, and (3) China and Taiwan. Each of these tales-of-two-countries focuses on states that adopted constitutions at the same time and within the same geographic or ideological milieu, but whose *average* level of constitutional stability has been markedly different. Chapter Eight, on the other hand, analyzes a set of countries from a most-different systems sample. In that chapter, we explore paired comparisons of (1) Haiti and the Dominican Republic (which we consider jointly) with Thailand, and (2) Mexico with Japan. Besides our analytic considerations, we chose countries whose constitutional history is particularly noteworthy or for which we have some prior knowledge and experience.

INDIA AND PAKISTAN: STABILITY AND CRISIS

India and Pakistan form an interesting paired constitutional comparison: joined at birth, the two have provided contrasting environments for constitutional development. India's constitution has succeeded in unifying a centrifugal nation against strong odds, making Pakistan's constitutional instability all the more stark. The three wars and myriad other minor clashes between the two countries form a set of common shocks. Although Pakistan's constitutions seem to die with some frequency, India's constitution has bent but not broken. What explains the divergent histories of these neighboring descendents of the British Raj?

The birth of India and Pakistan marked both the success and failure of one of the more audacious constitutional negotiations in history. On the success side, a group of committed nationalists won independence from the world's largest empire, and did so under the banner of constitutional democracy. Democracy and, after 1934, a constituent assembly to draft a constitution, had been the central demands of the Congress Party in India. At the same time, the founding of the two states marked a profound failure of another negotiation, that between the founders of India and the leaders of the Muslim League, who preferred to remain outside the bargain rather than submit to perceived Hindu domination. The Muslim League ended up boycotting the Indian constitutional assembly once it materialized, making partition inevitable.

One can think of partition as the least unattractive solution to a set of incompatible preference orderings between the two main political forces, the Congress Party and the Muslim League. The Congress' overriding goal was for the British to leave, and their first preference was for India to stay united thereafter. This, however, was the least favorite outcome from the perspective of the Muslim League, whose members felt the British needed to stay to guarantee minority rights (Austin 1972). The Muslim League's preferred outcome was for partition with the British gone, but, if that could not be obtained, the continuation of colonial rule was better than Hindu domination. The Congress Party's second favored position was for the British to leave and India to be partitioned, and their least favored outcome was for the British to stay. Partition meant that neither side got its worst outcome, and the Muslim League obtained its best.

Alas, what was best for the elites of the Muslim League was not necessarily best for the citizens of their nation in the long run. Although initially conditions seemed similar in India and Pakistan given the shared historical process leading up to independence, later, a number of important differences arose, which affected subsequent constitutional development. One can think of these as congenital defects that have undermined Pakistan's ability to create an enduring, inclusive, self-enforcing constitutional bargain. This inability is more painful given the enduring success of the Indian Constitution against what some perceived to be long odds.

India: Robust at Birth

India is poor and ethnically diverse, two characteristics that some have associated with constitutional instability. Yet, the Indian Constitution, described by one leading analyst as "The Cornerstone of a Nation" (Austin 1972), has endured for six decades and been internalized by both elites and masses. It has provided the basis for limitations on ambitious executives and provided a language of politics for various groups in society.

According to the predictions of our epidemiological model, India's framers have built a document to last generations. We can begin with the inclusive drafting process that gave the constitution its start. The universal franchise had long been embedded in nationalist demands for self-determination (Bhargava 2008). For Jawaharlal Nehru, India's first Prime Minister, and his Congress Party, the idea of a directly elected constituent assembly empowered to draft a constitutional document was itself a major demand – and thus took on symbolic value even before the first draft was completed. The assembly embodied a "nation on the move, throwing away the shell of its past political and possibly social structure, and fashioning for itself a new garment of its own making" (Nehru 1947: 35). In a society of continuing inequalities, the assembly's product constituted a formal commitment to eradicating ascriptive hierarchy.

In the end, India's Constituent Assembly was constituted through indirect election by the existing provincial legislatures, mainly because of considerations of speed (Sarkar 1999). Although largely a one-party affair, it was an inclusive one because the Congress itself was an ideologically diverse party. As Nehru described it in 1939, "The Congress [Party] has within its fold many groups widely differing in their viewpoints and ideologies. This is natural and inevitable if the Congress is to be the mirror of the nation" (Austin 1972: 11). The Assembly included designated representatives from many minorities: Christians, Parsis, Anglo-Indians, and the so-called Backward Castes. Although some groups were not represented – communists, socialists, and the Hindu Right being the most prominent outside the Muslim League – their views were largely reflected in various representatives of the Congress Party (Austin 1972: 14–15; Austin 1999 ; Sarkar 1999). And, there was substantial input from civil society and private individuals in communications to the Assembly.

The drafting process produced an extremely detailed document, with an explicit recognition of the value of specificity. Lawyers dominated the Assembly, and this led to an emphasis on legal language, including borrowings from the 1935 Government of India Act designed to facilitate the transition to independence.[3] The transformative agenda for the constitution and the distrust of the hierarchical basis of Indian society were also responsible for some of the details. For example, Dr. B. R. Ambedkar, the legal expert who served as head of the Constituent Assembly, argued that there was no option but to spell out the rights of minorities in great detail in the constitution (Mane 2005: 257–258). He drafted a long list of detailed rights and an elaborate social scheme, only some of which made it into the final document. Articles 330 and 332 call for the reservation of seats in the national and state legislatures for members of the scheduled castes and scheduled tribes (Singhvi and Swarup 2006: 40–41; Revankar 1971: 83).[4] The Indian constitution was both detailed and of broad scope; of the ninety-two topics that we count in our measure of constitutional scope, the Indian constitution had provisions on sixty of them when it was born. Only two earlier constitutions – Cuba 1940 and Brazil 1946 – had covered more topics. Ambedkar, again, was part of this expansive push. In addition to his concern for rights, he was also a champion of the national judiciary and insisted on entrenching details of judicial power and structure into the constitution, where they would be somewhat safer from politicization. All the detail has been subject to criticism (Jennings 1953: 9–16), but, in the end, seems to have stood the test of time. The detail has also provoked use of the amendment procedure, another mechanism to ensure vital constitutional politics.

Like the Pakistani constitution, the Indian constitution included a flexible amendment procedure, or procedures to be exact. As an empirical matter, our analysis even suggests that India's amendment provision strikes the optimal balance between flexibility and commitment – at least as far as longevity is concerned (see Chapter Six). The founders knew that they could not anticipate all the challenges the new state would face; indeed, they drafted it during a time of extraordinary turmoil in international affairs. The drafters, including Ambedkar, Nehru, and Rau, were explicit about the need for flexibility (Austin 1972: 261–63). Rau tied flexibility to accommodation and co-optation and saw easy amendment as a device to deal with complex questions of minority and linguistic demands. Ambedkar viewed flexibility as key to responsive federalism.

---

[3] Austin's list of the twenty-one most important members of the Assembly contains only seven (Azad, Deo, Kripalani, Krishnamachari, Mookerjee, Sinha, and Sitaramayya) who were neither lawyers nor educated in law (Austin 1972: 337–44).

[4] These were limited temporally to a ten-year period, but have subsequently been extended.

Another central participant in the constitutional debates, P.S. Deshmukh, noted that simple modification was an attractive bargain if it could forestall wholesale constitutional change. Finally, a general mood of imperfection and a recognition that, in the process of drafting, certain mistakes were inevitable helped carry the day for flexibility.

As a result, the drafters set up a variable amendment formula, by which some provisions can be amended by a vote of 2/3 of members present in both houses of parliament, so long as an absolute majority is represented, and some provisions require an additional ratification by half of the states.[5] An additional set of individual provisions in the constitution was designated for modification by simple majority in parliament.

The Constitution thus included all three of our key factors for constitutional endurance. Within a few years, most major groups in society – including those that had not participated in the drafting process – were committed to working through constitutional institutions. Adjustments from the founding bargain were needed, and certain actors exploited drafting ambiguities to advance their interests. But, this participation produced an overwhelmingly inclusive brand of high politics, in which the constitution was the terrain of battle, and thus of increasing relevance to Indian society.[6]

An illustration comes from the complicated politics leading up to the First Amendment of the Constitution in 1951, an omnibus amendment involving freedom of speech, property, and affirmative action policies. The Congress Party had long adopted socialist leanings and sought to achieve a revolutionary reordering of a fundamentally unequal society. The constitution itself included a list of nonjusticiable *Directive Principles* designed to guide state policy in the realm of social and economic justice. As a result, early Congress policies included nationalizations, takings (understood as the appropriation of land without compensation), and the abolition of rights of large landholders known as *zamindars*. Many of these policies had been extensively debated during the constitutional assembly itself, with substantial discussion around the level

---

[5] Article 368.
[6] Some of the debates concerned the text itself. The first head of state, President Rajendra Prasad, read the constitution literally, and assumed that his functions of promulgating laws, serving as head of the armed forces, and making appointments were to be somewhat discretionary, notwithstanding provisions that he would act with the aid and advice of the cabinet (Austin 1999: 19–26; Basu 1994: 184). Art. 74 ("There shall be a Council of Ministers with the Prime Minister at the head to aid and advise the President who shall, in the exercise of his functions, act in accordance with such advice"). Others, including Nehru, viewed the constitution as embodying implicit limits associated with the parliamentary system. These issues triggered extensive constitutional dialogue, but were resolved mostly through political mechanisms in favor of traditional parliamentary prerogatives.

of compensation and whether it ought to be justiciable (Austin 1972: 87–99; 1999: 83). When the policies began to be implemented, however, property owners did not remain silent. In various courtrooms around the country, they challenged the constitutionality of land reform and other acts. Relying on the rights to property, they met with some success. These cases triggered a demand for constitutional amendment to overrule the courts and provide for some grounds on which takings would be presumptively valid. The result of this debate was the Ninth Schedule of the Constitution, which detailed acts that would be valid and not subject to judicial challenge. The particular result of these dialogues was a more detailed articulation of the rights to property and the scope of judicial review. The unintended consequences of the amendment was a constitutional trump card, in which interest groups would have a golden key to protect their legislation from court scrutiny, and the Ninth Schedule became used for all kinds of unanticipated bills. This card was played again to refine the issue of compensation in the Fourth Amendment in 1955, after further litigation by the *zamindars*.

The theme of dialogue between courts and the constitutional amendment process pervades Indian constitutional history. The founders had seen courts as essential for a social revolution and a necessary device to protect minority and individual rights inspired by American experience, among others (Austin 1972: 169, 171). The courts have played this role, but the flexibility of the formal document has meant that their decisions have at times been overruled. Even in the darkest days of Indira Gandhi's dictatorship, however, the courts continued to function and were a locus for challenges to the regime. The constitutional dialogues, too, have played a role in constitutional refinement and articulation and have produced an even more detailed formal document supplemented with detailed jurisprudence as to what the constitutional understanding entails.

A central debate concerned the limits on the scope of the amending power itself. In a series of cases, beginning with *Golak Nath*, the Indian Supreme Court considered the constitutionality of the property amendments and, without retrospectively overruling them, announced the doctrine of implied limitations on the constitutional amendment powers.[7] Certain "basic features" of the constitution could not be amended even by procedurally proper amendments, because such amendments were bound by provisions in the Constitution not to abridge rights.[8] The decision prompted counterattacks in the form of "restoring" parliamentary supremacy through constitutional amendment. The Supreme Court, called on to consider the constitutionality of

---

[7] *I.C Golak Nath and Others, petitioners v. State of Punjab and Another* 1967 (2) SCR 763.
[8] In elaborating this doctrine, the justices were influenced by a German scholar who had given lectures on the implied limitations of the amending power.

these amendments, upheld them in the landmark *Kesavananda* case, but also revived the idea of a constitutional "basic structure," which was not to be subject to amendment.[9]

The confrontation with the judiciary continued after Indira Gandhi declared a state of emergency in 1975. After passing amendments restricting emergency declarations from judicial purview and hoping to limit the courts from reviewing a case involving her own election, Gandhi transferred judges who had ruled against the government in various cases. The judiciary's unwillingness to overturn *Kesavananda* prompted the Forty-Second Amendment in 1976. This amendment excluded the courts from election disputes, strengthened the center vis-à-vis the states, raised the threshold for judicial findings of constitutionality, and stated that constitutional amendments could not be questioned in court on any ground. For example, the fifth and last clause of Article 368, the article on amendment powers, has since stated rather provocatively:

> For the removal of doubts, it is hereby declared that there shall be no limitation whatever on the constituent power of parliament to amend by way of addition, variation or repeal the provisions of this constitution under this article.

Interestingly, during the debate, allies of Gandhi seem to have floated the idea – in the form of several resolutions of state assemblies – of a new Constituent Assembly to draft a new constitution from scratch (Austin 1999: 377–381). There is some indication that they would have suspended elections entirely and done away with the democratic trappings of the constitution (Austin 1999: 380 n. 31). Reaction was swift and negative, and the proposals went nowhere. This is an illustration of a near-fatal experience for the constitution, in which enforcement dynamics came into play, and prevented a power-hungry executive from achieving extra-constitutional change. The executive, in this case, would be satisfied with intra-constitutional change via the Forty-second Amendment, which passed easily given the flexibility of the formal document.

Mrs. Gandhi's dictatorship came to an end shortly thereafter, because of miscalculations and internal tensions in her coalition. The new coalition government that replaced her, led by the Janata Dal, set about undoing many of her excesses in two amendments. As information on the abuses of emergency rule began to become more widely available, the amendments passed with the support of the Congress Party. These amendments restored judicial review and allowed the president to request reconsideration of bills by the cabinet. Although Gandhi returned to power in 1980, the courts resumed their stance.

[9] *Kesavananda Bharati v. State of Kerala* AIR [1973] SC 1461.

They overturned parts of the Forty-second Amendment in 1980, and restored the *Kesavananda* principle, thus reestablishing a balance of powers.[10] The tide had turned, and the Constitution was restored. It had bent, but had not broken.

India's Constitution accommodated many different visions of the state, but one central innovation was its early embrace of affirmative action, which was meant to extend the inclusiveness of the constitution-making process into the future.[11] Article 334 provides for reserved seats in legislatures for scheduled castes and tribes, and Article 335 provides for advantages for these groups in state employment. The very term *scheduled caste*, created by the constitution, has become a central category in India's public life. Article 340 extends the set-asides to the ambiguous category of *Other Backward Classes* (Jaffrelot 2008). The result again is the investment of interest groups, including the poorest members of society, in the constitution. Although social inequality remains a profound reality, the institutional structures of the constitution have provided more than mere aspiration for the lower strata – they have provided concrete benefits in the set-asides and reserved seats (Kohli 2001).

The Indian Constitution has also accommodated shifts among different institutional structures (Basu 1994; Rudolph and Rudolph 2001). We have already referred to claims of presidential and judicial power vis-à-vis parliament. It has generally allowed for a centralizing federalism and the emergence of a powerful Electoral Commission, which served to protect the integrity of elections against a number of challenges in the 1990s (Rudolph and Rudolph 2001: 154–161). Federalism has also accommodated linguistic diversity that might have otherwise broken up the state (Choudhry 2009). Several times, commissions have been formed to review the constitution, including most recently in the late 1990s (Rudolph and Rudolph 2001). But, these have never gone far toward any comprehensive reform. Rather, the day-to-day incremental processes of constitutional governance have played the role of ensuring continuing fit between the constitution and its social and political environment.

India's Constitution has become owned by many – property holders, Tamil speakers, Muslims, Brahmins, and *dalits* (the scheduled castes). It provides aspiration for many of those left behind as well as protection for those who already have secured their position. This element embodies the principle of accommodation, as leading scholar Granville Austin noted, between apparently incompatible goals.[12] But, it also involves a strong dose of co-optation.

---

[10] *Minerva Mills Ltd. and Others* vs. *Union of India and Others* (1980) 2 S.C.C. 591.

[11] See Jacobsohn (2003) for an extended discussion of issues of ethnic and religious identity in Indian constitutional politics.

[12] Not all politics of accommodation are good politics, and not all constitutionalist accommodations are good accommodations. Rajeev Bhargava, for example, writes about how the secular, liberal democratic discourse (associated with the constitution) shaped discursive strategies of all new groups, including the illiberal Hindu nationalists (Bhargava 2003; 2004).

It is constitutional alchemy when groups with conflicting agendas all believe they are better off with existing rules than in overturning them, and therein lies the key to India's constitutional endurance. The Indian Constitution has been, in Austin's phrase "the source of the country's political stability and its open society" (Austin 1999: 635).

Pakistan: Congenital Defects

The state of Pakistan was born on August 14, 1947, the day before India gained formal independence. This occurred as the result of a new set of demands from the Muslim League. As one scholar notes, it is not clear what percentage of India's Muslims harbored sovereign ambitions but "there is no doubt that the most prominent community leaders wanted a separate state – or at least staked out a claim for Pakistan in the hope of winning concessions in the final round of negotiations" (Cohen 2004: 29). A central fear was that democracy – which was a demand of the Congress Party – would leave the Muslims as a permanent minority in India. As Muhammad Ali-Jinnah stated in reply to Gandhi's assertion that all Indians were brothers, "[t]he only difference is this, that brother Gandhi has three votes, and I have only one vote" (Cohen 2004: 36). Ironically, this distrust of democracy lingered in the newly independent state, as the Punjabi core of West Pakistan feared domination by the numerically larger Bengali-speaking East Pakistan.

Partition led to very different endowments in the two new states. Most of the senior civil service remained in India. The industrial base in Pakistan was weak, there were few raw materials, and much of the commercial elite in the areas that became Pakistan fled to India during partition. In addition, Pakistan inherited the Pashtun and Baluchi areas in the far west, which had never been governed directly by the British (or any other government) and look to be inherently ungovernable from the vantage point of the early twenty-first century. Pakistan was, at first, split into two territories separated by more than a thousand miles. The majority of the population was concentrated in culturally distinct East Pakistan (later to become Bangladesh), whereas the capital city, the military, and elites were concentrated in West Pakistan. The mass movement that had pushed for the creation of the state, the Muslim League, had little organizational capacity or support in the territory of West Pakistan. Finally, the emergence of the Kashmir problem created a thorn in the side of West Pakistan and provided what was seen as an existential challenge for a state whose sole *raison d'etre* was the inability of Muslims to live in India. These factors highlight that, despite superficial similarity of starting conditions, Pakistan's environment may have been more challenging for the development of constitutional endurance.

Another contrast with India is that Pakistan was a truly new state, formed as a result of an elite-driven project and agreed to rather suddenly by the British, whereas India was an ancient civilization with a strong identity. That Pakistan was a new creation, and a two-headed one at that, meant that there were few shared norms among its population, and so state building and the creation of a national identity were crucial. But, from the beginning, efforts to create a constitution to unite the country failed. The national founder Jinnah, along with his close associate Liaquat Ali Khan, died early, denying the strong hand of a founding figure.[13]

Pakistan's Constituent Assembly first met four days before independence was granted, and continued to serve as a federal parliament until framing of the constitution was complete. In 1949, it issued an *Objectives Resolution* setting out a series of goals for the state and providing a foundation for subsequent developments.[14] But, drafting went slowly, despite its inclusive structure. The first constitution was approved a full nine years after the state's creation, on March 23, 1956.[15] The first President, the soldier Iskander Mirza, abrogated the constitution just two years later and was subsequently replaced in a coup by General Ayub Khan. From this point on, political life in Pakistan has alternated between military rule and tentative civilian political governance. Pakistan's lawyers and courts have continually found ways to justify military coups in legal ways, and have provided some veneer of constitutionalism through the doctrines of necessity.[16] Essentially, the courts pretended that the coups were required (Maluka 1997; Newberg 1996). Alas, an expectation of constitutional enforcement, a happy and reinforcing consequence of endurance, would not run in the Pakistani family.

In 1962, the 1956 Constitution was formally replaced in a backroom process with a document that sought to remove the military from active politics and centralize power in an indirectly elected presidency to be held by Ayub. This document was only moderately inclusive by our measure (with a score half a standard deviation below average). Both the 1956 and the 1962 documents were rather long and reasonably comprehensive documents with a flexible amendment procedure moderately more rigid than that of the Indian

---

[13] Whereas Pakistan's leaders died early, India's founding triumvirate of Jawalharlal Nehru, Sardar Vallabhbhai Patel, and Rajendra Prasad provided a stable hand for the early years, and personal continuity with the father of the nation, Mahatma Gandhi.

[14] It was eventually incorporated into the operative constitution in 1985.

[15] Until this time, the India Act of 1935 continued to provide the fundamental legal basis for the state, regulate the federal balance, and define government organs.

[16] A key lawyer here was Syed Sharifuddin Pirzada, who had served as Jinnah's personal assistant and helped advise military dictators through President Musharraf. Jane Perlez, "On Retainer in Pakistan, To Ease Military Rulers' Path." *The New York Times.* Dec. 15, 2007.

constitution. Indeed, in terms of the formal constitutional design factors under consideration here, we do not find that much of a difference between the Pakistani and Indian documents of the post-war era.

When Ayub committed a crucial error in going to war with India in 1965, he made clear that the core of Pakistan was in the West, triggering pressures from Sheikh Mujibur Rahman and the Awami League in East Pakistan to renegotiate the constitutional bargain and allow for democratization. That sort of revision was hardly tolerable to West Pakistan elites who controlled the less populous segment of the country. Attempts at accommodation were lukewarm, and alienated the Bengalis in East Pakistan. When West Pakistan rejected the Awami League's triumph in the long-delayed first elections of 1970, the breakup of the country followed. The 1971 War of Independence led to a loss of 54 percent of Pakistan's territory to the new state of Bangladesh and shifted the balance of power within the remaining section of Pakistan, thus undermining the constitutional bargain. The military defeat resulted in a return to civilian authority in the form of Zulfikar Ali Bhutto, who presided over the drafting and passage of the current Constitution of Pakistan, adopted in 1973. This is one case, at least, that seems to belie the finding that defeat in war and a loss of territory does not lead to a new constitution. Certainly, in Pakistan it did.

The 1973 document featured a stronger prime minister and a figurehead president, although this balance would be subject to amendment with the vagaries of the country's political oscillations between military and civilian leaders over the next decades. The amendment procedure did not change much from provisions in the earlier incarnations of the Pakistani constitution, which as we have noted, were very similar in design to the Indian constitution. The legislature maintained almost exclusive power to amend the document with a two-thirds majority and the assent of the President. Gone were earlier provisions that protected certain aspects of the constitution from amendment. Like the Indians, the Pakistanis also added a phrase that guaranteed the legislature's power to amend over and above any objections from the judiciary.

The Constitution was suspended with the blessing of the courts by military leader Zia al Huq in 1977, and he, in violation of the clear text of the constitution, assumed the office of president without giving up his military post. Furthermore, he interfered with the judiciary, and stripped their jurisdiction when courts began to review martial law orders. In 1985, Zia held elections without parties and restored the Constitution, as amended to provide for substantially enhanced presidential authority. When Zia died in a plane crash, the Constitution served as the basis for the election of Benazir Bhutto as Prime Minister, and the next decade featured her alternation in power with rival Nawaz Sharif, until General Musharraf's coup in 1999.

All this is a story of democratic failure. No successive elected governments have ever taken power, and only one prime minister ever completed a term of office (Cohen 2004: 59).[17] The military remains the central institution of the state. Yet, Pakistan is not wholly a story of constitutional failure. Albeit halting, legal continuity has been maintained through sometimes tortured interpretations of the constitution involving the notion of "state necessity" (Huq 2006). Judicial review has been used for flexibility but it has not served to provide focal points for enforcement of constitutional norms (with the recent exceptions of lawyers' demonstrations in 2007 and 2008).

The constitution has also been used by the military to accomplish internal coordination and describe the institutions of government. For example, Musharraf used constitutional amendments to create a new National Security Council in 2004, and thereby institutionalized a basis for a military role in governance. The constitution has facilitated elite accomodation at times, as when Musharraf resigned from active duty and, in accordance with the constitution's stipulations, took the more figurehead role of the presidency in late 2007.

But, all in all, constitutional life has been cheap in Pakistan and, as a consequence, constitutional limits on executives have been porous. The longest period a Pakistani constitution has remained in force appears to be the fourteen years from Zia's reinstatement in 1985 through Musharraf's coup in 1999, and this was hardly a period of stable democratic governance. The earlier constitutions died following the loss of territory in the 1971 war or were suspended by military coup. All this despite a highly specific, relatively inclusive document that is quite easy to amend – a document that is much like India's long-standing constitution. The preliminary lesson from Pakistani constitutional history, it seems, is that crises and a destabilizing state structure will upend a constitution despite any design virtues.

However, the events of 2007, in many ways, represent a very strong indicator of constitutional health. As we have emphasized throughout the volume, citizens and elites who think to stand up and enforce the constitution are extremely vulnerable and will likely not do so unless they expect others to join them. In Pakistan, a group of vigilant lawyers was able to coordinate to prevent a breach of the constitution by General Musharraf in the form of extended emergency provisions. This is exactly the sort of enforcement that comes with common knowledge of the constitutional limits and widespread attachment to these limits. Thanks in part to such enforcement (and crucial intervention from the United States to nudge Musharraf toward constitutional conformity),

---

[17] Zulfiqar Ali Bhutto in 1977.

the original 1977 document, reborn in 1985, has now surpassed the global life expectancy of nineteen years. Given the rapidly declining hazard rates for constitutions in that part of their life cycle and the extremely healthful design characteristics of the Pakistani document, the 1985 reinstatement is now projected to last another sixty years or so.

Summary

This tale of two entwined nations highlights the central importance of inclusion. India's constitution-making process was public, inclusive, and supported by most segments of the population. It symbolized the moment of independence. Pakistan's founding moment, in contrast, was not embodied in an effective constitution, with only the partial and inoperative Objectives Resolution providing a symbolic basis for unifying the state. Its elites have never sought to expand public involvement in constitution making or governance.

Flexibility and specificity appear to have been less central in explaining the difference in outcomes as the Pakistani and Indian documents are quite similar on these scores. Nevertheless, it appears that these elements have played a role in India's success and will quite possibly facilitate constitutional stability in Pakistan going forward. The flexibility of India's constitutional process has led to ongoing elaboration, both through judicial review and formal amendments, producing ever-greater specificity in such areas as property rights, so essential for social transformation. The constitution has been used as a redistributive device, containing elaborate schedules of various groups granted benefits under the state's affirmative action programs. It has also been a terrain of institutional conflict and adjustment between parliament and judiciary, state and center, and individual and government.

Pakistan's economy and politics have faced more external and internal shocks than has India's. Loser of every war with India, Pakistan's army is nevertheless the dominant institution in the country's politics. Yet, this domination has led to frequent coups, another risk factor for constitutional death. Military interference in politics has meant that Pakistan's courts have faced far more difficult antagonists in their attempts to adjust to ongoing circumstances. Pakistan's courts are rightly recognized as being generally accommodating of coups, until the conflict between Musharraf and Chief Justice Chaudhry in 2007. In our terms, the courts have readily blessed placing the constitution on life support and have attempted to preserve formal continuity and ignore the content. This is a form of flexibility, to be sure, but, it is not an inclusive form that accommodates new social and political forces. Rather, it is a flexibility of convenience for myopic executives who desire the legitimization of the constitution without its constraint.

In short, India's constitution is more participatory and more highly articulated than those in Pakistan's history, both with regard to the formal text and informal elaboration by the Supreme Court. It has continually accommodated new groups and provided a framework for government. It has become the world's longest constitution in words and is now one of the longest lasting.

THE UNITED STATES AND FRANCE: ENDURING VERSUS EPISODIC LIBERALISM

We began this volume contrasting the United States and France, two countries which adopted constitutions within two years of each other in the late eighteenth century, each animated by the republican spirit and reflecting new ideologies of human rights and democratic inclusion. Both are stable constitutional democracies today. Yet, their constitutional histories have diverged dramatically. Although the current constitution of France is 50 years old, it is exceptional in French history. By contrast, the current U.S. document is an example of constitutional superlongevity.

Does our theory help to account for the divergent histories? Partially. French political life has been buffeted by internal and external shocks, whereas the United States has been free of foreign invasion, coups, and loss of territory. Still, Americans sometimes overlook the various crises the Constitution has had to confront, including the election of 1800, the disputes over slavery leading to the Civil War, the Great Depression, and various other conflicts. The U.S. Constitution has survived and has come to represent and foster Americans' sense of shared national identity.

United States: Youthful Experimentation and Increasing Returns

We must begin with a story of failure. The first national constitution, the Articles of Confederation, was ratified in 1781 and died, in our terms, with the promulgation of the U.S. Constitution in 1789. Many of the defects of the Articles were substantive, such as the insufficient power of the national government to tax, provide for an army, and facilitate internal free trade among the states. Perhaps the more crucial problem, however, was structural. Because amendment required unanimous approval, the Articles were no more flexible than a typical international treaty (Martin 2007). Indeed, the Articles may be the poster child for our rule against excessive rigidity in amendment rules. As the new nation faced increasing challenges, including threats from abroad and home in the form of Shays's Rebellion in Massachusetts, some states began to call for adjustments. The Congress subsequently convened the Constitutional Convention in Philadelphia and empowered it only to propose amendments to the Articles. Alas, the delegates did not take long before agreeing to violate their charge and draft a completely new document.

Why has the American Constitution survived? A central difference between the new document and the Articles was improved flexibility through the formal amendment process, but, even this modification produced a relatively rigid procedure. Many scholars also emphasize the importance of judicial review in renewing the Constitution over time. For more than two and a quarter centuries, the United States has experienced technological, economic, and social changes, which could not possibly have been anticipated by the founders (although as Federalist 23 makes clear, they fully understood the inevitability of change). Such changes have led to pressures for formal amendment but, as many scholars have emphasized, Article V is neither necessary nor sufficient to explain constitutional change (Strauss 2001; Levinson 1995). Judicial review (as well as evolution of popular understandings) has provided a mechanism for updating the Constitution, thus ensuring that its allegedly timeless principles are applied to modern realities, and has demonstrated the importance of flexibility.

Inclusion is also a factor in the American case and has been a theme of American constitutional history. But, by our measure, initial levels of inclusion were low. The U.S. Constitution emerged from Philadelphia without an especially high degree of consensus. Sixteen of the fifty-five delegates who participated in drafting the document declined to sign it, and Rhode Island, predisposed against the convention from the beginning, did not even send a delegation. Nonetheless, a rather high-minded campaign and debate, well catalogued in the Federalist and anti-Federalist Papers, went great lengths toward increasing the visibility and ultimate acceptance of the Constitution's provisions. As imperfect as the initial document was according to democratic criteria, it still represented an attempt to bridge a broad range of social interests, including sectional cleavages, small and large states, and urban and rural areas. As new social forces have arisen, they have, after long and sometimes bloody struggles, been accommodated in the constitutional order. Some of these changes have been manifested in the text of the document, such as the Civil War amendments seeking to overturn the antebellum order. Although not fully implemented for a century, the Fourteenth and Fifteenth Amendments presented an aspiration that supported claims to equality. Constitutional demands for inclusion have also been accommodated through judicial decisions such as *Brown v. Board of Education* and its progeny during the Warren Court. Yet, others have left their legacy in popular and legislative struggles over the constitution: Jacksonian democracy and Progressivism, which are reflected in constitutional practice if not text.

Many Americans believe that the document has endured precisely because it is not very specific (but see Hammons 1999). A *framework* constitution, it is argued, allows for adjustment over time. It has also allowed competing interests to lay claim to the constitutional mantle in support of their positions: that both Frederick Douglass and John Calhoun could believe that the Constitution reflected their positions is rather amazing (Graber 2006). Yet, the very vagueness of the document has forced the Supreme Court to articulate the boundaries of the Constitution, sometimes well beyond the four corners of the text. Specificity has been provided by the courts and political process, rather than the text.

It is also worthwhile to recognize that some provisions of the Constitution are very precise. Article V, for example, provides that no bill banning slavery may be passed before 1808. No doubt this provision helped the Constitution to survive its early crises, as both Northerners and Southerners wrongly anticipated that the period after 1808 would be one in which it had a clear majority (Graber 2006: 92; Whittington and Maclean 2002). The rather specific provision helped take an important issue off the bargaining table. By the time 1808 came around, population shifts had made it possible for Congress to ban the importation of slaves, and this development indirectly triggered the series of legislative compromises that preserved bisectionalism through the mid-nineteenth century. The compromises, in turn, marked temporary (and relatively informal) solutions to constitutional crises that might otherwise have derailed the nation.

Perhaps the best way to understand specificity in the American context is that the Constitution is specific about some matters and not others. The framers' distrust of parchment barriers led to an unwillingness to specify a set of rights for citizens (Graber 2006: 98). On the other hand, they believed that government institutions required careful articulation and so provided sometimes great detail about the powers and composition of government. To be sure, the Constitution does not seem to do much in terms of providing benefits to interest groups, which was part of our argument about specificity in Chapter Four. Nor have interest groups been able to secure gains in the formal text through constitutional amendment, with the exception of Prohibition (Boudreaux and Pritchard 1993) and the expansion of the franchise.

In short, our account helps to explain some aspects of American constitutional history but not others. It is not surprising, for example, that the Northern victors in the Civil War chose to retain the Constitution, which had been the symbol of their struggle. Furthermore, through the manipulation of constitutional rules, they were able to impose Reconstruction on a recalcitrant South. The civil war completely reset the bargaining positions of South and North and that power vacuum allowed Northerners to overcome what would otherwise have been a very difficult amendment process. Without that vacuum, the Thirteenth, Fourteenth, and Fifteenth Amendments or their equivalent may well have met the same fate as the Equal Rights Amendment. For several years, at least, the Article V rules on amendment were effectively flexible.

Moreover, the flexibility of constitutional practice is apparent in the great shift of the 1930s in which the constitutional regime changed dramatically, even without a change in the written text. Unlike Bruce Ackerman (1993), we do not believe that these major shifts associated with the rise of the modern administrative state amounted to an entirely new constitution. To further a point developed in Chapter Three, one cannot understand American politics today without understanding crucial decisions taken in 1789: the Senate, the Electoral College, and the Article V amendment process itself. But, we agree that the Constitution is very different in character today, precisely because of its informal flexibility.

The survival of the constitution through misfirings of the electoral system in 1796 and 1800, on the other hand, does not seem to be at all well explained by our theory. The founders had not anticipated the rise of parties and had simply imagined a Vice President who would be runner-up in an election in which electors cast two ballots each. This system clearly required some coordination if a dominant party were to avoid a tie of their top two candidates, but also guarantee that its number two would not come in third (one and only one elector had to *not* vote for the agreed-upon second preference). But, how would they determine which candidate would be second and which elector would drop him from the ticket? In 1796, the Federalists did not coordinate well enough and too many electors dropped Pinckney from the ticket, thereby allowing the Republican candidate Jefferson to sneak into second place. A Vice President from the opposing party, of course, is not necessarily a crisis, but there is an obvious potential for mischief, and at the very least a conflict of interest in such a situation. Elections in 1800 produced the opposite problem. Afraid of a repeat of 1796, none of the Republican electors dropped Aaron Burr from the ticket. When the electoral ballots were counted in that election, Thomas Jefferson (the Republicans' clear favorite) and Burr were tied. According to the terms of the Constitution, this sent the election to the House of Representatives, which deadlocked thirty-five times before electing Jefferson on the thirty-sixth ballot.

These constitutional crises illustrate the importance of uncertain information, as emphasized in Chapter Four. The founders had devised a carefully
constructed, if idiosyncratic, system to identify the best candidates for president, but had not anticipated the rise of political parties. The system featured
pooled votes for president and vice-president, cast by an electoral college. First
round voting that did not produce a majority winner would go to the House
of Representatives, with each state delegation casting a single collective vote.
Given the lack of truly national candidates, the founders expected nearly all
elections to be ultimately decided in the House, where the single delegation
vote would mean that small states would have a disproportionate advantage.
Of course, the Twelfth Amendment – part of the solution to the crisis – created
separate elections for President and Vice President, thereby institutionalizing
the party system and insuring that small states would lose a critical part of the
original bargain. Not only, then, had the founders not anticipated parties and
the coordination required to operate the election system as designed, but a
critical part of their presidential election machinery – and a piece of a carefully
crafted bargain – was dropped within the first twenty years of the constitution.
There were also many logistical ambiguities in the provisions, setting up a vacuum that actually materialized in 1800. Was it acceptable for the President of
the Senate to preside over the counting of the votes if, as it turned out, he was
one of the candidates (Jefferson, in a position repeated by Al Gore in 2000)?
What was to happen in the event of a House deadlock? Was the government
to come to an end when the term of the previous administration expired?

The risk of not finding a solution to these questions was grave. Ackerman
(2005: 3, 244–45) notes how our very notion of a written constitution hung in
the balance. Had the Constitution failed and been replaced, the United States
and France would be seen as having similar rather than disparate constitutional
histories.

Specificity, inclusion, and flexibility do not necessarily explain the successful outcome of these crises. The U.S. Constitution's detail was, in some sense,
the source of the problem, although it is unclear whether a vaguer formulation
such as majority rule would have prevented either crisis. Inclusion is also not
a helpful concept in the midst of a true deadlock – one side or the other
will be excluded by whatever decision is rendered. Nor was the crisis of 1800
solved by constitutional amendment or interpretation. The courts did not play
a role: the Republican Congress postponed the session of the Supreme Court
to prevent it from becoming involved.

Instead, Ackerman (2005: 6) attributes the resolution to "inspired states-
manship and plain good luck." Much of the debate over how to resolve the
stalemate drew on textual arguments about the written constitution (Ackerman

2005: 14–16). But, the ultimate solution lay in prudent accommodation after intense rivalry. The result was a transformed constitutional order, with the president at the center of the political system in ways unanticipated by the constitutional text.[18]

It was this revised system, however, that endured through massive social changes. And, in part, the notions of specificity, inclusion, and flexibility seem to play a role in explaining subsequent survival. To be sure, various other factors no doubt help to explain American constitutional endurance. The frontier allowed for increasing returns and the reinforcement of incentives to remain in the bargain for some time; territorial isolation insulated the country from foreign invasion; and the Constitution was established as the embodiment of the nation fairly early. Perhaps the lesson of the United States, then, is that the Constitution was strengthened by having survived an initial crisis. To be sure, it was a very different constitution that emerged. But, the revised one was tempered by experience and was the stronger for having overcome its genetic defects. As it ages, it seems to grow stronger, and the risk of death recedes.

France: Underlying Instability, but Gradual Crystallization

If the American constitutional experience has been marked by stability and continuity, French constitutional turnover has reflected the underlying instability in French political institutions. As one scholar put it, the French Revolution of 1789 "set something in motion that nobody could effectively control; the French nation was like a driver of a motorbike who has lost control over the handlebars at high speed, helplessly zigzagging along the street, left-right-left-right – until he drops" (van Nifterik 2007: 477).

---

[18] This order withstood another crisis shortly thereafter. In the winter of 1814–1815, a group of prominent New Englanders gathered in Hartford for a discussion of the future of their region. Although no record of their debate exists, it was widely reported that the agenda included a plan to secede from the United States and form a new union with England. Such concern about segmentation of regions to join foreign powers was widespread in the early years of the republic (LaCroix 2005). Republicans, who admired the French Revolution, and Federalists, who feared radicalism and admired England, each saw the other as potential traitors. After Madison's Declaration of War against Britain in the War of 1812, federalist New England found itself bearing a disproportionate share of the costs with the disruption of transatlantic trade. The final report of the Hartford Convention does not call for secession, but rather sought to amend the federal constitution to abandon the 3/5 clause, require a 2/3 vote of congress to admit new states or declare war, and require the presidency to be held by a citizen from a different state than that of the incumbent (to end Virginia's near-monopoly on the presidency.) In short, the delegates at Hartford considered the costs and benefits of secession versus amendment and decided on the latter. Flexibility induced them to remain in the Union for sufficient time for the storm to blow over.

Each of these zigzags has been marked with a new constitution. The initial constitution of September 1791 reflected the last gasp of the monarchy, as revolutionary leaders made peace with the king and retained him out of a desire for detente. But, within two years, the king was guillotined and the republican Constitution of June 1793 came into force, with its promises of equality and commitment to democracy. It was, however, suspended quickly in favor of a revolutionary government. A new constitution rose in its place in 1795. Written mostly to dispel the Terror, the 1795 document harkened back to the 1791 constitution, albeit with some changes such as a shift to a single chamber in the legislature. The 1795 constitution would not last long either. The year 1799 brought with it yet another new constitution marking the period known as the consulate, in which the government was centered around three consuls (with Napoleon Bonaparte as first consul). Napoleon's fall saw the return of the monarchy and a constitution granted by Louis XVIII, which endured a then record fifteen years. When the Bourbons were overthrown in 1830, a new constitution was introduced, and then another in 1848 with the introduction of the Second Republic. France, then, is an example of a country with a tight fit between regime survival and constitutional survival.

What explains this congruity? One point not much noticed in the literature is that French constitutions, particularly the early models, have been relatively inflexible. In terms of informal amendment, French constitutionalism has been characterized for more than 200 years by a fear of *government du juges*. Parliamentary supremacy has been a theme of the democratic constitutions, and the authoritarian ones similarly disempowered judges (Stone 1992).[19] This meant that there was no nominally disinterested body able to adjust the constitution over time. The closest thing was the *Conseil d'Etat*, the administrative organ that supervised the administration. But this body could not constrain the political authorities.

Formal amendment too has typically been rigid, when it is specified at all, and most French constitutions score low on our measure of formal flexibility. To be sure, the French radical democratic tradition has an ideological bias in favor of revision. The people as the ultimate sovereign should not be restrained from adjusting to changing circumstance. Practically, however, French constitutions have alternated between specifying significant barriers to amendment and silence about revision. The barriers tend to take the form of temporal requirements rather than high thresholds. The 1791 Constitution (Part VII), for example, allowed revision after a proposal to that effect was adopted by three successive legislatures. A fourth legislature was then elected

---

[19] This came to an end with constitutional amendments in 2008, allowing the Conseil Constitutionnel to set aside legislation for unconstitutionality after it had been promulgated.

and supplemented with additional members to serve as an Assembly of Revision (whose members could not include those from the proposing legislature). The Assembly had to vote on amendments after which special members retired. In the turmoil of the French Revolution, however, there was simply no chance for these provisions to be implemented.

The Constitution of 1793 was silent on revision, though it was allowed. But the Constitution of the Year III, adopted in 1795, reverted to the temporal barriers. A proposal had to be ratified three times with each vote three years apart before an Assembly of Revision could be formed. Needless to say, no amendment proposal would have had a chance to complete this gestation period before the adoption of the Constitution of the Year VIII in 1799, which was again silent on amendment, as were its successors in 1815 and 1830. The 1848 Constitution followed the three-vote system, but this time proposals could be made by the same assembly over intervals of a month, after which an Assembly of Revision actually modified the text. The Constitution of 1852 allowed relatively easy amendment but, as with many other constitutions, died shortly after a military defeat when the French lost the Franco-Prussian war in 1871.

France's most enduring constitution to date emerged in 1875 in the midst of political turmoil, class conflict, and economic decline. Three different candidates sought to claim the throne of the Empire, and politicians were appointed to a placeholder presidency while the conflict was resolved and a constitution drafted. Republican groups were nearly as divided as the monarchists. When an amendment was introduced in the drafting assembly calling for a presidency to be elected by the assembly for a seven year term, it passed by one vote and the republic was established. In the words of one of these politicians, Louise-Adolphe Thiers, there was "only one throne and three men cannot sit on it. . . . The Republic divided us least" (Shirer 1969: 3). The constitution that emerged was a compromise that combined a strong chamber of deputies elected by universal suffrage and an upper house composed of senators selected by local notables or appointed for life terms. Combining both popular and conservative impulses, these institutions nevertheless facilitated the dominance of republicanism, and eventually the life-term seats were eliminated after several amendment attempts (Currier 1893).

The 1875 constitution was an unusual one in our terms because it did not consist of a consolidated document, but rather a series of laws setting up institutions of republican governance, centered on parliamentary sovereignty. The boundaries of the 1875 Constitution were thus more open and flexible than others in the French tradition. This constitution survived many challenges, including political crises, the Dreyfus Affair, anarchist violence, and World War I. It also saw the triumph of secularism as a fundamental principle for the state, with the disestablishment of the Catholic Church. Political instability was a feature of the period, later blamed by many historians as causing the defeat in World War II.[20] Yet, from the perspective of endurance, the Third Republic was a great success, dying only with the German invasion of 1940. Flexibility seems to have been the key, but it took the form of unconstrained parliamentary sovereignty: the traditional hostility to judicial review was maintained (Stone 1992: 27–28).

The Third Republic also illustrates the role of constitutional luck in endurance (Scheppele 2008). Largely defeated in the constitutional bargaining process, the right wing found a champion in General Boulanger in the late 1880s. His movement, known to historians as *Boulangisme*, called for revision of the constitution and a return to monarchy. In January 1889, he won an election and marched on Paris, in what his supporters hoped was a coup. Rather than go to the palace of government, however, Boulanger returned home to his mistress and the government survived, regaining its footing and undermining his movement. Boulanger's failure of nerve ensured that the constitution endured (Shirer 1969), although it was a near-death experience averted only through luck. Later, in the Dreyfus affair, the right again called for the overthrow of the constitution, but at a crucial moment, a general arrested a leader of the challengers, rather than join them (Shirer 1969: 63–84). Had different personnel been in place, the constitution might have died. By 1905, however, the Third Republic had consolidated definitively.

Arguably, France's most successful constitution is the current one, now more than five decades old. It features relatively easy amendment procedures and scores well on our measure of flexibillity: the president has the option of seeking a 60 percent vote of both houses of parliament or can use a referendum to pass a constitutional amendment. The document has been amended eighteen times as of this writing, thus providing for adjustments to changing circumstances.

The current constitution came into being because of the failure of the 1946 constitution of the Fourth Republic. Adopted inclusively by referendum, and proposed by a grand coalition of the so-called three party alliance, the 1946 constitution suffered from internal divisions that some assert were exacerbated by the parliamentary form of government. Although democratic, the Fourth Republic is usually seen as being unable to handle the instability of the times. The amendment formula was complex, involving proposal by two consecutive votes of the National Assembly, and then consideration by the Parliament, followed by submission to referendum unless certain thresholds were met. In any case, this was irrelevant given parliamentary instability.

---

[20] Although there was a good deal of governmental instability, many of these governments consisted of the same sets of politicians in different positions (Haine 2000: 123).

The Algiers crisis of 1958 proved too much for the constitution to handle. Faced with a loss of territory and the war of liberation in Algeria, French political institutions became gridlocked. Unable to form a government, the last Parliament dissolved itself and called a constitutional convention. General Charles de Gaulle, who had opposed the 1946 constitution, called on France to create a new constitution with a strong presidency. His draft was overwhelmingly approved by those who voted, demonstrating an inclusive founding. Once he occupied the office of president, de Gaulle further modified the document through referendum and created a system of direct presidential elections (and also a new system of constitutional amendment through referendum, not provided in the original text.) This expanded inclusion in our terms.

Unique in French constitutional history, the Fifth Republic has been marked by intense judicial politics centered around the Conseil Constitutionnel (Stone 1992). Although originally intended to play a moderate role of preserving executive lawmaking authority from legislative encroachment, the Conseil has expanded its role and in the process allowed a new channel for flexibility. French politics has been constitutionalized, in turn giving interest groups a further stake in constitutional politics. These changes seem to help explain French constitutional endurance. No longer will our proverbial librarian be able to characterize the French constitution as a periodical.

The French case also illustrates an important factor that has not received attention in our other cases. In many ways, the fundamental legal document in French legal culture is not the constitution, but the Code Civil of 1805. This document, which created the modern individual and empowered her with legal capacity, establishes a private sphere distinct and largely autonomous from public governance. The French civil service, centered around the Conseil d'Etat, has also maintained a good deal of autonomy and professionalism. Whether the French government has been imperial, republican or fascist, the Code Civil and the administration remain, and might be considered to have unwritten constitutional status in some sense. With an enduring set of background norms, formal constitutional endurance becomes less important.

CHINA AND TAIWAN: ENDURANCE OF IDEOLOGICAL CONSTITUTIONS

What are the dynamics of constitutional endurance work in nonconstitutionalist settings? China and Taiwan (the Republic of China or ROC) form an interesting paired comparison, illustrating the various ways constitutions can die, but also demonstrating the logic of endurance in both communist and capitalist contexts. The two jurisdictions are like fraternal twins, sharing some but not all genetic material, and were actually governed by the same document for two years from the establishment of the Taiwan Provincial Government of the ROC in 1947 until the establishment of the People's Republic of China (PRC) in 1949. The current Constitution of the Republic of China was drafted in Nanjing in 1946 and came into force in December of 1947. With the end of the Chinese civil war, it ceased to apply in the mainland. Meanwhile, in Taiwan, many provisions of the Constitution were suspended by the so-called Temporary Provisions or rendered inoperative by martial law.

In 1949, the two jurisdictions diverged sharply into communist and capitalist systems, but neither was characterized by genuine constitutionalism. The PRC adopted its own constitutional document in 1954 and replaced it in 1975, 1978, and 1982. Taiwan, on the other hand, had a good deal of constitutional stability until 1991, when its National Assembly amended the constitution as part of the country's transition to democracy. Six rounds of further amendments through 2005 adjusted the political system to various needs and to the reality that the government no longer controlled mainland China. China's own constitutional updating practice shifted in 1982 from replacement to amendment, and there has been formal continuity since then. This reflects Deng Xiaoping's turn to law as a tool to provide an institutional basis for rule by the Chinese Communist Party.

Although the two regimes were hostile ideological opponents, each claiming to be the sole government of China, they shared the feature that in neither jurisdiction could the constitution be said to provide a real constraint on government for much of the period. Notwithstanding Chiang Kai-shek's claim to be "Free China," Taiwan was a one-party state until 1986, and it was only afterwards that the ROC Constitution was regularly enforced in the courts. The PRC Constitution has been described as the *least* important document in the Chinese legal system (Clarke 2003). As with earlier Chinese constitutions, it is not meant to be legally enforceable. Courts are not able to enforce its rights or to set aside laws on its basis, and its interpretation is monopolized by the legislature.

It would be wrong to suggest, however, that the constitution does not matter. Indeed, if it were irrelevant, why would the Chinese Communist Party amend the document four times since 1982 (in 1988, 1993, 1999, and 2004)? The constitution plays an important role as an authoritative ideological statement and communicative act (Nathan 1986; Cao 2004: 122–40). The Chinese Communist Party uses constitutional amendments to signal new directions in policy. Elevation of a particular policy into the constitutional text marks it as a legitimate basis for governance and usually follows, rather than precedes, implementation. The constitution thus serves as a coordination device for internal discourse within the authoritarian regime.

The two cases suggest a number of questions about constitutional death. Why did the ROC Constitution not die in 1949 following the defeat of the Kuomintang (KMT) in the Chinese civil war? And, why was it not replaced in the transition to democracy in the 1990s? Why was the PRC Constitution replaced several times before the adoption of the present document in 1982? And, why has that document endured? We address these questions below.

Taiwan

Sometimes, but not always, defeat in war and the loss of territory are factors that can trigger constitutional demise. The survival of the ROC Constitution in 1949, however, made some sense given the need for Chiang Kai-shek to secure international and domestic support for his regime. Chiang faced a hostile enemy across the Taiwan straits and needed the United States to guarantee his security. This required a certain democratic form, if not substance. Chiang based his claim to external legitimacy on the fiction that his government was constitutionally constrained, in contrast with that of communist China. In addition, Chiang harbored the dream of retaking the mainland. Preserving a constitution that claimed to govern all of China provided ideological direction for his regime and ensured the loyalty of his political base of Kuomintang officials who had retreated from the mainland. Meanwhile, the local Taiwanese citizenry was completely excluded from power.

Chiang faced a crucial juncture in the 1950s, when it became clear that retaking the mainland was a fantasy and inconsistent with America's Cold War policies. Committed to both a nominal constitutionalism and the preservation of the one-China paradigm, Chiang had to deal with the problem of elections. Three constitutional bodies, the National Assembly, Control Yuan, and Legislative Yuan, had been directly elected on the mainland in 1947. What would happen when their terms expired? The KMT regime faced three options. It could sponsor elections in the areas under its control, namely Taiwan and some small islands, and thereby limit the electorate to those present there. However, limiting the electorate to Taiwan would have ensured the defeat of the KMT regime, which was perceived as a brutal occupying force by the majority of the Taiwan-born population. Another option would be to simply suspend the Constitution entirely and cease holding elections. This was undesirable as well, as it would demolish the myth of constitutional government and endanger Chiang's support in the United States. Furthermore, the Constitution was so identified with the thought of modern China's founding father, Sun Yat-sen, that it could not simply be overturned.

Here, the institution of constitutional review proved useful in facilitating the necessary flexibility. Chiang asked the constitutional court, the Council of Grand Justices, to allow the suspension of elections, and it obliged in 1954 (Ginsburg 2003). Elections could be suspended during the allegedly temporary period when the mainland electoral districts remained in the hands of the Communists, and would resume thereafter. The Constitution bent (severely) and therefore did not need to break.

Because of this decision, Taiwan was governed into the 1980s by officials who were born on, and in some cases elected on, mainland China. The Constitution legitimated and facilitated this result. In the mid-1980s, faced with the rise of China and the impossibility of retaking the mainland, Chiang's son Chiang Ching-kuo initiated a policy of Taiwanizing the KMT and returning power to the people. Democratization continued under his designated successor, Lee Teng-hui, and several rounds of constitutional amendments facilitated the process. In addition, the amendments eliminated much of the constitutional infrastructure for governing the mainland and redesigned institutions for an island of 25 million instead of a nation of a billion. Democratization culminated in the first direct election of the president in 1996 and the transfer of the presidency to opposition figure Chen Shui-bian in 2000.

Why did the leaders of newly democratized Taiwan keep the ROC Constitution? Two related factors are important here: the gradual nature of the democratic transition and the international environment. Taiwan's transition took place over a decade and involved shifting alliances among various forces in the ruling KMT as well as some in the opposition Democratic Progressive Party. Those within the KMT were not eager for constitutional replacement as it would upset the traditionalist wing that believed in reunification and/or continuity with the ROC regime. On the other hand, opposition forces, particularly those around President Chen Shui-bian, sought to write a new constitution for Taiwan as a sign of its independence. Given that constitutional replacement would be seen as a provocative act by the mainland regime, this policy was unlikely to command a majority of support, and so attempts to redraft from scratch were thwarted. Preserving the ROC Constitution and flexibly amending it was a superior formula, allowing for the inclusion of the old guard, while increasing the congruence between the formal provisions of the text and the actual practice of government on the ground.

China

Communist China's first constitution, promulgated in 1954, reflected the borrowing from the Soviet Union that was the predominant mode. The ideological preamble recounts the history of the communist struggle and the establishment of the state under the leadership of the Chinese Communist Party and recounts the "indestructible friendship with the great Union of Soviet Socialist

Republics." The 106 articles of the document reflect significant borrowing from the 1936 Soviet document.

With the Sino-Soviet split, Russian influence declined, and China soon entered the tumultuous Cultural Revolution. This period saw an increasing cult of personality around Mao Zedong, who was included by name in the preamble of the new constitution adopted in 1975. (This is one of the few historical instances in which an individual is named in a national constitution while still alive.) The 1975 document is short (30 articles) and overwhelmingly ideological in character, extolling Marxism-Leninism-Mao Zedong thought as well as proletarian internationalism and containing a promise that China would never become a superpower. It also elevates the Communist Party to a constitutional role, giving it direct control over the armed forces. Following Mao's death in 1976, a new constitution was adopted in 1978. It nominally expanded the rights of citizens, but did not make a significant ideological break. (This constitution evoked the liberation of Taiwan for the first time.)

Shortly thereafter, Deng Xiaoping consolidated power and launched China's modernization program. Law played a central role in his thinking as he sought to provide greater institutional order to underpin China's development. The 1982 Constitution de-emphasizes the Communist Party and nominally places the Constitution above all organizations in the country. In Chinese terms, the Constitution is quite specific, providing details about the various governmental offices and the rights of citizens in 138 articles. But, in comparative terms, all Chinese constitutions since 1975 score low on our measures of specificity as well as flexibility. No doubt de facto flexibility is facilitated by the presence of a one-party dictatorship.

The Constitution has been revised four times, reflecting China's economic reforms. In 1988, the Constitution was revised to make reference to a private sector to complement the "socialist public economy."[21] It also provided for transfer of land use rights, even though land remained owned exclusively by the state or collectives. The 1993 amendments added the phrase "socialism with Chinese characteristics" to the preamble and introduced the "socialist market economy," thus incorporating Deng Xiaoping's formula for a market-friendly economy. In 1999, a reference to the recently deceased Deng was incorporated into the preamble.

In 2004, the Constitution was amended to guarantee private property rights and provide for compensation for expropriated land, an important signal for both foreign investors and China's own market sector.[22] Human rights are also included, reflecting the Party's ideological pushback against critics of

[21] Article 11.
[22] Article 13.

its practices.[23] In addition, in keeping with the tradition of each Chinese leader's leaving his mark on the Constitution, Jiang Zemin's theory of the *Three Represents* was introduced into the preamble.[24] This provided ideological coverage for inclusion of the business class ("advanced productive forces"). It seems highly likely that a future amendment will incorporate the latest formula of the *Harmonious Society* that is the mark of the current leaders, Hu Jintao and Wen Jiabao.

Why has the 1982 Constitution endured in China, whereas earlier constitutions were relatively short-lived? The 1982 Constitution seems to have adjusted to reflect ideological evolution during a period of tremendous social and economic change. Flexibility, however, is probably an inherent feature of constitutions in one-party states and cannot thereby explain endurance. The document is also relatively specific, but this does not seem to be an important feature for an explicitly unenforceable constitution, as we theorize that specificity helps endurance by providing for easier enforcement.

Ideological inclusion seems to be the key factor in this case (and the document scores well on structural measures of inclusion as well). The 1982 Constitution recognizes the contributions of non-party groups to China's modernization and can thus be seen as inclusive within the socialist ideological framework. As new political forces have arisen with China's modernization, they have also been accommodated in the official ideology and found their place in the Constitution. Thus in 1999, Jiang Zemin incorporated businessmen into the official structure of the Constitution. Furthermore, ideological continuity is attractive for a regime presiding over such rapid change. New leaders after Deng have not sought to produce new constitutions, but have used amendments to leave their mark on the fundamental document. It seems possible that China's 1982 Constitution will play a role not unlike that of Mexico's 1917 document (described in the next chapter shortly), which gradually expanded to co-opt and include new social forces.

No doubt structural factors are at play as well. China's economic growth means that few have the incentive to rock the boat. The document seems to provide for increasing returns and a sense of stability. Whatever social pressures exist on China's regime, they are not channeled through constitutional institutions.

---

[23] Article 23.

[24] The Three Represents theory provided that the Communist Party should represent "advanced productive forces, the orientation of the development of China's advanced culture, and the fundamental interests of the overwhelming majority of the people in China." This is read as providing for inclusion of the new capitalist classes, development of culture, and some theory of political representation.

Summary

Taiwan's Constitution is more than sixty years old, whereas China's is more than twenty-five years old. Both documents survived despite lack of enforcement for vast periods and played an ideological rather than constitutionalist function. In the Taiwan case, the fiction of a democratically elected regime temporarily prevented from governing all of China was a source of internal and external support for the KMT regime. The ROC Constitution provided ideological cover and thus was able to survive what might otherwise have been a fatal blow of the loss of the mainland in 1949. As the myth of retaking the mainland disappeared, the constitution adjusted to become more of a genuine blueprint for government and was modified accordingly. But, the particular political dynamics of the transition meant that the proponents of constitutional replacement never had sufficient strength to force a full renegotiation.

China's constitutions have reflected its ideological vagaries since the establishment of the PRC. The documents serve as a signal of policy and ideological continuity. Since 1982, stability and order have been explicit goals of the regime, even as it conducts one of the great transformations in world history. Constitutional stability itself furthers these aims, even if constitutionalism suffers.

CONCLUSION

These thumbnail histories present a diverse array of constitutional family histories. Each fits our central theory to various degrees, though none captures it perfectly. India is perhaps the paradigmatic case for our emphasis on design factors. Although the country is poor and diverse, the constitutional document has survived. It is both detailed and flexible and has sought to accommodate specific interest groups through constitutional language. It contrasts with Pakistan, whose constitutional order has been buffeted by a series of external shocks. Although flexible, Pakistan's constitutional tradition is hardly inclusive.

China and Taiwan present examples of ideological constitutions hardly meant to be applied. In authoritarian regimes, ideology matters, and the constitution can be a device to mark inclusion of particular groups, as in China's elevation of property holders in recent years. It can also be used to gain external legitimacy, as in Taiwan under the KMT dictatorship. The constitution endures, even without constitutionalism, but there is a logic to the system.

The United States presents a constitution with formal inflexibility but much informal flexibility. The U.S. Constitution was sustained through constitutional interpretation and the various bisectional compromises for many years.

As we have emphasized throughout this book, however, the United States structure is hardly to be emulated by countries looking for an enduring constitution. In contrast with the United States, France had no theory of informal amendment through judicial interpretation. Furthermore, the French state has suffered a series of shocks and wars, most of which led to new constitutions. The crucial case of the Fourth Republic, however, shows that when shocks interact with political institutions that are not sufficiently flexible, it can create conditions for failure. The Fifth Republic, in contrast, has benefited from the lack of war and adjusted through informal amendments, such as de Gaulle's innovation of direct election in 1962 and the interpretations of the Conseil Constitutionnel. It has been the most inclusive constitution in French history in terms of our formal measure.

One theme of the above historical account is that historical legacy is not destiny. Countries with a legacy of constitutional failure, such as the paradigmatic case of France, have over time, through luck and design, come into constitutions that have endured and been vital. Nor is the world as neatly divided into rich western democracies with low levels of constitutional mortality and poor countries with high levels. India and Mexico (which we will discuss in the next chapter) are a long way off from being considered rich countries. But they have each enjoyed vigorous, and enduring, constitutional politics.

8

Cases of Constitutional Mortality, Part II:
Contrasting Contexts, Similar Outcomes

This chapter continues our exploration of the constitutional histories of individual states, this time drawing from a sample of states selected with an inverse set of criteria from the previous chapter. In a variation of a most-different systems design (Przeworski and Teune 1970), we investigate a set of cases with a highly contrasting set of social and political conditions, but a similar set of outcomes. This set of cases includes some of the most intriguing constitutional chronologies from the standpoint of endurance.

We begin with a triad of cases – the Dominican Republic, Haiti, and Thailand – places where constitutions rarely survive more than seven or eight years. In some ways this amounts to a paired comparison (Haiti/Dominican Republic against Thailand), as the first two – both occupants of the Island of Hispaniola – have developed in parallel fashion. A focus on Haiti and the Dominican Republic takes on added significance as these two countries account for roughly 7 percent of the world's historical constitutions. Constitutions from the Island of Hispaniola, it seems, exhibit extremely high rates of infant mortality. We compare this duo to Thailand, where constitutional mortality has also been high. Key themes in the trajectory of the Hispaniola cases are the lack of inclusion and potentially overzealous constraints on executive power, which have tempted presidents to cast the written document aside repeatedly. Thailand is a somewhat anomalous case in which constitutional failure is arguably facilitated by unwritten rules around the country's long-serving monarch. The underlying stability of the unwritten rules may have mitigated the costs of constitutional failure – but, it has also undermined the willingness of elites to invest in written bargains, and so failure has become self-perpetuating.

We then consider the constitutional trajectory of Mexico and Japan, whose constitutions of 1917 and 1946, respectively, mark important and enduring landmarks in constitutional design. Alike in their formal endurance, the two

179

documents come from very different origins and have been maintained with contrasting levels of modification. As we note in Chapter 3, the Mexican constitution has been amended frequently, such that only about 75 percent of its structure remains intact today – a transformation that is comparable to constitutional replacement in most countries. By contrast, the Japanese document has never been amended, and stands as the longest running constitution currently in force without a single formal amendment.

HAITI AND THE DOMINICAN REPUBLIC: INTERLINKED CONGENITAL DEFECTS

We have referred to the constitutional graveyard that is the island of Hispaniola. Both Haitian and Dominican constitutional history is incredibly unstable, reflecting deeper political instability. In the Dominican case, this involves genuine ambivalence about independent statehood at various points in its history. Haiti has invaded, merged with, and separated from the Dominican Republic at various points in its history. It also reflects their status as *in-between* regimes, never fully consolidating democracy by some estimates, even though there have been attempts to institutionalize democracy (Hartlyn 1998: 14). Both countries, then, demonstrate the lingering threats of a legacy of instability to constitutional enforcement.

In the colonial period, Spain and France fought over the island of Hispaniola, ceding and relinquishing control over parts of the island to each other over a period of about two hundred years, and this pattern continued for the first part of the nineteenth century. Thereafter, instability was institutionalized, with a pattern in both countries of vacillation between liberal and authoritarian constitutions. Vacillation, which we sometimes refer to as constitutional toggling or cycling, results in part from a lack of inclusion. When one party takes power, it seeks to entrench all of its policies into the constitution, imposing the rules on the other side. This increases the stakes of politics and leads to conflict over the entire system. When this conflict produces a change in power, the new dominant force in turn imposes its own policies in the form of a new constitution. Such constitutions do not constrain, but instead merge with ordinary politics, with the added feature of creating an incentive for total conflict. Inclusion of opposing forces in a shared framework could resolve this problem.

Haiti

Haiti's first revolutionary constitution was promulgated in 1801, before formal independence, under Governor-General Toussaint L'Ouverture, the revolutionary hero. It named Toussaint governor for life and gave him the right to name his successor.[1] Independence was declared on 1 January 1804, the culmination of the only successful slave rebellion in world history. Toussaint's successor, Jean-Jacques Dessalines, became emperor of Haiti and authorized the constitution of 1805, a revolutionary document that called for freedom of religion, racial equality and nondiscrimination on the basis of color.[2] Property was sacred, but whites could not possess property.

Dessalines drew on Napoleonic, rather than liberal, constitutional tradition and provoked his own assassination engineered by his advisors. At the close of 1806, a replacement Constitution was adopted that empowered the legislature. The twenty-four member Senate had nine-year terms and the power to appoint an executive for a term of four years. Objecting to these constraints, Dessalines' co-successor, Henri Christophe, convened a constitutional assembly for the north of the country and engineered a more executive-centered document by transferring all the powers of the senate to the president. The country was then divided into two rival regimes associated with Alexandre Pétion and Christophe, each of whom promulgated a series of constitutions. In the south, a crucial innovation was Pétion's new Constitution of 1816, which revised the 1806 model to add a lower house of the legislature and changed the presidential term from four years to life. This draft became one of the prototypes for new constitutions as the country toggled back and forth between institutional variants for much of the next century (Steele 1952: 17).

The senate then elected Pétion president for life and gave him authority to choose his successor, who would be Jean-Pierre Boyer. Upon Pétion's death in 1816, Boyer took power and later reunified the country in 1820. Boyer responded to local interests in the Dominican Republic and occupied the eastern half of the island, uniting it under Haiti's rule. Boyer's overthrow by a joint group of Haitian and Dominicans in 1843 ushered in a new period of constitutional instability. Constitutional texts then alternated between liberal documents (1843) and imperial ones (1849). The major axes of variation were the issue of executive term limits and the power of the Senate.

A brief period of relative stability and prosperity ended in 1911, when revolution broke out. During the next four years, Haiti had six different presidents, each of whom was killed or forced into exile. With the imminent advent of World War I, the United States became concerned about the role of the German community in Haiti, who dominated international trade and infrastructure. Oddly, the foreign elite allegedly "served as the principal financiers of the nation's innumerable revolutions, floating innumerable loans – at high

---

[1] An early source on Haitian Constitutions is Steele (1952) 17.

[2] Constitution of 1805, Art. 14.

interest rates – to competing political factions" (Steele 1952). A revolt in 1915 prompted the United States to occupy the country for nineteen years until 1934. During this period, officials in the U.S. State Department and Navy Department, including Under Secretary for the Navy Franklin Roosevelt, played a major role in drafting a new constitution, which abolished the prohibition on foreign ownership of land. The elected National Assembly refused to adopt this draft and produced a document of its own; but, the military dissolved the National Assembly and a limited plebiscite adopted the U.S.-backed constitution in 1918 (Steele 1952: 32–33). The State Department justified this by saying "The people casting ballots would be 97 percent illiterate, ignorant in most cases of what they were voting for." The U.S.-backed constitution, however, proved to be an instrument of agglomeration of executive authority, a trend captured formally in the constitutional amendments of 1928. In 1932, a new constitution was passed, widely seen as a transitional document. Soon thereafter, the election of Franklin Delano Roosevelt as president and the adoption of his "Good Neighbor policy" led to the withdrawal of U.S. troops in 1934, although the United States retained control of Haiti's external finances until 1947. A new constitution adopted in 1935 then abandoned the separation of powers, asserting that the legislature and judiciary were to assist the president in his functions (Steele 1952: 36). After substantial amendment in 1944, a coup was launched in response to economic difficulties in 1946. The military junta handed over power to Dumarsais Estimé. A new constitution was adopted, reinstating a separation of powers, executive term limits, and civil and political rights. This period introduced major reforms in labor and social policy and greatly expanded civil and political liberties for the black majority.

In 1949, Estimé tried to change the constitution to allow for his own reelection, but, in 1950, this triggered another coup. A new constitution was again adopted, granting suffrage to women. General Paul Magloire then established a dictatorship that lasted until December 1956, when he was forced to resign by a general strike. After a period of disorder, elections were held in September 1957, which saw Dr. François Duvalier elected President, subject to a single seven-year term. Duvalier followed a long-standing pattern by engineering a life term in the new Constitution of 1964. On Duvalier's death in April 1971, power passed to his 19-year-old son "Baby Doc" Jean-Claude Duvalier, who celebrated his ascension with his own constitution. Widespread discontent in Haiti began in 1983, when Pope John Paul II condemned the regime during a visit. In February 1986, after months of disorder, the army forced Duvalier to resign and go into exile. In 1987, a new democratic constitution was ratified, providing for an elected bicameral parliament, an elected president, and a prime minister, cabinet, ministers, and Supreme Court appointed by the president with parliament's consent. The 1987 Constitution, however, was to be suspended frequently. The election of the charismatic priest Jean-Bertrand Aristide in 1990 promised redistributive policies, which prompted another violent coup in 1991 and the suspension of the constitution. A potential U.S. intervention in mid-1994 led the military to step down, and Aristide was able to return to finish his term. When Aristide's term ended in February 1996, René Préval, a prominent Aristide political ally, was elected president, marking Haiti's first-ever transition between two democratically elected presidents. A split between Préval and Aristide, however, has led to further crises since then.

Haiti's constitutional history has been marked by cycling among a range of institutional variants, with executive term limits providing a key factor in the death of constitutions. Haiti's pattern of constitution making reflects both the persistence of dictatorial tendencies but also resistance to them, prompting continuing conflict over the basic institutions of the country. The record on inclusion is mixed, and most constitutions score moderately on our measure of specificity. Flexibility also varies, but some constitutions appear to be fairly rigid. The 1950 document, for example, requires both houses of successive legislatures each to pass amendments to the document by 2/3 vote. From the beginning, then, revolutionary ideals in Haiti have been proclaimed by dictators who sought to consolidate power, and the country remains mired in the same basic pattern of serial constitutions with which it came into existence over two hundred years ago.

Dominican Republic

Instability preceded the birth of the Dominican Republic. Long a backwater in the Spanish colonial empire, with far fewer slaves than Haiti on the western part of Hispaniola, the colony of Santo Domingo gained some importance with the emergence of the Haitian slave rebellion in the late eighteenth century (Pons 1995). In a period of two decades, the colony that became the Dominican Republic was ceded to France (1795), invaded by Britain (1798) and the newly independent Haiti (1801, 1804–1805), before being retaken by Spain (1809–1821). Its first declaration of independence in 1821 produced the first constitution, but the country was promptly occupied by Haiti for the next two decades.

In the 1840s, political turmoil in Haiti led to a new constitutional assembly there, and this period provided Dominicans with an opportunity to secede. But different groups of separatists had different goals: a pro-Spanish group sought protection from Spain; another group wanted British protection, and a third wanted French protection. A fourth group, the so-called Trinitarios, allied with ranchers from the north under Ramon and Pedro Santana to overthrow the Haitian rulers.

Instability continued after the Dominican Republic again gained formal independence in 1844. The draft constitution of 1844, produced by an elected constitutional assembly was quite liberal and was modeled on the 1843 Haitian Constitution, as well as that of the United States. But *caudillo* Pedro Santana, out of fear that he would be overly constrained as president during an ongoing war, engineered amendments extending executive powers (Pons 1995: 163). Indeed, Santana was then elected to consecutive terms despite an explicit formal provision to the contrary (Hartlyn 1998: 34). A new, more liberal constitution was adopted in February 1854. Powers of the legislature were expanded and the infamous Article 210, which had allowed for extensive emergency powers, was deleted (Pons 1995: 177). But, under pressure from Santana, a new drafting process was soon initiated and another constitution promulgated on December 23, 1854 (Pons 1995: 179). Again in February 1858, after a short drafting process, a new constitution disallowed more than two consecutive terms of the president and initiated a broader set of rights; but, Santana engineered de facto and de jure amendments to restore the status quo ante with regard to restraints on executive power. The 1854 and 1858 constitutions would be the touchstones for authoritarians and liberals for much of the remainder of the nineteenth century.

Instability, combined with poverty and relative underpopulation during the colonial period, undermined Dominican institutions. The elite had "shallow roots" (Hartlyn 1998: 31). The church is a case in point, having been targeted by the Haitians during their early occupations. Until the rise of dictator Rafael Trujillo in 1930, there was no professionalization of a national army to centralize the provision of order. Political parties emerged relatively late. All this meant that there were few devices to aggregate interests and deliver a stable constitutional bargain. As Lowenthal put it, "From the time of independence until the U.S. occupation of 1916 ended the period of *caudillo* politics . . . the Dominican Republic was not characterized by a powerful triad of oligarchy, church and military, but rather by exactly the reverse: an insecure grouping of elite families, a weak and dependent church, and no national military institution" (Lowenthal 1969: 53).

Another interesting factor contributing to constitutional instability is that Dominican factions have been ambivalent about statehood itself. There was a faction at independence that desired unification with France (Hartlyn 1998: 27). Santana, the country's *caudillo* strongman, renegotiated a merger with Spain in 1861, but this too was contested and, with Haitian help, the country regained independence in 1865. The elites continuously turned to foreign powers, including the United States, to try to provide security, and indeed, the United States operated the customs authority through the mid-1940s.

In theoretical terms, the possibility of an outside alliance or secession raises the reservation price of factions to a constitutional bargain; that is, the default position of no internal agreement is relatively less costly. This has the effect of reducing the scope of a constitutional bargain, making it less inclusive. It is also easy to see how this possibility would have feedback effects: if factions are unable to reach stable agreement internally, they will continually look outside for support. They will also, possibly, be reluctant to invest resources into the internal constitutional bargain because there is no record of one ever having been viable. This could form a kind of low-equilibrium trap for constitutions.

The half century after renewed independence from Spain in 1865 witnessed myriad changes in government, several dozen military uprisings, and sixteen constitutions (Hartlyn 1998). Most of these constitutions were associated with leadership change (the first president to serve a full term in office did not do so until 1882) or extensions of executive term. This period also saw fluctuation in the form of constitutions, between liberal and authoritarian institutions on the 1858 and 1854 models, respectively.

By 1880, the liberal tradition had won out as a formal matter, though democracy took another century to begin to take hold (Hartlyn 1998: 36).There followed a period of relative stability under Ulises Heaureaux, whose rule saw the emergence of proto-institutions. His primary interest in reform was to extend the presidential term. Heaureaux's assassination in 1899 set off a new period of instability and increasing involvement of the United States, which in the Roosevelt corollary to the Monroe Doctrine announced that it was prepared to both prevent European interference to collect its debts from the Dominican Republic and to assume police powers to ensure repayment. Eventually the United States occupied the Dominican Republic and stayed eight years, from 1916–1924.

The occupation was later followed by a non-intervention mode that eventually became Roosevelt's Good Neighbor Policy, which ironically facilitated Trujillo's accession to and exercise of power (Roorda 1998). Constitutional stability of a sort emerged, although it was dictatorial and not at all constitutionalist. This is consistent with the earlier argument about the effects of potential intervention as undermining self-enforcing bargains.

After the United States left the Dominican Republic in 1924, President Vasquez was elected to a four-year term, but then modified the constitution to extend his term for an additional two years, reestablishing a "neopatrimonial" attitude toward both the state and constitutions (Pons 1995: 348). The

United States apparently tolerated this, in part because constitutional formalities were observed (Hartlyn 1998: 41; 1991: 62). But Vasquez' manipulation of electoral law provoked a rebellion, and he was removed from the scene. The resulting instability, however, allowed Trujillo (who had secretly supported the rebellion) to take power. Trujillo had only four constitutions in his thirty-one-year rule, during which he served as president from 1930–1938 and 1942–1952, governing under puppet presidents (including his brother Hector after 1952) until his assassination in 1961.[3]

The United States eventually became disenchanted with Trujillo and supported a coup by some of his former associates. As with the earlier assassination of Heaureaux, the assassination of Trujillo in 1961 launched a period of instability, ending only with another American intervention (Lecce 1998). There were fourteen different governments in the Dominican Republic from 1961 to 1966, including the brief Bosch government that resulted from democratic elections and presided over the passage of a constitution in 1963. That document was drawn closely on a Western European model with separation of church and state, civil liberties, and a limited role for the military (Gleijeses 1978: 87–88). The 1963 Constitution allowed property expropriation with a balanced formula for compensation. It also allowed for cohabitation and protection of illegitimate children while ignoring any privileged status for the church.

Bosch's government fell in a coup after only seven months. But, in 1965, a "Constitutionalist" rebellion took root, trying to bring back Bosch and restore democracy. This time, worried about "another Cuba," the United States intervened with 23,000 troops and oversaw a new round of elections, in which a former Trujillo protégé, Joaquin Balaguer, took power (Lowenthal 1972). He quickly reengineered the constitution in a super-presidentialist direction, permitting unlimited reelection (Hartlyn 1998: 102). Hartlyn asserts that although the formal presidential powers in the constitution were relatively weak, presidents were able to set budgets and taxes by decree, and spend without limitation.

Pressures for democratization began to build in the Balaguer period and he lost power in 1978, only to be reelected in 1986 at the age of eighty years, after which he served another ten years (Atkins and Wilson, 1998: 220). In 1994, his narrow win prompted a political crisis and allegations of fraud. As a result,

---

[3] Trujillo cited the American practice of limiting the presidency to two terms when in 1938 he stated that he refused to run, despite the wishes of his people. After President Roosevelt ran for a third term in 1942, Trujillo ran again and reassumed the presidency.

and in part because of U.S. pressure, the opposition and Balaguer agreed to a "Pact for Democracy" and a set of constitutional amendments, limiting the eighty-eight-year-old Balaguer to a two-year term and prohibiting immediate reelection (Hartlyn 1998: 254). Other reforms established a judicial council for judicial appointments, and life tenure for all judges. These reforms established new institutions that led to more divided governance, with Balaguer's party constrained.

The new institutions seem to be operating as constraints on executive power, and a two-party system has emerged. Balaguer's successor, Leonel Fernandez of the PLD party, stepped down after his term ended in 2000, with the PLD running another candidate to obey the proscription on reelection. Fernandez' party lost the 2000 election to Hipólito Mejía of the PRD party; Mejia oversaw a new constitution that did away with the prohibition on reelection, but was then defeated by Fernandez in 2004. As a result, Fernandez was reelected to a third term in 2008.

In short, there appear to be three factors that explain virtually all the cases of Dominican constitutions: repeated *birth* of the state, both in the nineteenth century and after the interventions by the United States in 1916 and 1965;[4] underlying political instability;[5] and executive attempts to extend their own terms.[6] A leading observer summarized this history as follows: "For nearly all of Dominican history, unconstitutional regimes have utilized constitutionalism to augment their claims to legitimacy, rather than to employ them to establish general 'rules of the game' to which they or other major power-holders in society would commit themselves" (Hartlyn 1998: 34). But at the same time, there appear to be tentative moves toward real constraint and stability.

Summary

One can read this history as one in which the constitution was itself the object of political competition, rather than establishing rules under which political competition occurs. The nineteenth century, in both the Dominican Republic and Haiti, seemed to be marked by a kind of constitutional toggling between two models, autocratic and liberal. Neither side dominated the other enough to have an enduring constitution. Then, in the mid-twentieth century,

---

[4] This explains the 1821, 1844, 1865, 1924, and 1966 constitutions.

[5] This appears to explain the 1854, 1858, every case between 1866 and 1887, 1907, and 1908 documents.

[6] This appears to explain the 1896, 1927, 1929, 1934, 1966, and 2002 constitutions.

consolidated dictatorships emerged under Trujillo in the Dominican Republic and the Duvaliers in Haiti. At the close of the twentieth century, an uneasy
democratization seems to be emerging, with correspondingly increased stability in the Dominican Republic. As of this writing, democracy seems to be
holding in Haiti, although food riots in April 2008, and severe hurricanes in
September 2008, hardly invite predictions of continued stability.

One puzzle emerges from these materials. During periods when the presidents did have strong control, why did they choose to adopt new constitutions
rather than simply use amendment processes? They certainly used *informal*
retrofit techniques. But, why draft whole new documents? This puzzle applies
to the Duvalier regime, as well as a few of the many constitutions in Dominican history: 1942, 1947, and 1954 under Trujillo, and 1896 under Heaureaux.
The explanation may be simply that the dominant executives faced zero cost
in promulgating new documents.

The Dominican Republic and Haiti represent cases of regular death and
genetic defects. The pattern is one of churn: each incoming regime uses its
power to adopt a new constitution, without inclusion of the other side. This
in turn leads to a self-reinforcing pattern of constitutional death. Parties do
not invest in negotiation, and constitution making becomes an all or nothing
proposition. Constitutions are not devices for accommodation, but for dominance, and so are replaced whenever the particular dominant faction leaves.
This forms quite a contrast with the experiences of Mexico (as we shall see)
and Taiwan, two dictatorships whose constitutions have survived – and even
facilitated – transitions to democracy.

THAILAND: INSTABILITY SUSTAINED BY UNWRITTEN CONSTITUTIONAL NORMS

Thailand was an absolute monarchy until 1932, when a group of young army
officers led a bloodless coup d'etat and established a constitutional monarchy.
The political forces behind the coup included both right-wing elements in the
military and left-wing nationalists around the intellectual Pridi Banomyong.
The tension between the two (along with a third group, royalists who eventually
aligned with the military) dominated Thai politics, in one form or another,
for the next seven decades.

Pridi was one of the major drafters of the 1932 Constitution, and an anticolo-
nial nationalist, of the same generation and orientation as Aung San, Nehru,
and Ho Chi Minh. Unlike his more famous counterparts, Pridi did not face a
departing colonial power, but rather had adversaries that were domestic. When

Pridi's economic plan included elements of nationalization, he was attacked as being a communist, and successive coups by the military and royalists followed, until politics stabilized after the coup led by General Plaek Phibun-songkhram (Phibun). Phibun aligned with the Japanese during World War II. After the war, Pridi became the country's first elected prime minister, but Phibun soon managed to regain power, exiling Pridi. Phibun was deposed, in turn, by another coup in 1957, in which royalist elements allied with the army under Field Marshal Sarit Thanarat. The following five decades witnessed an oscillation between military rule and civilian government, accompanied by regular constitutional change.

Constitutional change is generally associated with regime change, which has been frequent. In the seventy-six years since the establishment of the constitutional monarchy, Thailand has had eighteen constitutions, somewhere between seventeen and twenty-three coups and coup attempts, and fifty-six governments. The pattern of constitution making seems to have involved cycling among a relatively small number of institutional variants. The 1932 Constitution, for example, was the basis for the 1952 document, just as the 1997 Constitution was the basis for the 2007 document. One of the chief axes of constitutional change has been whether the National Assembly, particularly the upper house or Senate, is to be elected or appointed by the government, military, or king.

Because of their ephemeral quality, Thai constitutions do little to constrain those in power in accordance with the constitutionalist ideal. Still, the very fact that constitutions are repeatedly promulgated suggests that they are playing some role in legitimating power holders, and may reflect what Engel (1975) describes as an "almost mystical faith that the promulgation of modern codes, statutes and constitutions would somehow produce a modern Thailand."

It is worth noting that Thailand's most enduring constitution, that of 1997, was also its most specific and inclusive. Adopted after one of the country's many coups, the 1997 "People's Constitution" made it to the ripe old age of nine before expiring in another coup in 2006. It was an incredibly detailed document and one of broad scope, which regulated many aspects of political practice, and has had some enduring impact on subsequent documents (Ginsburg 2009).

As in every country, underlying the formal constitutional text of the day in Thailand is a set of informal norms and rules that constrains the exercise of political power. Real constitutional constraint comes from unwritten constitutional norms, particularly those concerning the role of the country's long-ruling and widely respected monarch, King Bhumibol Adulyadej, who took the throne after the still-unsolved murder of his brother in 1946 (Handley 2006).

The unwritten constitutional status of the king did not emerge automatically in 1932 but was the result of decades of political battles between the monarchy, elected politicians, and the military. In 1956, for example, the king made a veiled criticism of the military junta, provoking a strong reaction from Phibun that threatened royal autonomy (Handley 2006: 134). Since Sarit's coup in 1957, however, the palace has gradually expanded its authority, and the royally endorsed coup has become a standard feature of Thai politics. It was most apparent in 1981, when coup leaders moved against Prime Minister Prem Tinsulanond (a former general) and took over much of Bangkok. The king's refusal to grant the leaders an audience was crucial in undermining the coup, which collapsed after three days (Suwannathat-Pian 2002: 57).

The king has developed ties with all the powerful groups in society, and the monarchy has established itself as the ultimate arbiter of political conflicts, sharing power with the politicians, bureaucrats, and generals who run the country on a day-to-day basis. The monarchy has remained a stabilizing factor, aloof from politics and yet intervening at crucial times to keep the system in some semblance of balance. This role has been played as a matter of informal politics rather than formal institutional authority. For example, the formal powers given to the king in the 1997 Constitution (adopted with great public fanfare and inclusion) were perhaps greater than what is accorded in comparable European constitutional monarchies, but not formidable.[7] In reality, the king's frequent though elliptical interventions in politics have meant that governance was bound by informal as well as formal constraints (Suwannathat-Pian 2003). At times, however, the monarch's interventions have gone well beyond his limited formal role. For example, in 1992, King Bhumibol appointed technocrat Anand Panyrachun as prime minister over elected MP Somboon Rahong, who had been nominated by the parliament. The choice was widely accepted, despite its utter lack of constitutional basis (Suwannathat-Pian 2002).

An incomplete listing of the unwritten constitutional rules is as follows: the monarch, head of state, is highly respected and will limit his interventions in the political sphere. However, on the occasions when he exercises his power, he will be respected. The military can step in to resolve perceived crises, and coups are a perfectly acceptable method of leadership change. However, coup leaders should always seek a private blessing from the throne before, and a public

---

[7] These include refusing to assent to bills and calling for further deliberation (§ 94); dissolving the House of Representatives (§ 116) and convoking extraordinary sessions of the national assembly (§ 162).

one immediately after, any coup.[8] Meanwhile, violence against the people is rarely, if ever, legitimate, and no political force is entitled to excessively restrict the freedoms of the people. Furthermore, there seems to be a constitutional understanding now that coup leaders should restore democracy by promising new elections and a new constitution. The coup leaders invariably promulgate a new interim text – the fact that Thailand has had so many constitutions attests to the tradition of blessing coups in this fashion. As one commentator has observed, Thailand has accepted constitutional processes without accepting constitutional ideals and practices, repeatedly adopting new texts that fail to endure or constrain (Wongtrangan 1990: 289).

The unwritten constraints, however, ensure that Thai authoritarianism is, in relative terms, not very authoritarian. Compared with neighboring Myanmar or Indonesia, repression by the Thai military has been relatively mild, even in its darkest hours. One can conclude that, although proceeding from a different historical tradition from Western liberal constitutionalism, Thai society operates on the basis of quasi-constitutional understandings of limitation on government, which do not proceed from a written text.

The monarch does not view constitutions as enduring or permanent institutions that constrain and channel power; in fact, he has spoken of constitutions as foreign imports, based on textbook notions of democracy that are not appropriate for Thailand's unique political culture.[9] Drawing on the Buddhist idea of impermanence, the king has emphasized that unworkable institutions can easily be changed and that constitutions are impermanent human creations (Harding 2007). Thailand's constitutional monarchy thus differs significantly from that of the United Kingdom or the Netherlands. There, *constitutional* monarchy suggests that both constitution and monarch are enduring, and that the former constrains the latter. The monarch is the embodiment of the nation, but not a force in politics. In Thailand, the monarchy is permanent whereas constitutions are ephemeral. Constitutions may not regulate the monarchy; nonetheless, they *are* used to legitimate temporal power holders (Harding 2007).

This unstable constitutional scheme in Thailand is workable in large part because the state is autonomous and continues to function without much interference from the political classes. Thailand has been influentially, if

---

[8] Even the antiroyalist Phibun sought the king's formal approval (Handley 2006: 91). In 1977, the Kriengsak coup did not seek go-ahead approval in advance, and was not received warmly by the king. (*Id.* at 267–268).

[9] In a 1992 speech, he mischaracterized the United States as providing a constitutional right to welfare, which he argued would not be fiscally sound if imported to Thailand. (Handley 2006: 344).

elliptically, described as a *bureaucratic polity*, to emphasize the relative autonomy of the state and the idea that political organization tends to occur in
pervasive patron-client relations with state elites (Riggs 1966). The political
parties are viewed as almost parasitic on the society, using money to organize
their constituents rather than representing organic interests from the bottom
up. There has been limited local involvement in decision making, as governors
are appointed Ministry of Interior bureaucrats. In short, Thailand's stabilizing
institutions – monarchy, bureaucracy, and Buddhism – all derive their power
from extra-constitutional sources and are constrained by a set of informal norms
rather than by formal rules. This suggests that, oddly, Thai constitutions are
weak in part because of the constitutional monarch (Handley 2006).

One can imagine a counterfactual history of Thailand in which the
monarch had embraced constitutionalism in 1932. The pattern of unstable
struggles among royalists, the military, and civilian leadership was established
in Pridi's era, and we argue that it has been exacerbated by the monarch's
ambivalence toward written documents. To be fair, by the time the current
king assumed the throne, the pattern of instability was clear and the survival
of the monarchy could not be guaranteed by mere parchment.

In sum, Thailand's formal constitutional instability has reflected, and in
part resulted from, a deeper stability in the unwritten constitution around the
role of the monarchy. The monarch has served as an external enforcer of the
unwritten norms, intervening sometimes to topple written constitutions. This
pattern might change with the death of the current monarch, who is widely
respected, in which case some of the normative risks of constitutional turnover
may come into play.

MEXICO AND JAPAN: FLEXIBLE COOPTATION AND POLITICAL STABILITY

Mexico and Japan would seem to be an odd pairing. The countries share
the experience of being run during the period under review by single non-
communist political parties, the Mexican Party of the Institutionalized Revolution (PRI) and the Liberal Democratic Party (LDP) of Japan. The Mexican
case shares some features with those of Taiwan and China in that the constitution, at least initially, played a role as an ideological document more than one
that constrained government. As with the case of Taiwan, democratization
in Mexico has been accompanied by greater constitutional constraint. The
Japanese case, in contrast, is one in which constitutional limits had more bite
in their infancy, owing in part to the U.S. shadow. As we shall see, although
the two cases have experienced similar levels of endurance, the Mexican

document has evolved dramatically, whereas the Japanese document appears to be frozen in time, at least formally.

Mexico: Flexible Co-optation

A particularly important category of cases to consider in understanding constitutional endurance are those constitutions that survive across regime types. We have noted, for example, the intriguing survival of the Pinochet-drafted constitution in a post-Pinochet democratic Chile. Mexico, whose transition has been decidedly less abrupt, presents something of the same question. How can a set of institutions serve both democrats and authoritarians?

In part, because of its stable constitutional structure, Mexico under the PRI is often described as a semi-dictatorship. When pressed to employ binary categories, scholars almost universally consider Mexico to be a case of authoritarianism prior to 1994, when the PRI's dominance broke down (Przeworski et al. 1999). Elections would occur at regular intervals, but they were subject to manipulation by the dominant PRI, which held power continuously since its organization around 1929.[10] The elections provided for a modicum of political competition, and the media and courts maintained nominal independence. In addition, repression was selective and localized rather than a central instrument of regime power (Greene 2007; Magaloni 2008). At the same time, the PRI remained comfortably in control. It was a responsive dictatorship, a precursor of the phenomenon that would later be identified as *competitive authoritarianism*.

The Constitution of 1917 has its roots in earlier constitutional instability and emerged after a long period of autocratic rule in which Porfirio Diaz had amended the constitution to extend his term indefinitely, notwithstanding his own election on a promise of "no re-election." It also reflected the broad and somewhat antagonistic coalition that toppled Diaz in 1910. The coalition included nationalists, liberals, Jacobins, socialists, and military strongmen (Saravia 2008: 132), demonstrating inclusion. The 1917 Constitution was adopted during a period of internal struggle among these forces and incorporated much of the language of the 1857 Liberal Constitution, which like the 1824 constitution, borrowed many elements from the U.S. document.[11] In his inaugural address, the president of the 1917 Constitutional Congress went so

---

[10] The predecessor to the PRI was created in 1929 as the Party of the National Revolution (PNR), renamed as the Party of the Mexican Revolution (PRM) in 1938, and finally taking the name of the Party of the Institutional Revolution (PRI) in 1946.

[11] Ironically, the document included even many *porfirista* amendments that the "constitutionalists" earlier had rejected in the negotiation process.

far as to call the new constitution an amendment to the old one (although in the same speech he also described the 1917 Constitution as a radical departure from the earlier constitution).[12]

In reaction to Diaz' excesses, the Constitution provided for non-reelection after a single four year term, later amended to six years. Substantively, the Constitution was redistributive, providing for nationalization of the country's resources and restricting the power of the church. Mexico's emerging coalition sought to provide a more stable means of transferring power, an issue that (as we have seen) has bedeviled regimes throughout Latin America (see, for example, Hartlyn and Valenzuela 1998). Yet, the early years after the revolution proved tumultuous, as they frequently do, with violent struggle over power. Emerging triumphant was President Alvaro Obregón, who assumed the presidency in 1920, for a four-year term. He was succeeded by Plutarco Elias Calles, whose anti-Catholic fanaticism provoked a rebellion. In 1927, Obregón successfully pushed to modify the Constitution to allow for his own reelection after a term out of power, notwithstanding the cardinal importance of the norm proscribing reelection. Shortly after winning reelection, Obregón was murdered.[13]

From this point onward, PRI insiders agreed that succession should be handled through peaceful mechanisms and sought to develop more stable means of governance. The core feature of PRI rule – the absolute power of the president, who would nevertheless step down after a single six-year term – did not develop until the 1940s. It would be wrong to say that ballots replaced bullets, for the convention that emerged was that the president himself would choose his successor (the famous *dedazo*, or finger tap). Still, the stability of the system and its successful solution to the chronic problem of executive tenure is worth exploring. This is particularly true given the high stakes involved: total power for a limited duration.[14]

The Mexican PRI regime's survival hinged on a large-c constitutional rule – no re-election – supplemented by numerous unwritten rules. Most important among the latter are the rules within the PRI governing the *dedazo*. The decision was a personal one, and the choice was unfailingly ratified by the PRI and the electorate as a whole for six decades from 1940 through 1994. By convention, successors were always drawn from the cabinet, but the written

[12] This section owes much to Michael S. Werner.

[13] Although it is tempting to attribute this to the enforcement of the non-reelection norm, his assassin was a young Catholic fanatic who had come to see Obregón as the anti-Christ. Some scholars, however, do believe that enforcement of the constitutional norm was part of the motive for the murder.

[14] As Jorge Castañeda has said, "The presidential succession unleashes abnormal ambition and greed for many reasons, but one is foremost: there is too much power at stake. It is, or was, all the power in the entire country, all the time, for six years" (2001: 126).

constitution imposed additional requirements regarding age (a minimum of 35 years old) and nonmembership in the clergy, military, or certain government positions. Article 82 also required resignation from the cabinet six months before elections, a constraint taken seriously in the succession following President Carlos Salinas de Gortari.[15] Another unwritten constitutional norm concerned election losers: those who were not chosen would be dealt with fairly, usually rewarded with lesser positions, but never fully purged or killed. Finally, a political convention required some fluctuation among factions within the PRI. A right-wing president would be followed by a left-wing one for the first several decades of PRI rule.

Constitutional endurance made sense for the PRI for three reasons: ideology, internal coordination, and co-optation. Ideologically, the 1917 Constitution provided a continuous link to the revolution that it helped to consolidate, rendering less incongruous the party's odd designation as the embodiment of the institutionalized revolution. As in other programmatic or ideological constitutions, many of the provisions were not meant to be formally implemented in practice, but rather to provide aspirational goals for the regime to strive to meet. Internal coordination was facilitated by the stability of certain core provisions, most prominently the non-reelection norm embodied in Article 83. Article 83 provided a focal point that ensured that incumbents would step down after a single *sexenio* (six-year term), with the background enforcement threat placed in sharp relief by Obregón's assassination.

The Constitution was also a device for internal co-optation. The PRI was subject to challenge from various social forces during its long rule. A typical response was to provide a constitutional amendment embodying the demands of the group. For example, Article 123 on labor and social security rights was modified several times, including nine times between 1960 and 1986. These modifications provided for a number of distinctive benefits for particular interest groups, including expanding the scope of federal labor regulation to particular industries ranging from movies to glass-making to vegetable fats,[16] providing for detailed rules about working hours, the rate of overtime pay, the duration of leave, and social security. The result is a mega-article that looks more like a labor code than a constitution; but all the detail allowed for continuing payoffs to labor, a central element of the PRI coalition. This illustrates our theme of specificity – broader constitutions, with detail, help to co-opt interest groups and ensure loyalty to the bargain.

---

[15] Salinas' designated successor, Luis Colosio, was murdered, and a leading candidate was PRI insider Pedro Aspe. Aspe, however, was constitutionally disqualified because he was serving in the cabinet (Castañeda 2001: 93–94).

[16] Article 123 XXXI.

Flexibility was another structural feature of the document that promoted endurance. The Constitution was amended some 103 times between 1921 and 1996, because the PRI had the ability to do so unilaterally (Oropeza 1997: 332–33).[17] Formal amendment requires a two-thirds vote in both houses plus approval of the majority of state legislatures. This was not much of a constraint during the period of PRI dominance, until it lost its two-thirds majority in the Chamber of Deputies in 1988.[18] Amendment, thus, reflected shifts in policy, such as Miguel Aleman's alignment with capitalists in 1946 and de la Madrid's privatization program in the 1980s.

Why were the opposition and social movements mollified with constitutional amendments whose enforcement was hardly certain? Here, one can also see focal points at work. Movement leaders could demand constitutional amendments as a way of mobilizing their supporters and then claim credit when the amendment was passed. Even if the constitution was not fully implemented, the inclusion of the demand in the pantheon of aspirations provided a basis for subsequent claims. Yet, in embedding the demand in the constitution, the opposition became co-opted through a stake in the constitution's survival.

For example, in the late 1930s, President Lázaro Cárdenas (1934–1940) sought to complete the land reform program that had been a central promise of the 1917 Constitution. However, the Supreme Court disagreed with his program, siding instead with large landowners who sought to protect their property rights. Cárdenas responded by interfering with the court, replacing the membership, and ending life terms in favor of six-year terms. Changing the court required a constitutional amendment, easy enough for Cárdenas with his large majorities in both the national Congress and state assemblies. The amendment disciplining the Supreme Court represented an expansion of the constitutional coalition of the PRI, bringing in peasants and landless workers as supporters.

Many of the amendments expanded the scope of the Constitution in terms of the issues that it regulated. The Constitution thus grew in scope over time as it co-opted more and more groups. The most frequently amended provision was Article 73, dealing with the enumerated powers of Congress and the fiscal basis of the center (Oropeza 1997).[19] The combination of flexibility and

---

[17] Compare Magaloni, 2008 (450 amendments, but Magaloni counts the number of provisions that were amended rather than instances of amendment).

[18] It then entered into a pact with the opposition PAN party, which would allow the PRI to govern in exchange for reforms to the electoral law.

[19] Constitutional amendments were seen as entrenching policies politically even if not formally. For example, President Jose Lopez Portillo, when faced with opposition to his economic policies of nationalizing the banks, decided to amend the Constitution (Castañeda 2001: 170).

specificity played the essential role in endurance, and the expansion of the zone of inclusion mattered as well.[20]

In short, constitutional amendment during the PRI regime was frequent, and amendments provided political goods. The PRI used the Constitution to incorporate social insurgencies and political dissidents while limiting their effective power. Our account of inclusion, specificity, and flexibility seems to explain constitutional endurance in this case. The process of gradual reform has given the Mexican Constitution a measure of stability but has created certain other tensions. First, the accumulation of constitutional amendments has inverted many of the original intentions of the 1917 Constitution's framers, shifting power from Congress toward the president and from states to Mexico City (Valadés 2007: 811–43). Second, the document is considered by some to be too complex for the average citizen to comprehend (Valadés 2007).

Mexico's political system is now in the midst of a gradual but dramatic transition, which is building momentum as the opposition parties begin to win elections at the state and local levels (Greene 2007). Institutional adjustment laid the seeds for a more profound transformation. If the roots of *presidencialismo* can be traced to the assassination of Obregón in 1928, the system's decline intensified with the assassination of Salinas' designated successor Luis Donaldo Colosio in early 1994 (Castañeda 2001: 113). Colosio's designation had violated an implicit norm of rotation within the PRI, as both Salinas and de la Madrid had come from the more conservative wing of the party (Apreza 1997: 1184). Colosio's killing led to a crisis in which President Salinas briefly contemplated amending the Mexican Constitution to allow sitting governors and cabinet ministers to run for president (Castañeda 2001: 116).[21] In the end, however, he appointed Ernesto Zedillo as his replacement, with historic consequences. Zedillo immediately announced a judicial reform to increase judicial independence, ending unilateral presidential appointment. Zedillo

Apreza (1997: 1182) reports that this nationalization made the public begin to question the wide discretion of the presidency.

[20] Constitutional discourse increased during the regime of Miguel de la Madrid (1982–88), a constitutional lawyer who saw himself as bound, in some loose sense, to embody policies in the constitutional text. Thus, he nationalized the banks and introduced a notion of "strategic" state industries into the text. He also introduced new social and economic rights, namely the rights to health and housing. His view of the Constitution, as described in his autobiography, was one of defining ends, as a programmatic document rather than one constraining power in a meaningful way.

[21] Interestingly Castañeda (2001: 123) notes that many PRI insiders were, in fact, unaware that this provision applied to governors. Salinas explored the possibility of amending the constitution, or alternatively postpone the election for some weeks to allow the six-month period to expire. These options were opposed by powerful forces inside and outside the PRI and so were not pursued.

also initiated economic reforms and appointed an opposition PAN member as attorney general. He became the last PRI president designated unilaterally from within the party as Vicente Fox of the opposition PAN party won power in the 2000 elections (Saravia 2008).

The PRI has fallen from power and a stable three-party system has taken hold, with significant constitutional implications (Zamora and Cossio 2006). Congress is emerging as a major locus of decision making and policy initiation, and the president's power has declined significantly. Mexico's Supreme Court has begun to emerge as a powerful player, although it is most influential in disputes among different levels of governments rather than claims for protection of human rights (Navia and Rios 2005; Ruibal 2008; Zamora and Cossio 2006). With the decline of the PRI supermajority, the primary mechanism of constitutional change has shifted from formal constitutional amendment toward informal judicial amendment through interpretation to refine constitutional ambiguities.

Why did Mexico not adopt a new constitution after democratization in the 1990s? Some proposals to this effect were put forward by the left-wing PRD, and academics explored the issue.[22] In 2003, the Supreme Court initiated a discussion of possible reforms to the Constitution, producing a white paper of options after an extensive consultation process. But, the general consensus seems to have been that a new constitution could in fact produce a worse outcome than the current imperfect one (Carpizo 1999: 85–104; Valadés 2007 811–843). The fact that no political force has sufficient political strength to dictate a new constitution suggests that risk-aversion is reasonably high. The status quo provides a form of political insurance against radical shifts in either the left- or right-wing direction, and so, the current institutions are stable, notwithstanding their possible suboptimality. Scholars have instead called for *reforging* the Constitution (Valadés 2007: n.20)[23] or engaging in more major integral reforms without a new constitutional assembly (Carbonell 1999: 33–51).[24]

More broadly, the Mexican Constitution survives because it has now allowed for alternation in power, as well as domestication of the *presidencialismo* system. Mexico has become a more complicated place, with the presidency no longer so dominant. Furthermore, constitutional politics are alive and well under the 1917 document. When President Calderon recently introduced a plan for the partial privatization of PEMEX, the national oil monopoly, it was

---

[22] Instituto de Investigaciones Jurídicas (1999).

[23] Compare Andrade 1999: 5–12 (arguing for a constitutional culture under the existing document rather than a new draft).

[24] See also Joseph and Nugent 1994 (crisis in government results from more long-term and structural problems).

the left wing that made arguments that the proposal was unconstitutional. Consistent with our notion of inclusion, constitutional politics has been embraced by most major political forces.

Finally, it is worth speculating on the benefits of constitutional endurance in the Mexican case. It has provided for an inclusive if not always democratic political process. It has domesticated the power-seeking executive, providing for a series of peaceful transitions from power. And, it has arguably ensured a stable environment for Mexico's remarkable economic growth over several decades. In short, it has in many ways grown into the lofty ambitions inscribed in the document in 1917. It seems unlikely that periodic replacement of the document would have allowed for such development.

Japan: The Unlikely Endurance of an Imposed Constitution

The Japanese constitution would seem to be a paradigmatic case of imposition, as the document was largely drafted by the occupation authorities in the wake of World War II in February 1946. But, the facts are more complex, and recent scholarship has emphasized the collaborative nature of the enterprise (Beer and Maki 2002: 84–85; Dower 2000; Miwa and Ramseyer 2009). Moore and Robinson (2002), in their recent magisterial study, use the term *conspiracy* to describe the production of the final Japanese document. In large part, the conspiratorial element was necessitated by the need for secrecy with regard to the authorship of the draft. From the American side, General MacArthur needed the Japanese government to represent that the draft was its own, not only to make it legitimate locally but also to convince the other Allied governments, who were calling for Emperor Hirohito's head, that the matter was out of MacArthur's control. The Japanese, reluctant to cede all autonomy or at least to appear to have done so, had an interest in deemphasizing U.S. involvement as well. Thus, the two sides had a common interest in secrecy.[25]

Once in place, Japan's constitution has been incredibly resilient and has become genuinely entrenched in the public imagination (Beer and Maki 2002). It has been intensely contested, but also remarkably stable – never amended, occasionally adjudicated, and ultimately grounded in a set of principles that the people understand and many accept. How has the Constitution been so resilient? The key factor is that Japan's Constitution has been largely self-enforcing during the immediate post-war period. Importantly, the forces keeping it in equilibrium are in flux today, and it is possible that a coalition

---

[25] The Japanese concept of *tatemae* (public presentation as contrasted with true inner feelings) resonates here.

will indeed be able to introduce changes in the next few years. The Japanese case thus provides an excellent case study of how an imposed constitution can become self-enforcing, as well as the conditions under which constitutional change can occur.

The Japanese Constitution has been under attack from political conservatives from the very beginning, and this intensified when the true story of its origins emerged some years later. Domestic revisionists sought for Japan to become a "normal country" with armed forces. Since its formation in 1955, the Liberal Democratic Party (LDP) has sought to make changes to the constitution but has never been able to muster the two-thirds support in the Diet. In 1956, it created a Commission on the Constitution to study revision but after several years of deliberations, the Commission was unable to reach consensus and its recommendations were never implemented (Maki 1980; 1993). The Constitution was also attacked from abroad. The Far Eastern Commission (FEC) attacked it almost immediately as not having gone through the process of FEC approval that it believed was required by the Moscow Declaration. But, despite promises, the Japanese government never formally tried to change it.

One clue as to why the Constitution was stable lies in the Japanese debates over its adoption. In the debates in the Diet, two issues stood out: the treatment of the emperor and the pacifism of Article 9, which banned the maintenance of armed forces (Moore and Robinson 2002: 334). The former issue was an unconditional demand of the American occupiers, faced as they were with the Allied powers demanding harsher treatment of the emperor. The latter, though of uncertain origin, also constituted a major imposition and was quite controversial.

The bargain could be struck through *gaiatsu* (outside pressure). But, it could only be maintained through *naiatsu* (internal pressure). Here, a key factor was that the Japanese were not in fact united on the key issues. The left wing wanted Article 9 to prevent a return to militarism. The right wing, on the other hand, was concerned with the treatment of the emperor and the maintenance of his prerogatives. Japanese elites were thus split on the two key issues of the postwar constitution. Had they united, they could certainly have rejected the draft, with the likely outcome that the FEC would have become involved and imposed a settlement on Japan. That settlement would no doubt have included hanging the emperor as a war criminal. One puzzle, then, is why the left wing did not seek to push this outcome. Perhaps it too, was sufficiently concerned with retaining a role for the emperor in some form, even a reduced one.

In any case, once adopted, postwar politics took over. After its foundation in 1955, the Liberal Democratic Party (LDP) governed Japan more or less continuously. The LDP was also split between revisionists, initially led by Hatoyama

Ichiro and later Kishi Nobusuke, and the pragmatic conservatives led initially by Yoshida Shigeru and later, Ikeda Hayato, Sato Eisaku, and Miyazawa Kiichi (Samuels 2004). The party system as a whole, however, was fairly stable during the Cold War, with the Socialists consistently getting a fairly substantial minority of the vote. This meant that the Socialists retained sufficient power to block the LDP from engineering constitutional amendments to abolish or modify Article 9. Of course, the socialists also lacked a majority to propose any amendments to the economic system or to abolish the imperial house entirely. They nevertheless were able to share in some spoils of the system and always were better off than they would have been in proposing a complete constitutional revision, which might have led to the replacement of Article 9. Thus, the Constitution succeeded because it also gave the *losers* a stake in maintaining it. This is the key quality of self-enforcing constitutions.

A critical juncture arose during the great protests surrounding the US-Japan Security Treaty in 1960. The Japanese government at the time was led by the revisionist Kishi Nobosuke, who sought to revise the Security Treaty to give Japan a larger role in its own defense. Faced with opposition among Diet members who saw a threat to Article 9, Kishi rammed through the Treaty in a secret session when the opposition was absent. This led to massive political protests, with several hundred thousand citizens taking to the streets. Kishi eventually resigned and was replaced with the pragmatist Ikeda. The incident illustrates an executive threat to transgress the constitutional order that provoked enforcement by the public. The public was able to overcome its collective action problem and effectively enforce the Constitution. Even though the Security Treaty survived, effectuating a de facto reinterpretation of Article 9, Kishi was punished for his procedural violation. One can imagine an alternative ending to this story in which the Constitution was overturned, either by leftist protest, rightist reaction, or Kishi's routinization of the practice of calling secret sessions. But, the Constitution survived and Japan entered the high-growth era of the 1960s.

The Cold War is now over and the socialists all but dead as a political force. Their last gasp was a brief period in government in the mid-1990s, in which they performed so poorly they ensured their demise as a political factor. At the same time, intrafactional politics within the LDP shifted power toward the constitutional revisionists associated with Yasuhiro Nakasone, Shintaro Abe, and others. This group consolidated its position with the popular Koizumi prime ministership; Koizumi also established a new politics based more on public relations than the traditional pork barrel.

These changes had severe consequences for the self-enforcing nature of the Constitution. As the party system recalibrated after an electoral reform, a new opposition Democratic Party (DPJ) emerged, made up in part of former LDP hawks who had left the party. When the LDP proposed constitutional reform again in the mid-1990s, the DPJ and other small parties did not oppose reform, but scrambled to come up with proposals of their own. The self-enforcing equilibrium has fallen apart, and reform of the key bargain may occur in some form in the next few years. The consensus view is that the bulk of the 1946 document will remain intact, and crucial features such as the rights provisions will not be threatened. Japan will remain a constitutional democracy. But, the point is, that the particular bargain will change, and Japan will enter a (post–) post-occupation era.

IMPLICATIONS OF CASE STUDIES

Having reviewed a wide range of family histories and a smaller number of constitutional autopsies, we are now in position to make some comparative observations about their implications for our inquiry. The case study approach allows us to tease out the various explanatory factors offered in the statistical analysis and evaluate some of the assumptions that underlie their causal power. Table 8.1 summarizes some of the features of these cases.

Although not a universal pattern, it seems at first glance that constitutions adopted by new nations just after state formation *can* succeed, such as those of India or the United States. But, just as often, countries require some trial and error (and in unreported robustness checks in the hazard analysis, we do not find that *first* constitutions endure longer). Indeed, the United States had one false start; other new states such as Haiti and Mexico had periods of constitutional instability early on, with the Haitians never recovering. Older states that adopt new constitutions in the modern period also exhibit a varied pattern. Thus, although France, Thailand, and China were unable to find stable constitutions once they began the effort, Japan's 1889 Constitution was quite enduring. In short, issues of constitutional birth order and the relative age of the state do not seem crucial for outcomes.

A second point is that state-level instability, such as that experienced by France and China, may yield constitutional instability but is not a permanent curse. Notwithstanding the joke about the French Constitution being a periodical, the current document has been stable, nurtured by (and contributing to) the remarkable postwar political and economic stability of Europe. Legacies of instability, it seems, can be overcome, but only in a sufficiently benevolent environment. International conditions seem to matter.

Even China, whose constitutions are uniformly ideological and programmatic rather than constraining (Nathan 1986), seems to be settling into a pattern

			Structural features				
Case	Years	Crisis level[1]	Legacy of enforcement[2]	Inclusiveness[3]	Flexibility[4]	Detail[5]	Outcome[6]
Pakistan	Early years	High	Low	Low	Moderate	High	Premature Deaths Mean Age = 4
	1973	High	Low	Moderate	Moderate	High	Still alive in 2009 (frequently suspended)
India	1949	High	None	High	Optimal	High	Still alive in 2009 Age = 61
United States	1781	High	None	Low	Suboptimal	Low	Premature death Age = 8
	1789	High	Low	High	Moderate	Low	Still alive in 2009 Age = 221
France	Early years	Mixed	Low	Varied	Suboptimal	Moderate	Premature Death Mean Age = 5
	1815	Moderate	Low	—	—	—	Premature Death Age = 15
	1830	Moderate	Low	—	—	—	Expected Lifespan Age = 18
	1848	High	Moderate	Moderate	Suboptimal	Low	Premature Death Age = 4
	1852	High	Moderate	Moderate	Moderate	Low	Expected Lifespan Age = 23
	1875	High	Moderate	High	Moderate	Low	Long Life Age = 65
	1940	High	Moderate	—	—	—	Premature Death Age = 6
	1946	High	Moderate	Moderate	Moderate	Moderate	Premature Death Age = 12
	1958	Moderate	Moderate	High	Optimal	Moderate	Still alive in 2009 Age = 52

(continued)

TABLE 8.1 (continued)

Case	Years	Crisis level[1]	Legacy of enforcement[2]	Inclusiveness[3]	Flexibility[4]	Detail[5]	Outcome[6]
China/Taiwan	Early years	High	Low	Low	Mixed	Low	Premature Deaths Mean Age = 4
	1928	High	Low	Moderate	Suboptimal	Low	Expected Lifespan Age = 19
	1947	Moderate	Moderate	Varied	Optimal	Moderate	Premature Death in China Age = 2; Still alive in 2009 in Taiwan Age = 62
	1954	Moderate	Moderate	Low	Suboptimal	Moderate	Expected Lifespan Age = 21
	1975	High	Moderate	Moderate	Suboptimal	Low	Premature Death Age = 3
	1978	Moderate	Moderate	Low	Suboptimal	Low	Premature Death Age = 4
	1982	Moderate	Moderate	Moderate	Suboptimal	Low	Still Alive in 2009 Age = 28
Mexico	Early years	Mixed	Moderate	Low	Suboptimal	Moderate	Premature Deaths Mean Age = 8
	1867	Moderate	Moderate	Low	Suboptimal	High	Long Life Age = 50
	1917	Moderate	Moderate	Moderate	Moderate	High	Still alive in 2009 Age = 93
Japan	1889	High	None	Low	Suboptimal	Low	Long Life Age = 57
	1946	Moderate	High	Moderate	Moderate	Moderate	Still Alive in 2009 Age = 64

Haiti	All	Mixed	Low	Mixed	Suboptimal	Moderate	Premature Death Age = 64
Dominican Republic	All	Mixed	Low	Mixed	Suboptimal	Moderate	Premature Death Mean Age = 6
Thailand	All	Mixed	Low	Low	Mixed	Moderate	Premature Death Mean Age = 4

1 Crisis level refers to the number of crises experienced in the country per year of the constitution's life. Scores of low are those with crisis numbers under the 25th percentile (1.8), moderate is between the 25th and 75th percentiles (1.8–7), and high is above the 75th percentile (7).

2 Legacy of enforcement represents the mean lifespan of all previous constitutions. None is listed for first constitutions, as they have no legacy. For all subsequent constitutions, low the scores are those below 25th percentile (5), moderate is between the 25th and 75th percentiles (5–22), and high is above the 75th percentile (22).

3 In general, inclusiveness represents levels of the inclusiveness index, where low is a score of 0 or 1 on the index, moderate is a score of 2, 3, or 4 and high is a score of 5 or higher. However, we have changed some of these values based on our reading of the historical record in order to capture details of the constitution that may have been missed by our coding of the documents.

4 Flexibility is a combination of the ease of amendment and judicial review. The scores for flexibility are referred to as suboptimal, moderate, and optimal, because of the curvilinear relationship between the ease of amendment and endurance suggested in Chapter 6. A constitution has suboptimal flexibility if it has an estimated amendment rate of less than 0.35 or greater than 0.75, moderate flexibility if it has an estimated amendment rate of between 0.35 and 0.45 or 0.65 and 0.75, and optimal flexibility if it has an estimated amendment rate between 0.45 and 0.65. Then, if the country has judicial review, the score is adjusted up one step (i.e. the United States is scored as moderate flexibility because of the presence of judicial review, even though its ease of amendment would place flexibility at suboptimal). The rationale for this rule is that amendment and judicial review are essentially substitutable methods of flexibility.

5 Detail is the number of words/scope item. Low scores are those less than the 25th percentile (241), moderate is between the 25th and 75th percentiles (241–502), and high is above the 75th percentile (502).

6 The outcome refers to the endurance of the constitutions. There are several possibilities here. Still alive in 2009 are constitutions that are still in force at the time of this writing. Premature death is the outcome for those constitutions that die well before the expected survival of constitutions from the baseline survival estimates in Chapter 6 (19 years). Expected lifespan is listed for those constitutions that die within five years of the expected survival of constitutions. Long life is for those constitutions that die long after the expected survival of constitutions.

of endurance. The twin constitutional histories of the People's Republic of China and Taiwan illustrate that enforceability is hardly a necessary condition for endurance, as each reflects a need for ideological continuity. Nevertheless, on balance, countries that experience democratic stability do seem to enjoy constitutional stability, reflecting the result of the epidemiological analysis in Chapter Six.

Enforceability of a constitution is difficult to measure, and we do not tackle this question directly in this volume other than the introductory analyses in Chapters Two and Three. Intuitively, we know that some provision of a constitution may matter more than others. The autopsies here also show that this condition can vary over time. The Mexican and Indian constitutions both had a highly aspirational character at their founding but the polity and constitution have grown together in ways that seem to increase the alignment between de jure promise and de facto practice.

At least a moderate level of flexibility seems to be a necessary condition for enduring constitutions, but specificity is not a universal requirement. The French Constitution of the Third Republic and the U.S. Constitution are counterexamples that show specificity is not always a necessary condition for endurance. Inclusion, on the other hand, does seem to be a feature required at some level. Successful constitutions *do* give major and powerful groups a stake in their endurance, and adjust to accommodate new groups as they arise or become more powerful. They also allow some role for public involvement in governance.

Finally, we should emphasize the sheer variety of experience. Like human beings, constitutions are born and die in a wide array of circumstances. Their genetic codes include some family history, but also reflect the agency of their authors who can choose, within constraints, to make their bargains more inclusive, specific, and flexible. These features (particularly inclusion and flexibility) allow the constitution to adjust to the various changing environmental conditions of international society. Of course, even robust organisms can experience shocks so large as to die: the previously enduring French and Japanese Constitutions could not survive the trauma of World War II.

Conclusion

Thomas Jefferson's argument about the optimal endurance of constitutions turned out to be uncannily prescient: his proposed expiration date of nineteen years matches the predicted life expectancy for national constitutions since 1789. Since Jefferson's debate with Madison, constitutional endurance has been presumed and celebrated, but, with few exceptions (Hammons 1999; Niskanen 1990; Ordeshook 1992; Sutter 1997), rarely analyzed. This volume has sought to understand the phenomenon of constitutional endurance. Our analysis suggests that in too many cases in the real world, constitutional lives have been "nasty, brutish, and short," as Hobbes would put it. In Chapter Two, we provided some suggestive evidence to the effect that the lives of people living with frequent constitutional turnover may have a Hobbesian quality as well, in the sense that constitutional endurance is associated with other goods such as wealth and levels of democracy. That conclusion is decidedly qualified, as we have also uncovered suggestive evidence of some real benefits of periodic constitutional replacement.

Like those of human beings, constitutional life spans are the product of the interaction of many different factors. Some of these we have characterized as environmental and, thus outside the control of constitutional actors. Others, however, depend on decisions taken by those subject to the constitution in the course of constitutional design and thereafter. Our account thus emphasizes the role of politics in constitutional formation and maintenance. We focus on particular features, namely flexibility, specificity, and inclusion, which can facilitate constitutional endurance.

Flexibility, the ability of the constitution to adjust over time, allows it to adapt to changing circumstances and so prevents premature death. Specificity, which refers to both detail and scope, facilitates constitutional enforcement by facilitating agreement as to the contents and meaning of the constitution. Inclusion refers to the involvement of important groups in society in the design and maintenance of the constitution – broadly speaking, the more groups with a stake in the constitution, the more likely it is to endure.

For each of these factors, we recognize there are limits. Some of these effects have what we might call a Goldilocks quality. Specificity is helpful, but not if the constitution becomes a complete code governing every contingency. Inclusion is also beneficial so long as it does not degenerate into endless cycles of deliberative disagreement. The same goes for flexibility so long as it allows *some* reasonable degree of entrenchment, or *some* issues to be entrenched. There is, then, some non-linearity to these effects, but there is also some heterogeneity to them as well, in at least two senses. Specifically, the impact of these factors will differ across settings and will sometimes aggregate multiple effects, some complementary and some competing. This sort of heterogeneity is inevitable in any epidemiological study of a diverse population. Nevertheless, we repeat them here to emphasize that striking the proper balance is something that is quite local, dependent on the rate and type of exogenous and endogenous changes, the fragility and fragmentation of the polity, and other such factors. We certainly are not asserting a universally optimal level of these key factors. Even though red wine may be shown to have net benefits on human health, there are some people for whom, or quantities after which, the negative effects outweigh the positive. Constitutional design has a similar flavor, and always requires extensive tailoring to local conditions.

We also recognize that our key factors reflect features of constitutional design that may not, strictly speaking, be within the control of drafters. All of these features presuppose some level of prior agreement among those writing the constitution. This prior agreement is invisible to the social scientist, but may be the product of histories, interests, and constraints over which drafters have no real control. To the extent that bargainers can work within these constraints and develop a level of agreement embodied in the constitution, that document is more likely to endure. But, in some cases, it will be impossible to produce the detailed and inclusive agreements of the kind that have tended to flourish. In this sense, the variation we observe may reflect underlying political dynamics rather than the product of unrestricted design choices and processes.

IS ENDURANCE ALWAYS GOOD?

We have been careful not to treat long life with undue reverence. Surely, some constitutions *should* die, even if they were ideal at the time of their adoption. Exogenous and endogenous change means that some constitutions will grow out of alignment with their context and cease to fit. Sometimes this lack of fit indicates a problem of representation and sometimes it reflects a problem of outmoded institutions. Constitutions, like regulatory processes, can be captured by narrow groups and can entrench the past against the future. Furthermore, technologies of government evolve, and constitutional renewal can facilitate constitutional learning. For example, we contrasted the frequent updating of Latin American constitutions, which allowed many countries to shed institutions widely viewed to be suboptimal, with the constitutional stability of the United States, whose document retains some of the provisions abandoned by its southern neighbors. There is at least a plausible argument that the institutional updating associated with replacement constitutions involves improvement. Sometimes, we suspect, the process of re-writing higher law can be therapeutic and empowering for citizens and leaders.

Replacement can also be disruptive and costly in significant ways and, ideally, constitutions would adjust internally through amendments. Our empirical finding that flexibility fosters constitutional endurance is hardly surprising and is consistent with Jefferson's own suppositions about both the determinants and merits of frequent amendment. Jefferson was well aware that the alternative to flexibility was not permanence but disruptive change. As he wrote in 1824:

> The real friends of the Constitution in its federal form, if they wish it to be immortal, should be attentive, by amendments, to make it keep pace with the advance of the age in science and experience. Instead of this, the European governments have resisted reformation until the people, seeing no other resource, undertake it themselves by force, their only weapon, and work it out through blood, desolation and long-continued anarchy.[1]

Our finding vindicates the position of those analysts, such as Holmes and Sunstein (1995) who argued for flexibility in the drafting of constitutions. Locking in rules makes little sense when one is, as Elster and his co-authors (1998) put it, "rebuilding the ship at sea." Still, some degree of entrenchment is necessary and, indeed, in the nature of the beast. If pushed to an extreme, flexibility can undermine the very notion of constitutional politics, which implies a certain degree of rigidity. Only through entrenchment, it is often argued, are constitutions able to provide a stabilizing function for politics. Most constitutions that we examine are entrenched to *some* extent and, certainly, the solution to pathological entrenchment should not be full parliamentary sovereignty. But, we also think there are rapidly declining returns to rigidity: too much entrenchment leads the constitution to be ignored or overthrown. Constitutions with some level of flexibility draw interest groups into their functioning and provide enough incentive to maintain the document in the face of change.

[1] Thomas Jefferson to Robert J. Garnett, 1824.

Perhaps the ideal combination reflects the *appearance* of entrenchment with the fact of flexibility. The ideological distinction between constitutional and ordinary politics, then, may play a facilitative role, even if our analysis suggests that successful constitutions blur any such lines, as we describe shortly. A constitution that stretches to facilitate change nevertheless provides a framework in which new and old can interact and adjust, facilitating debate and political accommodation.

Our analysis provides qualified support for the notion of specificity. Much normative argument praises the merits of framework constitutions, which provide only general instruction without too much detail. We have argued, on theoretical grounds, that the opposite could be true. Constitutional detail can facilitate constitutional enforcement by providing for clarity when it comes to rules that need to be enforced. Furthermore, constitutional detail is likely to serve as a proxy for the level of investment in the constitutional bargain, something that is difficult to observe directly. There is some support for this from both anecdotal and more systematic empirical observation. The frequently amended, voluminous constitution of India provides a well-known example. Hammons (1999) finds that longer and more detailed state constitutions endure longer. On the other hand, the argument is subject to the same Goldilocks qualification. A constitution that is too prolix could be impossible for its subjects to understand and navigate and hence will be *more* difficult to enforce, not less.

Our empirical finding here is qualified. In the analysis of a sub-sample of cases, we found that longer constitutions do take longer to write, which suggests that they are products of deliberation rather than expediency. The multivariate analysis uncovered a strong positive association between detail (that is, words per topic) and constitutional endurance. On the other hand, we did not find that documents with more scope, meaning those that covered more topics, endured longer. Both increased detail and broader scope, through an interest group logic, reflect and contribute to groups' willingness to invest in constitutional maintenance. The discussion of the Mexican constitution under the PRI, for example, suggested that the constitution was used as a device to co-opt interest groups that might in other circumstances participate in an alternative governing coalition. Similarly, the Indian document specifies many details about the structure of benefits to interest groups, so that no coalition can emerge to overturn the current bargain.

We are not able to determine whether the association that we have identified between specificity and endurance has normative implications for real-world constitutional designers. We have emphasized that specificity may be a proxy variable that simply reflects the investment of groups in the process of constitutional design. If so, designers would not be able to self-consciously affect endurance simply by adding text, unless the text reflected the results of a meaningful bargaining process.

The Mexican and Indian stories also speak to the power of inclusion. Groups must have an interest in the constitution to maintain it. Inclusion in the making of constitutions can promote a unifying identity and invite participants to invest in the bargain; inclusion in ongoing constitutional provisions further facilitates the integration of new social forces through continued constitutional maintenance. Such maintenance involves rededication to constitutional principles. Inclusive constitutions are particularly important during pacted constitutional transitions, such as that of Spain in the late 1970s. The Spanish document was a carefully crafted compromise that integrated social forces that had previously engaged in violent conflict. The basis of the bargain restrained both sides for at least a generation, which is in our terms above the average level of constitutional endurance.

Our account is at odds with normative analysis associated with some expectations of public choice theory. Sutter (2003), for example, derives conditions under which durability will facilitate the general interest rather than the capture of constitutional institutions by particular narrow groups who engage in rent-seeking. Our own approach, in contrast, suggests that a certain amount of redistribution and rent-seeking may be tolerable and even valuable to the extent that it gives interest groups a stake in the enforcement of the bargain down the road. If constitutional endurance itself provides stability and facilitates long-term goods, then rent-seeking early on is not categorically to be frowned upon. Some rent-seeking may be necessary, and so we do not endorse the notion that judges should serve as guardians against it.

Our positive theory emphasizes the importance of enforcement for endurance, and in this sense is consistent with much recent positive and normative scholarship on constitutionalism. Constitutional limitation requires active enforcement, and our emphasis has been on factors that facilitate it. Yet, the overall thrust of our argument is to emphasize the similarities between constitutional politics and ordinary politics. Constitutions endure, we find, when they are more like statutes – flexible, detailed, and infused with self-interest – than the conventional image of constitutions would have it. Constitutions are supposed to be entrenched, to be general, and to embody higher-order principles of moral agreement. But, these features may render the constitution too rigid to adjust to changing conditions, too vague to provide meaningful guidance to subjects, and too high-falutin to induce costly investment by powerful actors in enforcing the terms of the bargain.

We have not purported to provide a complete model of the *effects* of constitutional endurance. Nevertheless, it is worth restating some of our demonstrated associations between democratic and constitutional endurance. Democrats, we have found, are more likely than authoritarians to write a new constitution after regime change. However, democrats are less likely to replace their constitution if the original was written in a democratic period than in an authoritarian period. Furthermore, there is no stable democracy that exhibits what we might call the Island of Hispaniola pattern of constitutional change. That is, stable democracies do not replace their constitution frequently, as Jefferson advocated. Together, these findings suggest that, while new democracies will be likely to initiate constitutional reform, the sustenance of democracy may require the absence of such reform.

IMPLICATIONS FOR CONSTITUTIONAL INTERPRETATION

Our theory does not speak directly to any particular theory of constitutional review. We see judges engaged in constitutional review as playing two crucial roles in constitutional maintenance, corresponding to two different normative theories of constitutional interpretation. On the one hand, judicial review facilitates common knowledge as to violations of the constitution, facilitating enforcement and thus inhibiting transgression. This allows the constitution to endure by preventing political actors from violating its terms. On the other hand, judicial review involves updating the constitution to keep pace with contemporary changes. The first function, that of identifying constitutional violations and facilitating enforcement, might be called a constitutionalist model of review. It loosely corresponds with the textualist position on interpretation in that it emphasizes fidelity to the past. The second function of constitutional review involves lawmaking and a looser construction of text.[2] The court can give voice to new intersubjective understandings of constitutional constraints. The court helps to modernize the constitutional text by ensuring its continued fit with the social and political environment. Both textual fidelity and modernizing lawmaking are important for different aspects of constitutional endurance.

IMPLICATIONS FOR THEORIES OF INSTITUTIONAL CHANGE

Constitutions are institutions, and particularly central ones at that. Our approach has fit squarely into the mainstream of institutional analysis, adopting an equilibrium approach. But, our account is distinct in the degree to which we argue that design choices matter. Environmental shocks, which can open windows to constitutional reform, are seen as a crucial determinant

---

[2] Jefferson is usually considered a textualist, yet he is in favor of constitutional updating to reflect each generation's values and circumstances.

of change in conventional institutional analysis. We show that constitutions are almost certainly subject to environmental shocks, but the power of these shocks is probably overstated. Structural and design features of the constitution appear to have direct effects on endurance and may even condition the effects of shocks.

Another theme of the book has been the effects of time, both from the perspective of constitutions and the states that they inhabit. With respect to the trajectory of states, we do not see any clear patterns with respect to state maturity or the birth order of their constitutional offspring. Older states do not necessarily have more enduring constitutions. Birth order effects vary considerably as well. The first or second constitutions of some countries, such as the United States, Sweden, and Belgium, have endured for quite a long time as a result of internal adjustments. In other countries, such as Mexico and China, it took time and the experimentation with a number of texts before one one took hold. Yet another pattern is an early model that endures, followed by breakdown and a failure to recalibrate (e.g., Uruguay). Finally, some countries seem to have found themselves in something of a low-equilibrium trap – self-fulfilling cycles of almost constant promulgation and replacement (e.g., the Dominican Republic).

From the perspective of the constitution, it makes sense to think of time in terms of life-cycle, period, and generational effects. Life-cycle effects are changes in mortality associated with the age of the constitution; period effects those associated with different eras regardless of the age of the constitution; and generational effects are those associated with the year of birth, which could be thought to instill whatever theories and provisions are in vogue.[3] With respect to the life-cycle, effects of decay or crystallization might seem equally plausible. Our theory of enforcement favors one of crystallization. As the citizenry becomes more attached, and more versed in, the provisions of the document, it will be more likely to defend it. In fact, life cycle effects are non-linear. There is a honeymoon period of low mortality rates at birth followed by increased rates as constitutions approach their mid-teens. Mortality peaks at age seventeen, after which rates decrease steadily as crystallization sets in. This pattern is the exact opposite of that of the human life span, in which one sees high infant mortality followed by a dramatic dip in mortality, followed again by a steadily increasing mortality rate with age. The constitutional mortality pattern, on the other hand, resembles almost perfectly that of marriage, to which constitutions are often compared. Not only does the pattern match, but so too does the predicted rate of mortality: as reported in Chapter Six, at its

---

[3] We did not test for generation effects. We leave this stone largely unturned for future researchers, or perhaps ourselves in future work if it remains unturned.

peak at age seven, the rate of divorce is 22 for every 1000 marriages, slightly less than the peak rate of constitutional death of 27 for every 1000. The proverbial seven-year itch simply comes ten years later for constitutions.

With respect to period, we find that the life expectancy of constitutions, if anything, has decreased over the last 200 years. That is, unlike human beings, the health of constitutions is not getting better with modernity. The effect is not pronounced, but still, it is towards increasing mortality rates. For scholars who expect the modern era to be associated with increased stability, these results need explaining. Recall that because our test for period effects controls for all other predictors in the model, we cannot look to secular increases or decreases in any of the included variables to explain the drop. Our best guess is that the changes in the sample are responsible. Over and above the level of development, geographic region, and levels of democracy, there is something about the states that emerged post-World War II, which is depressing global mortality rates. We speculate that a more benevolent international environment, in which small states are both more economically viable and less subject to outright conquest, has reduced the risk of exiting many constitutional bargains.

CONCLUSION

We close with an expression of modesty. The preceding paragraph ended intentionally with a bit of speculation about a set of findings that we devoted very little space to in this book. Those particular findings, regarding period effects, are just some of many to which we would wish to devote entire chapters. Alas, ours is not, nor could it be, a book that purports to explain all of the ways in which constitutions die, any more than those in the medical profession would set out to explain the many risks to human life. We have focused on a particular set of risks to constitutional life – those at the hands of constitutional drafters. At the same time, part of our objective is to call attention to an understudied phenomenon and invite others – with the use of our data or their own – to venture and test still other hypotheses. We hope, in summary, to have demonstrated that constitutional endurance is an important and engaging subject of analysis, mostly because constitutional designers have the ability to extend the life span of their products with careful attention to some key factors. In our view, these factors yield the benefit of redirecting the attention of scholars and practitioners to the art and science of constitutional design. Of the many pursuits of social scientists, the design of constitutional foundations would seem to merit a harder look. This is so even if – or perhaps *especially* if – these foundations are expected to last only a generation.

Appendix

TABLE A.1. *List of new, interim, and reinstated constitutions in the CCP sample (through 2005)*

Country	Constitutions[1]
Afghanistan	1923; 1931; 1964; 1973(I); 1977; 1978(I); 1979(I); 1980(I); 1985; 1987; 1990; 2001(I); 2004
Albania	1914; 1920; 1925; 1928; 1939; 1943(R); 1946; 1976; 1991(I); 1998
Algeria	1963
Andorra	1993
Angola	1975
Antigua and Barbuda	1981
Argentina	1816(I); 1819; 1826; 1853; 1956(R)
Armenia	1978; 1995
Australia	1901
Austria	1920; 1934; 1945(R)
Austria-Hungary	1848; 1867
Azerbaijan	1991; 1995
Baden	1818
Bahamas	1973
Bahrain	1973; 2002
Bangladesh	1972*; 1986(R)
Barbados	1966
Bavaria	1808; 1818
Belarus (Byelorussia)	1994
Belgium	1831
Belize	1981
Benin	1960*; 1964*; 1968; 1970*; 1979; 1990
Bhutan	1953; 2005(I)

(continued)

TABLE A.1 *(continued)*

Country	Constitutions
Bolivia	1826; 1831; 1834; 1836; 1839; 1843; 1851; 1861; 1868; 1871; 1878; 1880; 1938*; 1945; 1947; 1961; 1964(R); 1967
Bosnia-Herzegovina	1910; 1995
Botswana	1966
Brazil	1824; 1891; 1930(I); 1934; 1937; 1946; 1967; 1988
Brunei	1959
Bulgaria	1879*; 1883(R)*; 1938(R); 1947; 1971; 1991
Burkina Faso (Upper Volta)	1960*; 1970*; 1977*; 1983; 1988; 1991
Burundi	1962*; 1974*; 1981*; 1992; 1998(I); 2004
Cambodia (Kampuchea)	1947; 1972; 1976; 1981; 1989; 1993
Cameroon	1961; 1972
Canada	1867
Cape Verde	1980
Central African Republic	1959; 1964; 1976; 1979(I); 1981; 1986; 1994*; 2004
Chad	1960; 1962*; 1978; 1982(I); 1989*; 1993(I); 1996
Chile	1818(I); 1822; 1823*; 1826(I); 1828; 1833; 1925; 1980
China	1912(I); 1914; 1916(R); 1923; 1928; 1947; 1949; 1954; 1975; 1978; 1982
Colombia	1830; 1832; 1843; 1853; 1858; 1861(I); 1863; 1886; 1991
Comoros	1975(I); 1978; 1992; 1996; 2001
Congo	1961; 1963; 1969; 1973*; 1979; 1991(I); 1992; 2001
Congo, Democratic Republic of (Zaire)	1960; 1961(I); 1964; 1967; 1978; 1997; 2003; 2005
Costa Rica	1825; 1841; 1844; 1847; 1848; 1859; 1869; 1871; 1917; 1919(R)*; 1949
Cote D'Ivoire	1960*; 2000
Croatia	1991
Cuba	1901; 1933(I); 1934; 1935; 1940; 1952; 1953(R); 1959; 1976
Cyprus	1960
Czech Republic	1993
Czechoslovakia	1918(I); 1920; 1948; 1960
Denmark	1849; 1866; 1915; 1953
Djibouti	1977; 1992
Dominica	1978
Dominican Republic	1844; 1854.1; 1854.2; 1858*; 1865; 1866; 1868; 1872; 1874; 1875; 1877; 1878; 1879; 1880; 1881; 1887; 1896; 1907; 1908; 1924; 1927; 1929.1; 1929.2; 1934; 1942; 1947; 1955; 1961; 1962; 1963; 1966; 1994; 2002
East Timor	2002

Country	Constitutions
Ecuador	1830; 1835; 1843; 1845; 1851; 1852; 1861; 1869; 1878; 1884; 1897; 1906; 1929; 1935(R)*; 1939(R); 1945; 1946; 1967*; 1972(R)*; 1976(R); 1978; 1984; 1993; 1996; 1997; 1998*
Egypt	1923; 1930*; 1935(R)*; 1953(I); 1956; 1958(I); 1962; 1964(I); 1971
El Salvador	1840; 1841; 1859; 1864; 1871; 1872; 1880; 1883; 1886; 1939; 1945(R); 1950*; 1962(R); 1983
Equatorial Guinea	1968; 1973; 1982; 1991
Eritrea	1997
Estonia	1919(I); 1920; 1933; 1937; 1978; 1992
Ethiopia	1931; 1955; 1974; 1976; 1987; 1991(I); 1994
Fiji	1970; 1990; 1997
Finland	1919; 1999
France	1791; 1793; 1795; 1799; 1802; 1804; 1814; 1815; 1830; 1848; 1852; 1875; 1940; 1946; 1958
Gabon	1960; 1961; 1975; 1991
Gambia	1962; 1970*; 1996
Georgia	1992(R); 1995
German Democratic Republic	1949; 1968
German Federal Republic	1949
Germany (Prussia)	1848; 1850; 1871; 1919
Ghana	1957; 1960*; 1969*; 1979*; 1982(I); 1992
Great Colombia	1821
Greece	1827*; 1844; 1864; 1925; 1926; 1927; 1935(R); 1944(R); 1952; 1968; 1974(R); 1975
Grenada	1974*; 1991(R)
Guatemala	1839(I); 1845; 1851; 1879; 1944(R); 1945; 1954(I); 1956*; 1965; 1982(I); 1985
Guinea	1958; 1982*; 1990
Guinea-Bissau	1973; 1984
Guyana	1966; 1970; 1980
Haiti	1801; 1805; 1806; 1807; 1811; 1816; 1843; 1844(R); 1846; 1849; 1859(R); 1867; 1874; 1876(R); 1879; 1888; 1889; 1902; 1932; 1935; 1946.1; 1946.2; 1950; 1957; 1964; 1983; 1987
Hanover	1819; 1833; 1837(R); 1840; 1848; 1855(R)
Hesse-Darmstadt (Ducal)	1820
Hesse-Kassel (Electoral)	1831; 1852; 1860(R)
Honduras	1839; 1848; 1865; 1873; 1874(R); 1880; 1894; 1904; 1908(R); 1921; 1924; 1936; 1957; 1965; 1982
Hungary	1919; 1920; 1946; 1949

(*continued*)

TABLE A.1 *(continued)*

Country	Constitutions
Iceland	1944
India	1949
Indonesia	1945; 1949; 1950(I); 1955; 1959(R)
Iran (Persia)	1906; 1979
Iraq	1925; 1958; 1964(I); 1970(I); 1990(I); 2004(I); 2005
Ireland	1919; 1922; 1937
Israel	1948
Italy/Sardinia	1848; 1861; 1943(I); 1947
Jamaica	1962
Japan	1889; 1946
Jordan	1946; 1952
Kazakhstan	1993(I); 1995
Kenya	1963
Kiribati	1979
Korea, People's Republic of	1948; 1972
Korea, Republic of	1948
Kuwait	1961(I); 1962; 1980(R)*; 1992(R)
Kyrgyz Republic	1993
Laos	1947; 1991
Latvia	1919; 1920(I); 1922; 1940; 1991(R)
Lebanon	1926
Lesotho	1966*; 1983*; 1993
Liberia	1847*; 1986
Libya	1951; 1969
Liechtenstein	1818; 1862; 1921
Lithuania	1918.1(I); 1918.2(I); 1919(I); 1920(I); 1922; 1928; 1938; 1990(I); 1992
Luxembourg	1856; 1868
Macedonia (Former Yugoslav Republic of)	1991
Madagascar (Malagasy)	1959; 1972(I); 1975; 1992; 1998
Malawi	1964; 1966; 1994
Malaysia	1957
Maldives	1968; 1998
Mali	1960*; 1974; 1992
Malta	1964
Marshall Islands	1979
Mauritania	1959; 1961; 1978; 1980; 1985; 1991
Mauritius	1968
Mecklenburg-Schwerin	1849
Mexico	1814; 1822; 1824; 1836*; 1843; 1846(R); 1856(I); 1857; 1865(I); 1867(R); 1917

Country	Constitutions
Micronesia, Fed. Sts.	1981
Moldova	1978; 1994
Monaco	1911*; 1917(R)*; 1962
Mongolia	1924; 1940; 1960; 1990(I); 1992
Montenegro	1905
Morocco	1962; 1970; 1972
Mozambique	1975; 1990; 2004
Myanmar (Burma)	1947; 1962; 1974*
Namibia	1990
Nauru	1968
Nepal	1948; 1951(I); 1959*; 1962; 1990
Netherlands	1795; 1798; 1801; 1805; 1806; 1815; 1848
New Zealand	1852
Nicaragua	1838; 1848; 1854; 1858; 1893; 1905; 1911; 1937; 1939; 1948; 1950; 1974*; 1987
Niger	1960*; 1989*; 1992; 1996; 1999
Nigeria	1960; 1963*; 1975; 1978*; 1989; 1993(R); 1999
Norway	1814
Oman	1996
Orange Free State	1854; 1879
Pakistan	1956*; 1962; 1969(I); 1973*; 1985(R)*; 2002(R)
Palau	1981
Panama	1904; 1940; 1946; 1972
Papua New Guinea	1975
Paraguay	1813; 1844; 1870; 1940; 1967; 1992
Peru	1826; 1827(R); 1828; 1834; 1839; 1855(I); 1856; 1860; 1867; 1868(R); 1920; 1933; 1979; 1993
Philippines	1945(R); 1973; 1986
Poland	1919; 1921; 1935; 1944(I); 1947; 1952; 1976; 1992; 1997
Portugal	1822*; 1826*; 1838(R); 1911*; 1933*; 1976
Qatar	1970(I); 2003
Romania	1866; 1923; 1938*; 1944(R); 1948; 1952; 1965; 1991
Russia (Soviet Union)	1905; 1918; 1924; 1936; 1977; 1993
Rwanda	1962; 1978; 1995; 2003
Samoa	1962
Sao Tome and Principe	1975
Saudi Arabia	1926; 1992
Saxony	1820; 1831
Senegal	1959; 1963; 2001
Serbia	1869; 1888; 1894(R); 1901; 1903
Seychelles	1975(I); 1979; 1993
Sierra Leone	1961*; 1968(R); 1978; 1991*
Singapore	1959

(*continued*)

Appendix

TABLE A.1 *(continued)*

Country	Constitutions
Slovakia	1992
Slovenia	1991
Solomon Islands	1978
Somalia	1960*; 1979
South Africa	1909; 1961; 1983; 1993; 1996
Spain	1808; 1812*; 1820(R)*; 1834; 1836(R); 1837; 1845; 1861(R); 1869; 1876; 1931; 1936(I); 1967; 1978
Sri Lanka (Ceylon)	1946; 1972; 1978
St. Kitts and Nevis	1983
St. Lucia	1978
St. Vincent and the Grenadines	1979
Sudan	1955(I)*; 1964(R)*; 1971(I); 1973; 1985(I)*; 1998; 2005(I)
Surinam	1975*; 1981(I); 1982(I); 1987
Swaziland	1968; 2005
Sweden	1809; 1974
Switzerland	1798; 1802; 1803; 1815; 1848; 1874; 1999
Syria	1943(R)*; 1950*; 1953; 1954(R); 1958(I); 1961(I); 1964(I)*; 1969(I); 1973
Taiwan	1947
Tajikistan	1994
Tanzania/Tanganyika	1961; 1962; 1965(I); 1977; 1985
Thailand	1932; 1946; 1947; 1949; 1952(R)*; 1959(I); 1960(I); 1968*; 1972(I); 1974; 1976; 1977(I); 1978*; 1983(R); 1991(I); 1997
Togo	1960(I); 1961; 1963*; 1971; 1979; 1992
Tonga	1875
Transvaal	1856; 1906
Trinidad and Tobago	1962; 1976
Tunisia	1956(I); 1957(I); 1959
Turkey/Ottoman Empire	1876*; 1908(R); 1921; 1924; 1945; 1961; 1982
Turkmenistan	1992
Tuvalu	1978; 1986
Uganda	1962; 1966; 1967*; 1981(R); 1995
Ukraine	1978; 1996
United Arab Emirates	1971(I)
United Provinces of Central America	1824; 1835
United States of America	1789
Uruguay	1830; 1918*; 1934; 1952; 1966; 1985(R)
Uzbekistan	1992

Country	Constitutions
Vanuatu	1980
Venezuela	1821; 1830; 1857; 1858; 1864; 1874; 1881; 1891; 1893; 1901; 1904; 1909; 1914.1; 1914.2; 1922; 1925; 1928; 1929; 1931; 1936; 1945; 1947; 1948(R); 1953; 1961; 1999
Vietnam, Democratic Republic of	1960; 1980; 1992
Vietnam, Republic of	1956*; 1964(I); 1965(I); 1967
Wurttemberg	1806; 1815; 1819
Yemen (Arab Republic of Yemen)	1962(I); 1970; 1974(I); 1991
Yemen, People's Republic of	1970
Yugoslavia (Serbia)	1921; 1931; 1946; 1953; 1963; 1974; 1992; 2003
Zambia	1964; 1973; 1991
Zimbabwe (Rhodesia)	1965; 1969; 1979

Note: I = interim constitution; R = reinstated constitution; * = constitution died through suspension, not replacement by another new, interim, or reinstated constitution.

TABLE A.2. *List of items used in the scope and similarity indices*

Question ID	Question text
AMEND	Does the constitution provide for at least one procedure for amending the constitution?
ARTISTS	Does the constitution refer to artists or the arts?
ATGEN	Does the constitution provide for an attorney general or public prosecutor responsible for representing the government in criminal or civil cases?
BANK	Does the constitution contain provisions for a central bank?
BANKRUPT	Does the constitution mention bankruptcy law?
CABINET	Does the constitution mention the executive cabinet/ministers?
CAPPUN	How does the constitution treat the use of capital punishment?
CC	Does the constitution contain provisions for a counter corruption commission?
CENSUS	Does the constitution specify a census?
COMCHIEF	Who is the commander in chief of the armed forces?
COMMIT	Are legislative committees mentioned in the constitution?
CORPPUN	How does the constitution treat the use of corporal punishment?
CUSTLAW	Does the constitution refer to "customary" international law or the "law of nations?"
DEPEXEC	Does the constitution specify a deputy executive of any kind (e.g., deputy prime minister, vice president)?
ECONPLAN	Does the constitution mention the adoption of national economic plans?
EDUCATE	Does the constitution contain provisions concerning education?
EM	Does the constitution have provisions for calling a state of emergency?
ENV	Does the constitution refer to protection or preservation of the environment?
EXECNUM	How many executives are specified in the constitution?
EXSESS_98	Who, if anybody, can convene an extraordinary session of the legislature or extend an ongoing session?
FEDERAL_98	Does the constitution recognize any subnational governments?
FORTRAD	Does the constitution mention foreign or international trade?
GOVMED	How does the constitution address the state operation of print or electronic media?
HEADFORN	Who is the representative of the state for foreign affairs?
HOSDEC	Does the head of state have decree power?
HOSELECT	How is the head of state selected?
HOSIMM	Is the head of state provided with immunity from prosecution?
HOSSUCC	Should the head of state need to be replaced before the normally scheduled replacement process, what is the process of replacement?
HR	Does the constitution contain provisions for a human rights commission?

Question ID	Question Text
INTERP	To whom does the constitution assign the responsibility for the interpretation of the constitution?
INTLAW	Does the constitution contain provisions concerning the relationship between the constitution and international law?
INTORGS	Does the constitution contain provisions concerning international organizations?
JC	Does the constitution contain provisions for a judicial council/commission?
JREM	Are there provisions for dismissing judges?
JUDCRTS_1	Does the constitution provide for administrative courts?
JUDCRTS_2	Does the constitution provide for a constitutional court?
JUDCRTS_3	Does the constitution provide for courts of amparo?
JUDCRTS_4	Does the constitution provide for military courts?
JUDCRTS_5	Does the constitution provide for courts charged with cases against public office-holders?
JUDCRTS_6	Does the constitution provide for tax courts?
JUDCRTS_7	Does the constitution provide for labor courts?
JUDCRTS_8	Does the constitution provide for religious courts?
JUDCRTS_9	Does the constitution provide for other special courts?
LANG	Does the constitution specify either an official or national language?
LEGAPP	Who has the power to approve/reject legislation once it has been passed by the legislature (not including reviews for constitutionality)?
LEVJUD	Does the court system provide for a supreme court and/or other specified courts?
LHSELECT_98	How are members of the first (or only) chamber of the legislature selected?
MEDCOM	Does the constitution mention a special regulatory body/ institution to oversee the media market?
MILITARY	Is the military or armed forces mentioned in the constitution?
NAT	Does the constitution refer to nationals, subjects, or citizens?
NATCIT	Does the constitution provide for naturalized citizens?
OATH	Does the constitution stipulate that some public office holders take an oath to support or abide by the constitution?
OFFREL	Does the constitution contain provisions concerning a national or official religion or a national or official church?
OMBUDS	Does the constitution provide for an ombudsman?
OVERSGHT	Does the constitution provide for an electoral commission or electoral court to oversee the election process?
PART	Does the constitution refer to political parties?
PREAMBLE	Does the constitution have an introduction or preamble?
QUORUM	Is a quorum required for a session of the legislature to be official?

(continued)

TABLE A.2 *(continued)*

Question ID	Question Text
REMLEG	Are there provisions for removing individual legislators?
SOCCLAS	Does the constitution have any provisions with respect to social class?
SPECLEG_1	Does the constitution provide for organic laws?
SPECLEG_2	Does the constitution provide for budget bills?
SPECLEG_3	Does the constitution provide for tax bills?
SPECLEG_4	Does the constitution provide for finance bills?
SPECLEG_5	Does the constitution provide for spending bills?
TRANPROV	Does the constitution contain any transitional provisions?
TREAT	Does the constitution mention international treaties?
TRUTHCOM	Does the constitution provide for a commission for truth and reconciliation?
VOTERES	Does the constitution place any restrictions on the right to vote?
WAR	Who has the power to declare war?

Note: All questions recoded to dummy variables such that 1 indicates the presence of a specific provision.

Source: Comparative Constitutions Project.

TABLE A.3. *Descriptive statistics for country-year variables*

Concept	Raw data					Imputed data				
	Obs.	Mean	Standard deviation	Min.	Max.	Obs.	Mean	Standard deviation	Min.	Max.
Global Constitutional Events	13766	0.145	0.095	0	0.46	13766	0.145	0.095	0	1
Neighboring Constitutional Events	13766	0.054	0.122	0	1	13766	0.054	0.122	0	1
Territory Gain	13766	0.032	0.177	0	1	13766	0.032	0.177	0	1
Territory Loss	13764	0.02	0.14	0	1	13766	0.022	0.147	0	1
Defeat in War	13766	0.042	0.201	0	1	13766	0.042	0.201	0	1
Domestic Crisis	8711	0.106	0.308	0	1	13766	0.086	0.280	0	1
Economic Crisis	8970	0.072	0.259	0	1	13766	0.064	0.244	0	1
Democratic Transition	11306	0.047	0.211	0	1	13766	0.071	0.256	0	1
Authoritarian Transition	11305	0.032	0.177	0	1	13766	0.079	0.269	0	1
Extra-constitutional Leadership Change	10648	0.105	0.307	0	1	13766	0.171	0.377	0	1
Intra-constitutional Leadership Change	10595	0.235	0.424	0	1	13766	0.222	0.416	0	1
Democracy	11500	0.415	0.493	0	1	13766	0.343	0.475	0	1
Ethnic Heterogeneity	11717	0.420	0.257	0	1	13766	0.411	0.258	0	1
Economic Development	11077	0.014	0.062	0	1	13766	0.013	0.062	0	1
State Age	13766	0.129	0.197	0	1	13766	0.129	0.197	0	1
Latin America	13766	0.273	0.445	0	1	13766	0.273	0.445	0	1
Eastern Europe	13766	0.100	0.300	0	1	13766	0.100	0.300	0	1
Middle East	13766	0.078	0.268	0	1	13766	0.078	0.268	0	1
Africa	13766	0.150	0.357	0	1	13766	0.150	0.357	0	1
South Asia	13766	0.024	0.152	0	1	13766	0.024	0.152	0	1
East Asia	13766	.0069	0.253	0	1	13766	0.069	0.253	0	1
Oceania	13766	0.040	0.196	0	1	13766	0.040	0.196	0	1
1914–1945	13766	0.140	0.347	0	1	13766	0.140	0.347	0	1
After 1945	13766	0.589	0.492	0	1	13766	0.589	0.492	0	1

TABLE A.4. *Descriptive statistics for constitutional variables*

Variable	Raw data					Imputed data				
	Obs.	Mean	Standard deviation	Min.	Max.	Obs.	Mean	Standard deviation	Min.	Max.
Interim Constitution	935	0.094	0.292	0	1	935	0.094	0.292	0	1
Reinstated Constitution	935	0.062	0.241	0	1	935	0.062	0.241	0	1
Legacy of Endurance	935	0.077	0.072	0	1	935	0.077	0.072	0	1
Inclusiveness	411	0.367	0.225	0	1	935	0.161	0.235	0	1
Democratic at Promulgation	769	0.289	0.453	0	1	935	0.222	0.416	0	1
Occupation Constitution	935	0.067	0.251	0	1	935	0.067	0.251	0	1
Amendment Rate	454	0.377	0.375	0	1	935	0.374	0.394	0	1
Judicial Review in Authoritarian Regimes	576	0.559	0.497	0	1	935	0.646	0.478	0	1
Judicial Review in Democratic Regimes	502	0.225	0.418	0	1	935	0.166	0.372	0	1
Scope	576	0.491	0.114	0.10	0.79	935	0.467	0.119	0.08	0.79
Detail	572	0.110	0.089	0.01	0.62	935	0.098	0.080	0	0.62
Single Executive	557	0.585	0.493	0	1	935	0.446	0.497	0	1
Executive Term Limits	536	0.461	0.499	0	1	935	0.296	0.457	0	1
Parliamentary Power	575	0.337	0.125	0.05	0.67	935	0.337	0.132	0.03	0.84

TABLE A.5. *Duration models of constitutional endurance*[1]

Variable	Model 1	Model 2	Model 3	Model 4	Model 5
Global Constitutional Events	1.13**	1.17***		1.09	1.13**
	(0.05)	(0.05)		(0.11)	(0.06)
Neighboring Constitutional Events	2.13**	2.35***		1.03	2.44***
	(0.56)	(0.61)		(0.74)	(0.70)
Gain of Territory	1.19	1.12		0.88	1.22
	(0.24)	(0.22)		(0.38)	(0.29)
Loss of Territory	1.16	1.15		1.11	1.12
	(0.29)	(0.28)		(0.59)	(0.33)
Defeat in War	1.08	1.24		0.90	1.07
	(0.19)	(0.21)		(0.44)	(0.21)
Domestic Crisis	1.33*	1.23		1.54	1.20
	(0.21)	(0.18)		(0.45)	(0.22)
Economic Crisis	1.14	1.17		1.58	1.09
	(0.17)	(0.17)		(0.48)	(0.19)
Democratic Transition	1.48**	1.43**		1.39	1.45**
	(0.22)	(0.20)		(0.45)	(0.24)
Authoritarian Transition	1.30*	1.30*		2.08*	1.12
	(0.19)	(0.19)		(0.70)	(0.19)
Extra-constitutional Leadership Change	1.88***	1.98***		1.72*	2.02***
	(0.20)	(0.21)		(0.45)	(0.23)
Intra-constitutional Leadership Change	0.90	0.76**		0.74	0.97
	(0.11)	(0.08)		(0.17)	(0.14)
Interim Constitution	2.09***		2.39***	2.69*	2.00***
	(0.33)		(0.36)	(1.31)	(0.36)
Reinstated Constitution	0.73		0.82	0.72	0.67*
	(0.14)		(0.15)	(0.28)	(0.15)
Inclusiveness	0.32***		0.32***	0.21**	0.39***
	(0.07)		(0.07)	(0.12)	(0.10)
Democracy at Promulgation	1.12		1.01		
	(0.17)		(0.14)		
Occupation Constitution	1.07		1.01	1.46	1.11
	(0.19)		(0.17)	(0.94)	(0.21)
Amendment Rate	0.21**		0.26**	0.39	0.20**
	(0.12)		(0.15)	(0.58)	(0.12)
Amendment Rate Squared	1.15**		1.14**	1.09	1.15**
	(0.06)		(0.07)	(0.14)	(0.07)

(*continued*)

TABLE A.5 *(continued)*

Variable	Model 1	Model 2	Model 3	Model 4	Model 5
Judicial Review in Authoritarian Regimes	1.15 (0.15)		1.20 (0.14)	1.22 (0.76)	1.17 (0.17)
Judicial Review in Democratic Regimes	1.13 (0.26)		0.98 (0.15)	1.19 (0.69)	0.99 (0.36)
Scope	0.43 (0.26)		0.31* (0.20)	0.18 (0.36)	0.46 (0.30)
Detail	0.14** (0.11)		0.10** (0.09)	0.02** (0.03)	0.20 (0.20)
Single Executive	0.96 (0.10)		0.97 (0.10)	0.91 (0.30)	1.01 (0.11)
Executive Term Limits	0.75** (0.08)		0.80* (0.09)	0.90 (0.34)	0.69*** (0.08)
Parliamentary Power	1.00 (0.45)		1.02 (0.49)	0.46 (0.70)	0.93 (0.45)
Democracy	0.81 (0.16)			0.84 (0.45)	1.02 (0.27)
Ethnic Heterogeneity	1.52 (0.47)			1.02 (0.98)	1.67 (0.56)
Economic Development	0.11 (0.18)			0.00 (0.00)	0.16 (0.26)
Age of the State	1.73* (0.53)			1.01 (0.70)	2.09* (0.75)
Legacy of Endurance	0.01*** (0.01)		0.01*** (0.01)	0.06 (0.12)	0.01*** (0.01)
Latin America	2.68*** (0.45)	2.27*** (0.30)	2.39*** (0.34)	3.59** (1.64)	2.43*** (0.45)
Eastern Europe	2.09*** (0.42)	2.14*** (0.36)	1.60** (0.28)	1.57 (0.73)	2.14*** (0.50)
Middle East	1.17 (0.27)	1.71*** (0.34)	0.97 (0.21)	2.37 (1.50)	1.10 (0.29)
Sub-Saharan Africa	2.01** (0.49)	2.68*** (0.43)	1.89*** (0.32)	2.74 (1.75)	1.79** (0.49)
South Asia	1.60 (0.57)	1.88** (0.57)	1.54 (0.50)	3.65* (2.39)	0.98 (0.45)
East Asia	1.84** (0.39)	2.15*** (0.42)	1.56** (0.31)	2.01 (1.04)	1.82** (0.46)
Oceania	0.26**	0.23**	0.26**	0.98	0.10**

Variable	Model 1	Model 2	Model 3	Model 4	Model 5
	(0.16)	(0.14)	(0.16)	(0.84)	(0.10)
1914–1945	1.32*	1.09	1.50***	3.16**	1.12
	(0.18)	(0.14)	(0.20)	(1.14)	(0.18)
After 1945	1.15	0.71***	1.26	2.37*	1.07
	(0.16)	(0.08)	(0.17)	(0.91)	(0.18)
Failures	675	675	675	542	133
Observations	13,766	13,766	13,766	3717	10,049

Note: Cox proportional hazard models – hazard ratios reported with standard errors in parentheses; * significant at 10%, ** significant at 5%, *** significant at 1%; Model 1 – full model (estimates and predictions from this model reported in chapter 6); Model 2 – crisis variables only; Model 3 – constitutional structure variables only; Model 4 – democratic constitutions only; Model 5 – authoritarian constitutions only.

References

Aalen, Odd O. and Håkon K. Gjessing. 2001. Understanding the Shape of the Hazard Rate: A Process Point of View. *Statistical Science* 16: 1–22.

Aba-Namay, Rashad. 1993. The Recent Constitutional Reform in Saudi Arabia. *International and Comparative Law Quarterly* 42(3): 295–331.

Acemoglu, Daron and James Robinson, 2005. *Economic Origins of Dictatorship and Democracy*. New York: Cambridge University Press.

Achen, Christopher. 1987. *The Statistical Analysis of Quasi-Experiments*. Berkeley: University of California Press.

———. 2002. Toward a New Political Methodology: Microfoundations and ART. *Annual Review of Political Science* 5: 423–50.

Ackerman, Bruce. 1993. *We the People*. Cambridge, MA: Harvard University Press.

———. 2005. *The Failure of the Founding Fathers: Jefferson, Marshall and the Rise of Presidential Democracy*. Cambridge, MA: Harvard University Press.

———. 2007. The Living Constitution. *Harvard Law Review* 120(7): 1738–1812.

Ackerman, Bruce and James S. Fishkin. 2005. *Deliberation Day*. New Haven: Yale University Press.

Alesina, Alberto and Enrico Spolaore. 2003. *The Size of Nations*. Cambridge, MA: MIT Press.

Allison, Paul D. 2001. *Missing Data*. Sage University Papers Series on Quantitative Applications in the Social Sciences, 07-136. Thousand Oaks, CA: Sage.

Amar, Akhil. 2006. *America's Constitution: A Biography*. New York: Random House.

Anderson, Benedict. 2006. *Imagined Communities*. New York: Verso (revised edition).

Andrade, Eduardo. 1999. ¿Nueva Constitución? ¿Para Qué? In *Hacia Una Nueva Constitucionalidad*, edited by Celia Carreón Trujillo and Isidro Saucedo. Mexico City: Universidad Nacional Autónoma de México.

Apreza, Inés Castro. 1997. *Presidencialismo*. In *Encyclopedia of Mexico*, edited by Michael Werner. Chicago: Fitzroy Dearborn Publishers.

Arjomand, Said, ed. 2007. *Constitutionalism and Political Reconstruction*. Leiden: E.J. Brill.

Arthur, Brian. 1994. *Increasing Returns and Path Dependence in the Economy*. Ann Arbor: University of Michigan Press.

Atkins, G. Pope and Larman Curtis Wilson. 1998. *The Dominican Republic and the United States: From Imperialism to Transnationalism.* Athens: University of Georgia Press.

Austin, Granville. 1972. *The Indian Constitution: Cornerstone of a Nation.* Oxford, UK: Oxford University Press

———. 1999. *Working a Democratic Constitution: A History of the Indian Experience.* Oxford, UK: Oxford University Press.

Ayres, Ian and Robert Gertner. 1989. Filling Gaps in Incomplete Contracts: An Economic Theory of Default Rules. *Yale Law Journal* 99: 87–130.

Bailyn, Bernard. 2003. *To Begin the World Anew.* New York: Vintage Books.

Banks, Arthur S. 2001. *Cross National Time Series Data Archive.* Available at http://www.databanks.sitehosting.net/Default.htm.

Barro, Robert and José F. Ursúa. 2008. Macroeconomic Crises Since 1870. *NBER Working Paper No.* 13940.

Basler, Roy, ed. 1953. *The Collected Works of Abraham Lincoln* Vol 4. New Brunswick, NJ: Rutgers University Press.

Basu, D.D. 1994. *Introduction to the Constitution of India.* 16th ed. Delhi: Prentice Hall.

Beer, Lawrence and John M. Maki. 2002. *From Imperial Myth to Democracy: Japan's Two Constitutions 1889–2002.* Boulder: University Press of Colorado.

Berkowitz, Daniel and Karen Clay. 2005. American Civil Law Origins: Implications for State Constitutions. *American Law and Economics Review* 7(1): 62–82.

Bhargava, Rajeev. 2003. Liberal, Secular Democracy and Explanations of Hind Nationalism. In *Decentring the Indian Nation*, edited by Andrew Wyatt and John Zavos. Portland, OR: Frank Cass. First published in *Commonwealth & Comparative Politics* 40 (November 2002): 72–96.

———. 2004. India's Secular Constitution. In *India's Living Constitution*, edited by E. Sridharan, Zoya Hasan, R. Sudarshan. London: Anthem.

———. 2008. Introduction: Outline of a Political Theory of the Indian Constitution. In *Politics and Ethics of the Indian Constitution*, edited by Rajeev Bhargava. New York: Oxford University Press, 1–42.

Boudreaux, Donald and A. C. Pritchard. 1993. Rewriting the Constitution: An Economic Analysis of the Constitutional Amendment Process. *Fordham Law Review* 62(1): 111–62.

Box-Steffensmeier, Jan and Bradford Jones. 2004. *Event History Modeling.* New York: Cambridge University Press.

Brady, Henry and David Collier, eds. 2004. *Rethinking Social Inquiry.* Lanham, MD: Rowman and Littlefield.

Brennan, Geoffrey and Jose Casas Pardo. 1991. A Reading of the Spanish Constitution (1978). *Constitutional Political Economy* 2(1): 53–79.

Breslin, Beau. 2009. *From Words to Worlds: Exploring Constitutional Functionality.* Baltimore: Johns Hopkins University Press.

Brown, Nathan. 2001. *Constitutions in a Nonconstitutional World: Arab Basic Laws & the Prospects for Accountable Government.* Albany, NY: SUNY Press.

———. 2008. Reason, Interest, Rationality, and Passion in Constitution Drafting. *PS: Political Science and Politics* 6(4): 675–89.

Buchanan, James M. 1993. How Can Constitutions Be Designed so that Politicians Who Seek to Serve "Public Interest" Can Survive and Prosper? *Constitutional Political Economy* 4(1): 1–6.

————. 1990. The Domain of Constitutional Economics. *Constitutional Political Economy*, 1(1): 1–18.

Buchanan, James and Gordon Tullock. 1961. *The Calculus of Consent*. Ann Arbor: University of Michigan Press.

Burke, Edmund. 1790. Reflections on the Revolution in France. In Collected Works. Available at http://www.gutenberg.org/browse/authors/b#a842.

Burnham, Walter D. 1970. *Critical Elections and the Mainsprings of American Politics*. New York: W.W. Norton Publishers.

Cao, Deborah. 2004. *Chinese Law: A Language Perspective*. Burlington, VT: Ashgate Publishing.

Carbonell, Miguel. 1999. La Constitución de 1917 Hoy: Cinco Retos Inmediatos. In *Hacia Una Nueva Constitucionalidad*, edited by Celia Carreón Trujillo and Isidro Saucedo. Mexico City: Universidad Nacional Autónoma de México.

Carey, John. 2000. Parchment, Equilibria, and Institutions. *Comparative Political Studies* 33: 735–61.

————. 2009a. The Reelection Debate in Latin America. In *New Perspectives on Democracy in Latin America: Actors, Institutions and Practices*, edited by William C. Smith. Malden, MA: Blackwell Publishing, Inc.

————. 2009b. Does it matter how a constitution is created? *Is Democracy Exportable?* edited by Zoltan Barany and Robert G. Moser. New York: Cambridge University Press: 155–77.

Carpizo, Jorge. 1999. México: ¿Hacia una Nueva Constitución? In *Hacia una Nueva Constitucionalidad*, edited by Celia Carreón Trujillo and Isidro Saucedo. Mexico City: Universidad Nacional Autónoma de México.

Castañeda, Jorge. 2001. *Perpetuating Power: How Mexican Presidents were Chosen*. New York: The New Press.

Cheibub, Jose. 2007. *Presidentialism, Parliamentarism, and Democracy*. New York: Cambridge University Press.

Choudhry, Sujit. 2006. *The Migration of Constitutional Ideas*. New York: Cambridge University Press.

————. 2009. Managing Linguistic Nationalism through Constitutional Design: Lessons from South Asia. *International Journal of Constitutional Law*: __-__.

Chwe, Michael Suk-Young. 2003. *Rational Ritual: Culture, Coordination, and Common Knowledge*. Princeton, NJ: Princeton University Press.

Clarke, Donald. 2003. Puzzling Observations in Chinese Law: When is a Riddle Just a Mistake? In *Understanding China's Legal System: Essays in Honor of Jerome Cohen*, edited by C. Stephen Hsu. New York: New York University Press.

Cohen, Stephen. 2004. *The Idea of Pakistan*. Washington, DC: Brookings Institution Press.

Collier, David. 1993. The Comparative Method. In *Political Science: The State of the Discipline II*, edited by Ada W. Finifter. Washington, DC: American Political Science Association.

Congleton, Roger D. 2003a. *Improving Democracy through Constitutional Reform: Some Swedish Lessons*. Boston: Kluwer Academic Publishers.

———. 2003b. Social Science and History: How Predictable Is Political Behavior? Unpublished Manuscript.

Congleton, Roger D. and Birgitta Sweborg, eds. 2006. *Democratic Constitutional Design and Public Policy.* Cambridge, MA: Massachusetts Institute of Technology Press.

Cooter, Robert. 2000. *The Strategic Constitution.* Princeton, NJ: Princeton University Press.

Cortell, Andrew P. and Susan Peterson. 1999. Altered States: Explaining Institutional Change. *British Journal of Political Science* 29: 177–203.

Currier, Charles F. A. 1893. Constitutional and Organic Laws of France. *Annals of the American Academy of Political and Social Science.* 3(Supp. 4): 1–77.

Dahl, Robert. 1989. *Democracy and its Critics.* New Haven: Yale University Press.

———. 2001. *How Democratic is the American Constitution?* New Haven: Yale University Press.

Dahrendorf, Ralf. 1990. *Reflections on the Revolution in Europe.* London: Chatto and Windus.

David, Paul A. 1985. Clio and the Economics of QWERTY. *American Economic Review* 75: 332–37.

de Figueiredo, Rui and Barry Weingast. 2005. Self-enforcing Federalism. *Journal of Law, Economics, and Organization* 21: 103–35.

Derry, T.K. 1979. *A History of Scandinavia: Norway, Sweden, Denmark, Finland, and Iceland.* Minneapolis: University of Minnesota Press.

Dershowitz, Alan. 2001. *Supreme Injustice: How the High Court Hijacked Election 2000.* New York: Oxford University Press.

Dicey, Albert Venn. 1960. *Introduction to the Study of the Law of the Constitution.* London: MacMillan.

Dippel, Horst. 2005. *Index of European Constitutions 1850 to 2003.* Munchen: K.G. Saur Verlag.

———. 2008. *The Rise of Modern Constitutionalism 1776–1849.* K.G. Saur Verlag. Available at http://hc.rediris.es/04/Numero04.html?id=16.

Dower, John. 2000. *Embracing Defeat: Japan in the Wake of World War II.* New York: W.W. Norton & Company.

Durand, John D. 1960. Mortality Estimates from Roman Tombstone Inscriptions. *American Journal of Sociology* 65(4): 365–73.

Eisenstadt, Todd. 2004. *Courting Democracy in Mexico: Party Strategies and Electoral Institutions.* New York: Cambridge University Press.

Elazar, Daniel. 1985. Constitution-Making: The Preeminently Political Act. In *Redesigning the State: The Politics of Constitutional Change*, edited by Keith G. Banting and Richard Simeon. London: Macmillan Press.

Elkins, Zachary. 2009. Constitutional Networks. In *Networked Politics: Agency, Power, and Governance*, edited by Miles Kahler. Ithaca, NY: Cornell University Press.

Elkins, Zachary, Tom Ginsburg and James Melton. 2008. Baghdad, Tokyo, Kabul: Constitution-making in Occupied States. *William and Mary Law Review* 49: 1139–78.

Elkins, Zachary and Beth Simmons. 2005. On Waves, Clusters, and Diffusion: A Conceptual Framework. *Annals of the American Academy of Political and Social Science* 598: 33–51.

Elkins, Zachary and John Sides. 2007. Can Institutions Build Unity in Multiethnic States? *American Political Science Review* 101: 693–708.

Elliot, Jonathan, ed. 1784–1846. *Elliot's Debates.* 5: 508. Available at http://lcweb2 .loc.gov/ammem/amlaw/lwed.html.

Elster, Jon. 1995. Forces and Mechanisms in the Constitution-making Process. *Duke Law Review* 45: 364–96.

––––––. 1997. Ways of Constitution-making. In *Democracy's Victory and Crisis*, edited by Axel Hadenius. New York: Cambridge University Press: 123–42.

––––––. 2000. Arguing and Bargaining in Two Constituent Assemblies. *University of Pennsylvania Journal of Constitutional Law* 2: 345–421.

––––––. 2006. Legislatures as Constituent Assemblies. In *The Least Examined Branch: The Role of Legislatures in the Constitutional State*, edited by R. W. Bauman and T. Kahana. Cambridge: Cambridge University Press.

––––––. Forthcoming. *Unwritten Constitutional Norms.*

Elster, Jon, Claus Offe and Ulrich K. Preuss. 1998. *Institutional Design in Post-Communist Societies: Rebuilding the Ship at Sea.* New York: Cambridge University Press.

Engel, David. 1975. *Law and Kingship in Thailand during the Reign of King Chula-longkorn.* Ann Arbor: University of Michigan Center for Southeast Asian Studies.

Epp, Charles. 1998. *The Rights Revolution: Lawyers, Activists, and Supreme Courts in Comparative Perspective.* Chicago: The University of Chicago Press.

Epstein, Lee and Jack Knight. 1998. *The Choices Justices Make.* Washington, DC: CQ Press.

Eskridge, William and John Ferejohn. 2001. Super-Statutes. *Duke Law Journal* 50(5): 1215–76.

Fearon, James D. 2003. Ethnic and Cultural Diversity by Country. *Journal of Economic Growth* 8: 195–222.

Feldman, Noah. 2005. Imposed Constitutionalism. *Connecticut Law Review* 37: 857–89.

Ferejohn, John. 1997. The Politics of Imperfection: The Amendment of Constitutions. *Law and Social Inquiry* 22: 501–31.

Finer, S.E. 1979. *Five Constitutions.* Atlantic Highlands, NJ: Humanities Press.

––––––. 1988. Note Towards a History of Constitutions. In *Constitutions in Democratic Politics*, edited by Vernon Bogdanor. Aldershot, UK: Gower.

Finkel, Jodi. 2008. *Judicial Reform as Political Insurance.* South Bend, IN: University of Notre Dame Press.

Fish, M. Steven. 2006. Stronger Legislatures, Stronger Democracy. *Journal of Democracy* 17(1): 5–20.

Fish, M. Steven and Mathew Kroenig. 2009. *The Handbook of National Legislatures: A Global Survey.* New York: Cambridge University Press.

Fishkin, James S. 1991. *Democracy and Deliberation: New Directions for Democratic Reform.* New Haven: Yale University Press.

Freedom House. 2006. *Freedom in the World.* Washington, DC: Freedom House.

Fuller, Lon. 1977. *The Morality of Law.* Revised edition. New Haven: Yale University Press.

Geddes, Barbara. 1990. How the Cases You Choose Affect the Answers You Get: Selection Bias in Comparative Politics. *Political Analysis* 2: 131–50.

Gillette, Clayton. 1997. The Exercise of Trumps by Decentralized Governments. *Virginia Law Review.* 83(7): 1347–1418.

Gillman, Howard. 2001. *The Votes that Counted: How the Court Decided the 2000 Presidential Election.* Chicago: University of Chicago Press.

Ginsburg, Tom. 2003. *Judicial Review in New Democracies.* New York: Cambridge University Press.

———. 2009. Constitutional Afterlife: The Continuing Impact of Thailand's Post-Political Constitution. *International Journal of Constitutional Law* 7(1): 83–105.

Ginsburg, Tom, Zachary Elkins, and Justin Blount. 2009. Does the Process of Constitution-Making Matter? *Annual Review of Law and Social Science* 5: __-__.

Ginsburg, Tom and Nuno Garoupa. 2009. Reputation and the Industrial Organization of the Judiciary. *Unpublished Manuscript.*

Ginsburg, Tom and Richard McAdams. 2004. Adjudicating in Anarchy: An Expressive Theory of International Dispute Resolution. *William and Mary Law Review* 45(4): 1229–1340.

Ginsburg, Tom and Tamir Moustafa, eds. 2008. *Rule by Law: The Politics of Courts in Authoritarian Regimes.* New York: Cambridge University Press.

Gleditsch, Kristian S. and Michael D. Ward. 1999. Interstate System Membership: A Revised List of the Independent States since 1816. *International Interactions* 25: 393–413.

Gleditsch, Kristian S. and Michael D. Ward. 2006. *List of Independent States.* Last modified December 31, 2006. http://privatewww.essex.ac.uk/~ksg/statelist.html.

Gleijeses, Piero. 1978. *The Dominican Crisis: The 1965 Constitutionalist Revolt and American Intervention.* Baltimore: Johns Hopkins University Press.

Go, Julian. 2003. A Globalizing Constitutionalism? Views from the Postcolony. *International Sociology* 18(1): 71–95.

Goemans, H.E., Kristin Gleditsch, and Giacomo Chiozza. 2009. Introducing Archigos: A Dataset of Political Leaders. *Journal of Peace Research* 46(2): 269–83.

Goldstone, Lawrence. 2005. *Dark Bargain: Slavery, Profits, and the Struggle for the Constitution.* New York: Walker Publishing Company.

Graber, Mark. 2006. *Dred Scott and the Problem of Constitutional Evil.* New York: Cambridge University Press.

Greene, Kenneth F. 2007. *Why Dominant Parties Lose: Mexico's Democratization in Comparative Perspective.* New York: Cambridge University Press.

Grey, Thomas. 1975. Do We Have an Unwritten Constitution? *Stanford Law Review* 27: 703–18.

Haine, W. Scott. 2000. *The History of France.* Westport, CT: Greenwood Press.

Hamburger, Phillip. 1989. The Constitution's Accommodation of Social Change. *Michigan Law Review* 88: 239–327.

Hammons, Christopher. 1999. Was James Madison Wrong? Rethinking the American Preference for Short, Framework-Oriented Constitutions. *American Political Science Review* 93(4): 837–49.

Handley, Paul. 2006. *The King Never Smiles.* New Haven: Yale University Press.

Harding, Andrew. 2007. Buddhism, Human Rights and Constitutional Reform in Thailand. *Asian Journal of Comparative Law* 1, available at http://works.bepress.com/andrew_harding/1.

Harris II, William F. 1993. *The Interpretable Constitution.* Baltimore: Johns Hopkins University Press.

Hardin, Russell. 1989. Why a Constitution? In *The Federalist Papers and the New Institutionalism*, edited by Bernard Grofman and Donald Wittman. New York: Agathon Press.

Harnecker, Marta. 2002. *Hugo Chavez: Un Hombre, Un Pueblo*. San Sebastian, Spain: Editorial.

Hartlyn, Jonathan. 1991. The Dominican Republic: The Legacy of Intermittent Intervention. In *Exporting Democracy: The United States and Latin America*, edited by Abraham Lowenthal. Baltimore: Johns Hopkins University Press.

———. 1998. *The Struggle for Democratic Politics in the Dominican Republic*. Chapel Hill: University of North Carolina Press.

Hartlyn, Jonathan and Arturo Valenzuela. 1998. Democracy in Latin America Since 1930. In *Latin American Politics and Society Since 1930*, edited by Leslie Bethell. New York: Cambridge University Press.

Hathaway, Oona A. 2001. Path Dependence in the Law: The Course and Pattern of Legal Change in a Common Law System. *Iowa Law Review* 86: 601–65.

Hegel, G.W.F. 1952. *Philosophy of Right*. Translated by T.M. Knox. Oxford: Oxford University Press.

———. 1964. On the Recent Domestic Affairs in Wurtemburg. In *Hegel's Political Writings*. Translated by T.M. Knox. Oxford: Clarendon.

Hensel, Paul R. 2006. *International Correlates of War: Colonial History Data Set, Version 0.4*. Last Modified: June 13, 2006. Available at http://garnet.acns.fsu.edu/~phensel/icow.html.

Herbst, Jeffrey. 2000. States and Power in Africa: Comparative Lessons in Authority and Control. Princeton: Princeton University Press.

Heron, Melonie, Donna L. Hoyert, Sherry L. Murphy, Jiaquan Xu, Kenneth D. Kochanek, and Betzaida Tejada-Vera. 2009. Deaths: Final Data for 2006. *National Vital Statistics Reports* 57(14).

Hirschman, Albert O. 1970. *Exit, Voice, and Loyalty: Responses to Decline in Firms, Organizations, and States*. Cambridge, MA: Harvard University Press.

Holcombe, Randall. 1991. Constitutions as Constraints: A Case Study of Three American Constitutions. *Constitutional Political Economy* 2(3): 303–328.

Holmes, Stephen and Cass Sunstein. 1995. The Politics of Constitutional Revision in Eastern Europe In *Responding to Imperfection: the Theory and Practice of Constitutional Amendment*, edited by Sanford Levinson. Princeton, NJ: Princeton University Press.

Horowitz, Donald. 1990. Comparing Democratic Systems. *Journal of Democracy* 4(1): 73–79.

———. 2002. Constitutional Design: Proposals versus Processes. In *The Architecture of Democracy*, edited by Andrew Reynolds. New York: Oxford University Press.

———. 2009. The *Federalist* Abroad. In *The Federalist Papers*, edited by Ian Shapiro. New Haven: Yale University Press.

Horwill, Herbert W. 1925. *The Usages of the American Constitution*. London: Oxford University Press.

Howard, A.E. Dick. 1996. The Indeterminacy of Constitutions. *Wake Forest Law Review* 31(2): 383–410.

Hume, David. 1777. *Essays and Treatises on Various Subjects*.

Huntington, Samuel. 1981. *American Politics: The Promise of Disharmony*. Cambridge, MA: Harvard University Press.

Huq, Aziz Z. 2006. Mechanisms of Political Capture in Pakistan's Superior Courts. *Yearbook of Islamic and Middle Eastern Law* 10: 21–37.

Hutson, James and Leonard Rapport, eds. 1987. *Supplement to Max Ferrand's The Records of the Federal Convention of 1787.* New Haven: Yale University Press.

Immergut, Ellen M. 2002. The Swedish Constitution and Social Democratic Power: Measuring the Mechanical Effect of a Political Institution. *Scandinavian Political Studies* 25: 231–57.

Indian Parliament. 1948. *Constituent Assembly Debates.* Volume VII, p. 4a. Available at http://parliamentofindia.nic.in/ls/debates/vol7p4b.htm.

Instituto de Investigaciones Jurídicas. 1999. *Hacia una Nueva Constitucionalidad.* Serie Doctrina Jurídica, Núm. 8. Universidad Nacional Autónoma de México.

Inter-University Consortium for Political and Social Research. *Polity II Data.*

Jacobsohn, Gary Jeffrey. 2003. *The Wheel of Law: India's Secularism in Comparative Constitutional Perspective.* Princeton: Princeton University Press.

———. 2006. Constitutional Identity. *Review of Politics* 68: 361–97.

Jaffrelot, Christophe. 2008. Containing the Lower Castes: The Constituent Assembly and Reservations Policy. In *Politics and Ethics of the Indian Constitution*, edited by Rajeev Bhargava. New York: Oxford University Press, 249–66.

Jefferson, Thomas. 1930. *The Adams-Jefferson Letters: The Complete Correspondence Between Thomas Jefferson and Abigail and John Adams.* Edited by Lester J. Cappon. Chapel Hill: The University of North Carolina Press.

Jennings, Ivor. 1953. *Some Characteristics of the Indian Constitution.* Madras: Oxford University Press.

Joseph, Gilbert and Daniel Nugent, eds. 1994. *Everyday Forms of State Formation: Revolution and the Negotiation of Rule in Modern Mexico.* Durham, NC: Duke University Press.

Kahneman, Daniel, Jack L. Knetsch, and Richard H. Thaler. 1991. Anomalies: The Endowment Effect, Loss Aversion, and Status Quo Bias. *Journal of Economic Perspectives.* 5(1): 193–206.

King, Anthony. 2007. *The British Constitution.* New York: Oxford University Press.

King, Gary, James Honaker, Anne Joseph, and Kenneth Scheve. 2001. Analyzing Incomplete Political Science Data: An Alternative Algorithm for Multiple Imputation. *American Political Science Review* 95: 49–69.

Klug, Heinz. 2000. *Constituting Democracy: Law, Globalism and South Africa's Political Reconstruction.* New York: Cambridge University Press.

Kohli, Atul, ed. 2001. *The Success of India's Democracy.* New York: Cambridge University Press.

Koremenos, Barbara. 2005. Contracting Around Uncertainty. *American Political Science Review* 99(4): 549–565.

Krasner, Stephen D. 1984. Approaches to the State: Alternative Conceptions and Historical Dynamics. *Comparative Politics* 16(2): 223–46.

Krishnamurthy, Vivek. 2009. Colonial Cousins: Explaining India and Canada's Unwritten Constitutional Principles. *Yale Journal of International Law* 34: 174–239.

LaCroix, Alison. 2005. A Singular and Awkward War: The Transatlantic Context of the Hartford Convention. *American Nineteenth Century History* 6(1): 3–32.

Lake, David, and Angela O'Mahoney. 2004. The Incredible Shrinking State: Explaining the Territorial Size of Countries. *Journal of Conflict Resolution* 48: 699–722.

Law, David. 2008. A Theory of Judicial Power and Judicial Review. *Georgetown Law Journal* 97: 723–801.

Lecce, Major D.J. 1998. International Law Regarding Pro-Democratic Intervention: A Study of the Dominican Republic and Haiti. *Naval Law Review* 15: 247–62.

Leiber, Francis. 1865. *Amendments of the Constitution of the United States Submitted to the Consideration of the American People*. New York: Loyola Publishing Co.

Levinson, Sanford. 1988. *Constitutional Faith*. Princeton, NJ: Princeton University Press.

————. ed. 1995. *Responding to Imperfection: Theory and Practice of Constitutional Amendment*. Princeton, NJ: Princeton University Press.

————. 2006. *Our Undemocratic Constitution*. New York: Oxford University Press.

Lieberson, Stanley. 1991. Small N's and Big Conclusions: An Examination of the Reasoning in Comparative Studies Based on a Small Number of Cases. *Social Forces* 70: 307–20.

Lijphart, Arend. 1971. Comparative Politics and Comparative Method. *American Political Science Review* 65: 682–93.

————. 1999. *Patterns of Democracy*. New Haven: Yale University Press.

Linz, Juan and Alfred Stepan. 1996. *Problems of Democratic Transition and Consolidation*. Baltimore: Johns Hopkins University Press.

Lipset, Seymour Martin. 1959. Some Social Requisites of Democracy: Economic Development and Political Legitimacy. *American Political Science Review* 53: 69–105.

Llewellyn, Karl. 1934. The Constitution as an Institution. *Columbia Law Review* 34: 1–40.

Lorenz, Astrid. 2005. How to Measure Constitutional Rigidity: Four Concepts and Two Alternatives. *Journal of Theoretical Politics* 17: 339–61.

Lowenthal, Abraham. 1969. The Dominican Republic: The Politics of Chaos. In *Reform and Revolution: Readings in Latin American Politics*, edited by Robert Kaufman and Arpad von Lazar. Boston: Allyn and Bacon.

————. 1972. *The Dominican Intervention*. Cambridge, MA: Harvard University Press.

Lutz, Donald. 1994. Toward a Theory of Constitutional Amendment. *American Political Science Review* 88: 355–70.

————. 2006. *Principles of Constitutional Design*. New York: Cambridge University Press.

Macey, Jonathan R. 1988. Transaction Costs and the Normative Elements of the Public Choice Model: An Application to Constitutional Theory. *Virginia Law Review* 74 (1): 471–518.

Madison, James. 1787. Vices of the Political System of the United States. in *The Papers of James Madison*, edited by William T. Hutchinson, et al. Chicago: University of Chicago Press (1962–77), 9: 348–57.

Madison, James, Alexander Hamilton, and John Jay. 1826. *The Federalist: On the New Constitution*. Glazier & Co.

Magaloni, Beatriz. 2008. Enforcing the Autocratic Political Order and the Role of Courts: The Case of Mexico. In *Rule by Law: The Politics of Courts in Authoritarian Regimes*, edited by Tom Ginsburg and Tamir Moustafa. New York: Cambridge University Press.

Magliocca, Gerard. 2007. *Andrew Jackson and the Constitution: The Rise and Fall of Generational Regimes*. Lawrence, KS: University of Kansas Press.

Maki, John, ed. 1980. *Japan's Commission on the Constitution: The Final Report.* Seattle: University of Washington Press.

Maki, John. 1993. The Constitution of Japan: Pacifism, Popular Sovereignty and Fundamental Human Rights. In *Japanese Constitutional Law*, edited by Percy R. Luney Jr. and Kazuyuki Takahashi. Tokyo: University of Tokyo Press.

Maluka, Zulfiqar Khalid. 1997. *The Myth of Constitutionalism in Pakistan.* New York: Oxford University Press.

Mane, Suresh. 2005. Constitution and Dr. Ambedkar's Vision for Social Change. In *Ambedkar on Law, Constitution and Social Justice*, edited by Mohammad Shabbir. Delhi: Rawat Publications.

Marcus, Maeva. 1992. The Founding Fathers, Marbury v. Madison – and So What? In *Constitutional Justice Under Old Constitutions*, edited by Eivind Smith, 23–50. The Hague: Kluwer.

Martin, Forrest. 2007. *The Constitution as Treaty: The International Legal Constructionalist Approach to the U.S. Constitution.* New York: Cambridge University Press.

Marshall, Monty C with Jaggers, and Ted Robert Gurr. 2004. Polity IV: Political Regime Transitions and Characteristics, 1800–1999. Available at http://www.cidcm.umd.edu/polity/.

Marshall, Thurgood. 1987. Reflections on the Bicentennial of the United States Constitution. *Harvard Law Review* 101: 1–5.

Maskin, Eric and Tirole, Jean. 1999. Unforeseen Contingencies and Incomplete Contracts. *Review of Economic Studies* 66(1): 83–114.

Martineau, Robert J. 1970. The Mandatory Referendum on Calling a State Constitutional Convention. *Ohio State Law Journal* 31(3): 421–55.

Michelman, Frank. 1999. Constitutional Authorship by the People. *Notre Dame Law Review* 74: 1605–29.

———. 1998. Constitutional Authorship. In *Constitutionalism: Philosophical Foundations*, edited by Larry Alexander. New York: Cambridge University Press.

Mill, John Stuart. [1843] 1974. *A System of Logic.* Toronto: University of Toronto Press.

Miwa, Yoshiro & J. Mark Ramseyer. 2009. The Good Occupation. *Washington University Global Studies Law Review* 8: 363–78.

Moehler, Devra C. 2007. *Distrusting Democrats: Outcomes of Participatory Constitution-Making.* Ann Arbor: University of Michigan Press.

Moore, Ray and Donald Robinson. 2002. *Partners for Democracy: Crafting the New Japanese State under MacArthur.* New York: Oxford University Press.

Muller, Wolfgang C. and Kaare Strom. 1999. *Policy, Office, or Votes? How Political Parties in Western Europe Make Hard Decisions.* Cambridge, UK: Cambridge University Press.

Munro, William Bennett. 1930. *The Makers of the Unwritten Constitution.* New York: Macmillan.

Murphy, Walter F. 1993. Constitutions, Constitutionalism, and Democracy. In *Constitutionalism and Democracy: Transitions in the Contemporary World*, edited by Douglas Greenberg, Stanley N. Katz, Melanie Beth Oliviero, and Steven C. Wheatley.

———. 2007. *Constitutional Democracy: Creating and Maintaining a Just Political Order.* Baltimore: Johns Hopkins University Press.

Nathan, Andrew. 1986. *Chinese Democracy.* Berkeley: University of California Press.

Navia, Patricio and Julio Rios. 2005. The Constitutional Adjudication Mosaic of Latin America. *Comparative Political Studies* 38: 189–217.

Nehru, Jawaharlal. 1947. *Tryst with Destiny*. Speech made to the Indian Constituent Assembly on August 14.

Negretto, Gabriel. 2008. The Durability of Constitutions in Changing Environments: Explaining Constitutional Replacements in Latin America, Kellogg Institute, Working Paper #350.

Newberg, Paula. 1996. *Judging the State: Courts and Constitutional Politics in Pakistan*. New York: Cambridge University Press.

Nielson, Daniel L. and Matthew Soberg Shugart. 1999. Constitutional Change in Colombia: Policy Adjustment Through Institutional Reform. *Comparative Political Studies* 32: 313–41.

Niskanen, William. 1990. Conditions Affecting the Survival of Constitutional Rules. *Constitutional Political Economy* 1(2): 53–62.

North, Douglas and Barry Weingast. 1989. Constitutions and Commitment: The Evolution of Institutions Governing Public Choice in 17th Century England. *Journal of Economic History* 49(4): 803–832.

Norvell, Daniel. C. and Cummings, Peter. 2002. Association of helmet use with death in motorcycle crashes: a matched-pair cohort study. *American Journal of Epidemiology* 156: 483–87.

Nzelibe, Jide and John Yoo. 2006. Rational War and Constitutional Design. *Yale Law Journal* 115: 2512–41.

Ordeshook, Peter C. 1992. Constitutional Stability. *Constitutional Political Economy* 3(2): 137–75.

Oropeza, Manuel Gonzalez. 1997. The Constitution of 1917. In *Encyclopedia of Mexico*, edited by Michael Werner. Chicago: Fitzroy Dearborn Publishers.

Palmer, Matthew. 2006. What is New Zealand's constitution and who interprets it? Constitutional realism and the importance of public office-holders. *Public Law Review* 17: 133–62.

Parliamentary Monitoring Group. 2005. *Report of the Constitutional Review Committee, dated 28 October 2005*. Available at http://www.pmg.org.za/docs/2005/comreports/051101crcreport.htm.

Peaslee, Amos Jenkins. 1950. *Constitutions of Nations*. Concord, NH: Rumford Press.

Persson, Torsten, Gerard Roland, and Guido Tabellini. 1997. Separation of Powers and Political Accountability. *The Quarterly Journal of Economics* 112(4): 1163–1202.

Persson, Torsten and Guido Tabellini. 2003. *The Economic Effects of Constitutions*. Boston, MA: MIT Press.

Pierson, Paul. 2004. *Politics in Time*. Princeton, NJ: Princeton University Press.

Pitkin, Hanna Fenichel. 1987. The Idea of a Constitution. *Journal of Legal Education* 37: 167–70.

Pons, Frank Moya. 1995. *The Dominican Republic: A National History*. New Rochelle, NY: Hispaniola Books.

Posner, Eric A. and Adrian Vermeule. 2008. *Constitutional Showdowns*. University of Pennsylvania Law Review 156: 991–1048.

————. 2007. *Terror in the Balance*. New York: Oxford University Press.

Posner, Richard. 2001. *Breaking the Deadlock: The 2000 Election, the Constitution, and the Courts*. Princeton, NJ: Princeton University Press.

Powe, Lucas A. 2002. *The Warren Court and American Politics*. Cambridge, MA: Harvard University Press.

Przeworski, Adam and Henry Teune. 1970. *The Logic of Comparative Social Inquiry*. New York: John Wiley.

Przeworski, Adam. 1991. *Democracy and the Market*. Cambridge, UK: Cambridge University Press.

Przeworski, Adam, Michael E. Alvarez, José Antonio Cheibub, and Fernando Limongi. 1999. *Democracy and Development: Political Institutions and Well-Being in the World, 1950–1990*. Cambridge, UK: Cambridge University Press.

Putnam, Robert. 2003. *Making Democracy Work: Civic Traditions in Modern Italy*. Princeton, NJ: Princeton University Press.

Ragin, Charles. 1987, *The Comparative Method*. Berkeley: University of California Press.

Rakove, Jack. 1996. *Original Meanings: Politics and Ideas in the Making of the Constitution*. New York: Knopf.

Rasch, Bjørn Erik and Roger Congleton. 2006. Amendment Procedures and Constitutional Stability. In *Democratic Constitutional Design and Public Policy*, edited by Roger Congleton and Birgitta Sweborg. Cambridge, MA: MIT Press.

Reed Sarkees, Meredith. 2000. The Correlates of War Data on War: An Update to 1997. *Conflict Management and Peace Science* 18: 123–44.

Rees, Charles. 2007. Remarkable Evolution: The Early Constitutional History of Maryland. *The University of Baltimore Law Review* 36(2): 217–70.

Rehnquist, William. 1998. *All the Laws But One: Civil Liberties in Wartime*. New York: Alfred A. Knopf.

Revankar, Ratna G. 1971. *Indian Constitution: A Case Study of Backward Classes*. Rutherford, NJ: Farleigh Dickenson University Press.

Riggs, Fred. 1966. *Thailand: Modernization of a Bureaucratic Polity*. Honolulu: East-West Center Press.

Riker, William. 1964. *Federalism: Origins, Operation, Significance*. Boston: Little, Brown.

Ritchie, David T. 2005. Organic Constitutionalism: Rousseau, Hegel, and the Constitution of Society. *Journal of Law and Society* 6: 36–81.

Roeder, Philip. 2007. *Where Nation States Come From: Institutional Change in an Age of Nationalism*. Princeton, NJ: Princeton University Press.

Rohr, John. 2007. *Founding Republics in France and America: A Study in Constitutional Governance*. Lawrence, KS: University Press of Kansas.

Roorda, Eric. 1998. *The Dictator Next Door: Good Neighbor Policy and the Trujillo Regime in the Dominican Republic 1930–1945*. Durham, NC: Duke University Press.

Rousseau, Jean-Jacques. [1762] 1968. *The Social Contract*. New York: Penguin.

Rubenfeld, Jed. 2001a. The New Unwritten Constitution. *Duke Law Journal* 51: 289–305.

———. 2001b. *Freedom and Time: A Theory of Constitutional Self-Government*. New Haven: Yale University Press.

Rudolph, Lloyd and Susanne Hoeber Rudolph. 2001. Redoing the Constitutional Design: From an Interventionist Regulatory State. In *The Success of India's Democracy*, edited by Atul Kohli. New York: Cambridge University Press.

Ruibal, Alba. 2008. Definition of the New Institutional Role of the Supreme Court in Argentina, with Reference to the Mexican Case. At the seminar of the Doctoral Program at the Instituto de Investigaciones Jurídicas. May 21, Universidad Nacional Autónoma de México.

Russell, Peter. 1993. *Constitutional Odyssey: Can Canadians Become a Sovereign People?* Toronto: University of Toronto Press.

Rustow, Dankwart. 1970. Transitions to Democracy: Toward a Dynamic Model. *Comparative Politics* 2: 337–63.

Ryn, Claes G. 1992. Political Philosophy and the Unwritten Constitution. *Modern Age* 34(4): 303–09.

Sabato, Larry. 2007. *A More Perfect Constitution.* New York: Walker and Co.

Samaha, Adam. 2008. Dead Hand Arguments and Constitutional Interpretation. *Columbia Law Review* 108(3): 606–80.

Samuels, Richard. 2004. Constitutional Revision in Japan: The Future of Article 9. Speech at the Center for Northeast Asian Policy Studies, Brookings Institution, December 15.

Samuelson, William and Richard Zeckhauser. 1988. Status Quo Bias in Decisionmaking. *Journal of Risk and Uncertainty* 1: 7–59.

Saravia, Antonio. 2008. Institutional Change from an Evolutionary Perspective: The Mexican Experience. *Constitutional Political Economy* 19: 129–47.

Sarkar, Sumit. 1999. Indian Democracy: The Historical Inheritance. In *The Success of India's Democracy*, edited by Atul Kohli. New York: Cambridge University Press.

Sartori, Giovanni. 1970. Concept Misformation in Comparative Politics. *American Political Science Review* 64: 1033–53.

———. 1984. Guidelines for Concept Analysis. In *Social Science Concepts: A Systematic Analysis*, edited by Giovanni Sartori. Beverly Hills: Sage.

Scheiber, Harry, ed. 2006. *Earl Warren and the Warren Court: The Legacy in American and Foreign Law.* Lanham, MD: Lexington Books.

Schelling, Thomas. 1980. *The Strategy of Conflict.* Cambridge, MA: Harvard University Press.

Scheppele, Kim Lane. 2008. A Constitution Between Past and Future. *William and Mary Law Review* 49(4): 1377–1407.

Schwartzberg, Melissa. 2007. *Democracy and Legal Change.* New York: Cambridge University Press.

Scott, James. 1985. *Weapons of the Weak: Everyday Forms of Peasant Resistance.* New Haven: Yale University Press.

Shapiro, Martin. 1992. Federalism, the Race to the Bottom, and the Regulation-Averse Entrepreneur. In *North American And Comparative Federalism*, edited by Harry Scheiber. Berkeley: Institute of Governmental Studies Press.

Shapiro, Martin and Alec Stone Sweet. 2002. *On Law, Politics, and Judicialization.* New York: Oxford University Press.

Shirer, William L. 1969. *The Collapse of the Third Republic.* New York: Simon Schuster.

Simmons, Beth and Zachary Elkins. 2004. The Globalization of Liberalization: Policy Diffusion in the International Political Economy. *American Political Science Review* 98: 171–90.

Singhvi, L.M. and Jagadish Swarup. 2006. *Constitution of India: An Article-Wise Second Edition of Pioneer Commentary on the Constitution of India*. New Delhi; Modern Law Publications.

Skach, Cindy. 2005. *Borrowing Constitutional Designs*. Cambridge, MA: Harvard University Press.

Skocpol, Theda and Margaret Somers. 1980. The Uses of Comparative History in Macrosocial Inquiry. *Comparative Studies in Society and History* 22: 174–97.

Snyder, Richard. 2001. Scaling Down: The Subnational Comparative Method. *Studies in Comparative International Development* 36: 93–110.

Sollors, Werner. 1986. *Beyond Ethnicity: Consent and Descent in American Culture*. New York: Oxford University Press.

Steele, Martha. 1952. Constitutions of Haiti. *Revue de la Société Hatienne d'Histoire, de Géographie et de Géologie* 23: 84–99.

Stepan, Alfred and Cindy Skach. 1993. Constitutional Frameworks and Democratic Consolidation. *World Politics* 46: 1–22.

Stinchcombe, Arthur L. 1965. Social Structure and Organizations. In *Handbook of Organizations*, edited by James G. March. Chicago: Rand McNally.

―――. 1978. *Theoretical Methods in Social History*. New York: Academic Press.

Strang, David and Sarah A. Soule. 1998. Diffusion in Organizations and Social Movements: From Hybrid Corn to Poison Pills. *Annual Review of Sociology* 24: 265–90.

Stone, Alec. 1992. *The Birth of Constitutional Politics in France*. New York: Oxford University Press.

Strauss, David. 1996. Common Law Constitutional Interpretation. *University of Chicago Law Review* 877–935.

―――. 2001. The Irrelevance of Constitutional Amendments. *Harvard Law Review* 114(5): 1457–1505.

―――. 2003. Common Law, Common Ground, and Jefferson's Principle. *Yale Law Journal* 112: 1717–55.

Sturm, Albert L. 1982. The Development of American State Constitutions. *Publius* 12(1): 57–98.

Sunstein, Cass. 2000. *Behavioral Law and Economics*. New York: Cambridge University Press.

―――. 2001. *Designing Democracy: What Constitutions Do*. New York: Oxford University Press.

Sutter, Daniel. 1995. Constitutional Politics Within the Interest-Group Model. *Constitutional Political Economy* 6(2): 127–37.

―――. 1997. Enforcing Constitutional Constraints. *Constitutional Political Economy* 8: 139–50.

―――. 2003. Durable Constitutional Rules and Rent Seeking. *Public Finance Review* 31(4): 413–28.

Suwannathat-Pian, Kobkua. 2002. The Monarchy and Constitutional Change Since 1972. In *Reforming Thai Politics*, edited by Duncan McCargo. Copenhagen: Nordic Institute of Asian Studies.

―――. 2003. *Kings, Country and Constitutions: Thailand's Political Development 1932–2000*. Richmond: RoutledgeCurzon.

Tiedeman, Christopher Gustavas. 1890. *The Unwritten Constitution of the United States*. New York: G.P. Putnam's Sons.

Tir, Jaroslav, Philip Schafer, Paul F. Diehl, and Gary Goertz. 1998. Territorial Changes, 1816–1996. *Conflict Management and Peace Science* 16: 89–97.

Tolstoy, Leo. [1877] 1960. *Anna Karenina*. Translated by Joel Carmichael. New York: Bantam Books.

Treanor, William. 2006. Judicial Review Before Marbury. *Stanford Law Review* 58: 455–562.

Tribe, Laurence H. 2008. *The Invisible Constitution*. New York: Oxford University Press.

Tsebelis, George. 2002. *Veto Players: How Political Institutions Work*. Princeton: Princeton University Press.

Valadés, Diego. 2007. Las Funciones de la Reforma Constitucional. In *El Proceso Constituyente Mexicano: A 150 Años de la Constitución de 1857 y 90 de la Constitución de 1917*, edited by Diego Valadés and Miguel Carbonell. Mexico City: Universidad Nacional Autónoma de México.

Van Nifterik, Gustaaf. 2007. French Constitutional History: Garden or Graveyard? Some Thoughts on Occasion of *Les Grands Discours Parlementaires*. *European Constitutional Law Review* 3: 476–87.

Verney, Douglas V. 1957. *Parliamentary Reform in Sweden 1866–1921*. London: Oxford University Press.

Voigt, Stefan. 1997. Positive constitutional economics: A survey. *Public Choice* 90(1): 11–53.

———. 2003. The Consequences of Popular Participation in Constitutional Choice – Toward a Comparative Analysis. In *Deliberation and Decision*, edited by Anne van Aaken, et al. Aldershot, UK: Ashgate Publishing

———. 2007. Constitutional Garrulity. Manuscript.

Weber, Max. 1977. *Economy and Society*. Berkeley: University of California Press.

Webster, Noah. 1787. On Bills of Rights. *American Magazine* 1: 12.

Weingast, Barry. 1997. The Political Foundations of Democracy and the Rule of Law. *American Political Science Review* 91: 245–63.

———. 2005. Self-Enforcing Constitutions: With an Application to Democratic Stability in America's First Century. Stanford University. *Working Paper*.

———. 2006. Designing Constitutional Stability. In *Democratic Constitutional Design and Public Policy*, edited by Roger Congleton and Birgitta Swedborg. Cambridge: MIT Press.

Whittington, Keith and John Maclean. 2002. It's Alive! The Persistence of the Constitution. *The Good Society* 11(2): 8–12.

Widner Jennifer. 2005. Constitution Writing and Conflict Resolution: Data and Summaries. http://www.princeton.edu/~pcwcr/about/copyright.html.

———. 2007a. The Effects of Constitution Writing Procedures on Choice of Terms & Patterns of Violence: Some Data, Some Observations, and Many Reasons for Modesty. Paper read at Stanford Workshop in Comparative Politics, January 22, 2007, at Palo Alto, CA.

———. 2007b. Proceedings, "Workshop on Constitution Building Processes." Princeton University, May 17–20, 2007, Bobst Center for Peace and Justice, Princeton University, in conjunction with Interpeace and International IDEA.

———. 2008. Constitution Writing in Post-Conflict Settings: An Overview. *William and Mary Law Review* 49(4): 1513–41.

Williams, Robert F. 1996. Are State Constitutional Conventions Things of the Past? The Increasing Role the Constitutional Commission in State Constitutional Change. *Hofstra Law & Policy Symposium* 1: 1–16.

———. 2000. Is Constitutional Revision Success Worth its Popular Sovereignty Price? *Florida Law Review* 52(2): 249–74.

Williamson, Oliver. 1985. *The Economic Institutions of Capitalism*. New York: The Free Press.

Wongtrangan, Kanok. 1990. Executive Power and Constitutionalism in Thailand. In *Constitutional and Legal Systems of ASEAN Countries*, edited by Carmelo V. Sison. Manila: Academy of ASEAN Law and Jurisprudence, University of the Philippines.

World Bank. 2000. World Development Indicators 2000, Vol. 1.

Yarbrough, Jean M. 1998. *American Virtue: Thomas Jefferson on the Character of a Free People*. Lawrence, KS: University Press of Kansas.

Young, Ernest A. 2007. The Constitution Outside the Constitution. *Yale Law Journal* 117: 408–73.

Zamora, Stephen and José Ramón Cossío. 2006. Mexican Constitutionalism after Presidencialismo. *International Journal of Constitutional Law* 4(2): 411–37.

Index